Unsung Voices

PRINCETON STUDIES IN OPERA

Puccini's Turandot: *The End of the Great Tradition* by William Ashbrook and Harold Powers (1991)

Unsung Voices: Opera and Musical Narrative in the Nineteenth Century by Carolyn Abbate (1991)

Unsung Voices

OPERA AND MUSICAL NARRATIVE IN THE NINETEENTH CENTURY

Carolyn Abbate

PRINCETON UNIVERSITY PRESS

PRINCETON, NEW JERSEY

Copyright © 1991 by Princeton University Press
Published by Princeton University Press, 41 William Street,
Princeton, New Jersey 08540
In the United Kingdom: Princeton University Press, Oxford

Library of Congress Cataloging-in-Publication Data

Abbate, Carolyn.
Unsung voices : opera and musical narrative in the nineteenth
century / Carolyn Abbate.
p. cm.
Includes bibliographical references and indexes.
1. Opera—19th century. 2. Music—19th
century—Philosophy and aesthetics. I. Title.
ML3858.A2 1991 782.1′09′034—dc20 90–8972 CIP

ISBN 0-691-09140-4

This book has been composed in Linotron Baskerville

Princeton University Press books are printed on acid-free paper,
and meet the guidelines for permanence and durability of the
Committee on Production Guidelines for Book Longevity of the
Council on Library Resources

Printed in the United States of America by Princeton University Press,
Princeton, New Jersey

10 9 8 7 6 5 4 3 2 1

Sections of Chapters 2 and 3 were previously published as follows: "What the Sorcerer
Said," in *19th-Century Music* 12 (1989): 221–30; "Theories of Musical Narrative," in *Atti
del XIV congresso della società internazionale di musicologia*, ed. Lorenzo Bianconi, F. Al-
berto Gallo, Angelo Pompilio, and Donatella Restani (Turin: EDT, 1991); "Eric's
Dream and Tannhäuser's Journey," in *Reading Opera*, ed. Arthur Groos and Roger
Parker (Princeton: Princeton University Press, 1988), 129–67.

All translations in this book (unless otherwise noted) are by the author.

For LCM

CONTENTS

PREFACE

In *Opera, or the Undoing of Women*, Catherine Clément argues that women are killed off by the operatic plots they occupy so that their dangerous energy, contained by death, will be rendered innocuous.[1] The male observer, from his place in the audience, can thus gaze both upon these women and upon their defeat: a comforting pastime. A telling critique of Clément's thesis, however, comes from just such a male operagoer, Paul Robinson, who pointed out that in focusing on the women's fatal defeat by operatic plots, Clément neglected their triumph: the sound of their singing voices. This sound is (as he indicated) unconquerable; it cannot be concealed by orchestras, by male singers, or—in the end—by murderous plots. Robinson hears opera in a way that has nothing to do with the events that its libretto depicts; he hears it as sonorous texture, and he redirects our attention from opera's representation of dramatic action toward one aspect of its musical body.[2] His point was that women (though he could be speaking of any operatic character, regardless of apparent or real gender) tend to be interpreted as they are represented in plots: what is neglected is their voice, how the voice is depicted, how it is put to work—in the end, how this undefeated voice speaks across the crushing plot.

I start with this image of woman undone by plot yet triumphant in voice in order to underline a position taken in my own book, which explores the idea of voice. I deal not with the feminine but with music itself, which is caught in much the same matrix as Clément's operatic Woman. Music, conventionally defined in terms of its events (and often its plot), also sets forth speaking and singing voices. Plotted explanations of music—conceptualizations of music as process or series of events—are a familiar form of music-analytical discourse.[3] The metaphor of music singing, having a voice, though a commonplace of nineteenth-century musical aesthetics, is today more unusual; it is most familiar to Anglo-American readers from Edward Cone's 1974 book *The Composer's Voice*.[4]

For those outside music criticism, insistence upon voice may seem like painting the lily. Music has a voice whenever the human voice sings. What I mean by "voice" is, of course, not literally vocal performance, but rather a sense of certain isolated and rare gestures in music, whether vocal or nonvocal, that may be perceived as modes of subjects' enunciations.[5] By emphasizing voice, I hope to help restore to music criticism a sense for the *physical* force of music; music—like the human speaking voice—has the capacity to assail us with its sheer sound. This emphasis also facilitates a critical move from the monological authority of "the Composer," since what I mean by "voices" are potentially multiple musical voices that inhabit a work—not the creative efforts of the historical author, or even the utterance of a virtual author. This particular interpretive bias, of course, emphasizes music as embodied within the live performance of a work. Although I do not discuss (except in short asides) specific performers or performances, my discussion of performance in its figural sense— as the sound, through time, made by musical voices—may serve as a necessary reminder that music is written by a composer, but made and given phenomenal reality by performers. For this reason, I explore (if briefly) areas of literary criticism that focus on performance and voice, and that exploit assumptions about how *music* works to interpret literary texts.

This idea of voice is also unfolded within a more specific context: the question of music's narrativity. If we speak of music as "narrative," we realize that the word is metaphorical. Yet since the nineteenth century, musical works have been described as "narrative" and the word catches our attention. What does this mean? For what musical element, structure, gesture, effect, or device is "narrative" a satisfying descriptive characterization? In Chapter 1, a theoretical meditation on voice that also prepares my discussions of narrativity, I claim that "narrative" has generally been defined, since the nineteenth century, in terms of an analogy between certain linear elements of music (music proceeds through time, generates expectations based on one's instantaneous mental comparisons of music being heard with known types or paradigms, has tensions and resolutions, is a succession of sonic events that moves toward closure) and the events in a dramatic plot; that is, music has been perceived as enactment, as analogous to the event-sequences of theatrical or cinematic narrative. But, as I will argue, this analogy—while it has generated fascinating interpretive retellings—has its limitations. Chapter 1 looks in a general way at comparisons between music and narrative, examining interpretations from the nineteenth to the late twentieth century that, regardless of their differing vocabularies and methodological moves, tend to espouse this event-centered conceptual structure.

Where we can show that these analogies are arbitrary (in the broad linguistic sense), that alone is not reason for suggesting alternatives: all words about music are in that sense arbitrary: verbal constructions (themselves reflecting some cognitive configuration) placed upon musical reality that will seem, to a given listener, to assume a similar shape. Put another way, verbally couched interpretations of music are performances and can only be more or less convincing.[6] Indeed, in Chapter 2, in the course of reading Dukas's *Sorcerer's Apprentice,* I play a game with associations between sonorous events and narratological concepts, promising first this and then that musical equivalent for ideas such as "plot," "character," "cardinal function," "discourse," and the like. The money—an unambiguous ontology that identifies a given musical fact as *being* narrative—is pushed toward the reader, but then raked away again. A croupier's strategy like this one involves a tease, but it was chosen precisely for its capacity to demonstrate the limitations of arguments that propose analogies.

My reasons for moving beyond narrative as event-sequence and a plot-concept of music's narrativity nonetheless had nothing to do with the insecure nature of verbal imaginings to which the confrontation gives rise. That insecurity is endemic to interpreting music, endemic to my own readings, and I prefer to accept these uncertainties as a source of pleasure, rather than fear them as inimical to interpretive control. Musical narrative as a musical plot does nonetheless seem to me limited in certain ways; as paradoxical as the formulation may sound, one of its *limitations* is its interpretive *promiscuity.* Broad definitions of narrative (narrative as any event-sequence, or as any text that induces mental comparisons with a paradigm, for instance) are so broad as to enable almost all music, all parts of any given work, to be defined as narrative. Put bluntly: how much intellectual pleasure do we derive from a critical methodology that generates such uniformity and becomes a mere machine for naming any and all music? Is there no difference between narrative and nonnarrative music, as there is between text genres? My assumption was rather that music will have its nonnarrative expanses as well as its moments of narration (in which, so to speak, speakers' fantasies about causes, effects, and explanations create and fill out temporal gaps).[7] The notion of musical narration should, then, also raise questions about the contexts in which narration occurs, about narration's moral or performative suasions. I believe that the pleasures of narrational interpretation derive precisely from awakening a "second hearing" that enables us to sense *when* (for it happens but rarely) music can be heard as narrating, and more than this, to be aware of complex assumptions that encourage us to perceive such moments as narration.

To this end, I maintain certain distinctions throughout this book. Music is seen not merely as "acting out" or "representing" events as if it were a sort of unscrolling and noisy tapestry that mimes actions not visually but sonically, but also as occasionally respeaking an object in a morally distancing act of narration. Music has (in other words) moments of diegesis—musical voices that distance us from the sensual matter of what we are hearing, that speak across it. In both novels and film, the presence of this diegetic subject (even if that subject is deemed, as it were, at present absent) is taken for granted. It was precisely because most theorists of narrative had *denied* such a presence in music that I (in contrary fashion) wondered what would ensue if one listened for the sound of that voice.[8] My readings of Delibes, Mozart, Strauss, Dukas, Mahler, and Wagner attempt to recognize both voice and narrative acts in music, to identify when and by what means music narrates, and to suggest that such *loci* are far from being normal or universal. They are disruptive and charged with a sense of both distance and difference: narrating in music will contain elements of the fantastic. Certain nineteenth-century works can thus be conceived as oscillating between a normal musical state (*unscrolling*, which may well be described in terms of events, tonal unwindings, thematic development, or the like) and rarer moments of narrating. In Chapter 2, for instance, I associate this effect of narrating in Dukas's *Sorcerer's Apprentice* with a sense of narrative synthesis, a musical moment that reinterprets musical actions from a time already finished. These issues are taken up in many forms throughout the course of the book, which seeks this discursive distance or zone of noncongruence in music—whether it be a metaphysical abstraction like that developed in the preceding paragraphs, or the noncongruence of libretto and music in opera, or the noncongruence of gestures of narrating with some otherwise coherent piece that sets them forth.

The notion of music's narrativity, we can see, inevitably rebounds upon the larger questions raised by the general idea of musical voices: are the events of music simply *there*, or do we occasionally sense within them the voices of commentators that enunciate them? Does not the very notion of a musical work *narrating* construct a speaking presence behind that moment? I am not merely saying, of course, that some historical individual (Delibes, or Mahler) had to have organized sonorous thought into a piece, or even that we always assume that some virtual author created the sounds we hear. Yet in music above all—because music is live and present sonority—we cannot allude to narrative, yet elude voices by assuming a single speaker and dismissing him or her as identical to the author, by evoking the linguistics of Benveniste's "events that speak themselves,"[9] by making gestures toward poststructuralist characterizations of the subject as mere delusion, or simply by moving from the historical individual who wrote the piece to the piece itself as his dramatization, with themes as characters or actants, dissonant cadences as cardinal crises. I make a different, deliberately prosopopoeiac swerve; in effect I endow certain isolated musical moments with faces, and so with tongues and a special sonorous presence. I construct voices out of musical discourse. The questions that concerned me are: How does this constructed "they" seem to speak? Why do we hear them? What is their force? Precisely which musical gestures can be read as betraying their presence? All six of the succeeding chapters attempt to recover these voices, which—hence one sense of my title—have to me been overlooked, unsung. Sensitivity to this constructed presence means possessing that "second hearing" (an aural form of "second sight"), which reanimates, I hope, a sense for what is uncanny in music.

My speculation on voice (perhaps not surprisingly) weaves through an argument, set forth chiefly in Chapters 3 through 6, about the role of opera in creating modes of enunciated narration in music. The earlier nineteenth century saw expansion of scenes of dramatic action and narrative exposition in Romantic opera; formal and gestural experiments typical of musical modes for these scenes have long been considered one impetus for the overtly dramatic symphonic literature of the mid- to late nineteenth century.[10] Nineteenth-century opera, however, informed not only nineteenth-century symphonic music, but the writing of musical criticism as well. We could go even farther, and argue that opera—in which musical gestures are overtly and directly associated with brash, often melodramatic events—helped to engender our cultural tendency (endemic since the nineteenth century) to read dramas and plots into music, and to use dramatic and narrative metaphors in writing about music. Such large historical claims always seem banal, and I am deferring consideration of this one to some later time. I do, however, argue for one smaller point: that marks of musical narrating, as they existed in opera, can be revoiced in instrumental works of the late nineteenth century. In Chapter 4, one of Mahler's instrumental works (the *Todtenfeier* movement of the Second Symphony) is interpreted not as *plot*, but rather as enfolding the displacements typical of a certain operatic plot and operatic narrating voices alike within its symphonic march mode.

Richard Wagner figures importantly in these speculations. He included extensive scenes of narration and retrospection in his operas, and this alone set him apart from the librettists and composers who were his contemporaries. In Chapter 3, which discusses a theory of reflexivity in operatic narration, *Der fliegende Holländer* and *Tannhäuser* are seen as summarizing and exploding historical conventions for the music traditionally associated with narrative scenes in Mozartean and Romantic opera. Chapters 5 and 6 concern the *Ring*, and the immense complexities of its layered narrations. I suggest that the *Ring* contains musical narration that may speak both with and *across* the text, furnishing us with the opportunity to hear many narrating voices (both textual and musical), to separate the conflicting lines. Through repeated offerings of such polyphonic narration, Wagner undercuts the very notion of music as a voice whose purity is assured by virtue of its nonverbal nature. In Chapter 5, the history of the *Ring*'s genesis is set against a reception history of its narrative passages; both histories are critical to reading the longest narration— Wotan's Monologue in *Die Walküre*—as an enunciation emanating both textually *and musically* from Wotan, and hence as music that is itself unreliable. Chapter 6 returns to voice in a more general sense, in considering Brünnhilde, whose incarnation in the *Ring* is extremely complex. Her progressively developed hyperacusis for truth means that she can split both words and music into cross-talking strains. Yet even as the *Ring* foregrounds the hearing of this single character, it repeats a scene of narrating-as-lying (characters and music appear to describe *incorrectly* or differently certain events that we ourselves have witnessed) to become a morally radical work. The *Ring* undercuts security in the narrating voice even when that voice is musical, thus contradicting Wagner's own (Schopenhauerian) position on music as an untainted and transcendent discourse. Chapter 6 ends with Brünnhilde herself (not in her identity as a plot-character, but as what I call "voice-Brünnhilde") exemplifying Wagner's secret refusal of a Romantic tradition of musical metaphysics that originates with Rousseau and is still in force today.[11]

What unites the theoretical and historical strains of the book is a certain thematic concentration on voice, and on moments of noncongruence in opera and instrumental music. But I hope also to communicate an awareness of the difficulties of writing about music and hence of moving from a purely sonorous language to a discursive metalanguage. The metaphorical status of all words about music is not always self-consciously recognized by its interpreters. Music critics, analysts, and theorists often either imply or state outright that their "words about music" represent "what the composer" or "what musicians at the time" considered significant in a given work, thus at once invoking an authority that is not completely ours to possess and adopting a "poietic"[12] or "emic" strategy (reconstruction of the cultural or historical context that determined the work's production) to buttress interpretation. Many choose, on the other hand, to practice a form of musical New Criticism, to push aside genetic or historical considerations, and rest content in the faith that a particular analysis addresses some quality or configuration immanent in the work, a con-

figuration subject only to a process of discovery that—though mediated by and couched in verbal terms—is assumed to be uncorrupted
by culture or language.[13] Both are, needless to say, utopian visions of
interpretive certainty. There is nothing immanent in a musical work
(beyond the material reality of its written and sonic traces), and our
perceptions of forms, configurations, meanings, gestures, and symbols are always mediated by verbal formulas, as on a broader scale by
ideology and culture.[14] I have tried to embrace and acknowledge the
perils of interpretation, while remaining aware of two historical contexts for what I write: that of the music, and that of my own interpretive claims. Chapter 1 attempts, though only briefly, to situate the
act of writing about music within both historical traditions of musical
aesthetics and philosophy, and contemporary critical issues. Yet
speaking and writing about music should concern not only music critics (historians, analysts, and theorists), but all those involved with the
human sciences and caught up in fraught debates on the nature of
interpretation. Music, for many, is the sound over which one swoons
once the thoughtful labors of the day are done—but if so music
brings an ambiguous comfort. Far from being a refuge from worldly
questions of meaning, it is the beast in the closet; seemingly without
any discursive sense, it cries out the problems inherent in critical
reading and in interpretation as unfaithful translation. For interpreting music involves a terrible and unsafe leap between object and exegesis, from sound that seems to signify nothing (and is nonetheless
splendid) to words that claim discursive sense but are, by comparison,
modest and often unlovely. What is lost in the jump is what we all
fear: what must remain unsaid.

. . .

Unsung Voices began as a project on Wagner's operatic narratives; discussions with Reinhold Brinkmann, Harold Powers, and the late Carl
Dahlhaus shaped this initial phase, which was supported by an NEH
Fellowship in 1986–1987. Dr. Manfred Eger and Herr Gunter
Fischer of the Richard-Wagner-Archiv in Bayreuth put a number of
manuscripts at my disposal, and Egon Voss, Isolde Vetter, and
Christa Jost at the Richard-Wagner-Ausgabe in Munich listened encouragingly to assorted Wagnerian speculations. The book's mutation into a broader theoretical study began right away: parts were
presented as lectures in 1987 and 1988; I thank Lorenzo Bianconi,
director of the Bologna IMS Conference, Steven Paul Scher, director
of the Conference on Music and the Verbal Arts at Dartmouth, and
Esther Cavett-Dunsby, director of the Oxford Conference on Music

Analysis, for chance to try them out, and Hermann Danuser, Gary Tomlinson, and David Osmond-Smith for their comments on these lectures. Anthony Newcomb and Karol Berger kindly invited me to participate in a symposium on narrative and music at Stanford and Berkeley in May 1988; stimulating live exchanges on that occasion are echoed in small bursts throughout this book. My students at Princeton and in visiting seminars at Stony Brook and the University of Pennsylvania were instrumental in helping me to spin out my ideas; Carlo Caballero, Rose Mauro, and Sanna Pederson in particular have enriched my work in many ways. One of my students, Alice Clark, also served as an invaluable research assistant. Certain aspects of the book's theoretical bias go back many years to discussions with Edward Cone; his presence in these pages is a measure of my debt to his unique music-analytical vision. Walter Lippincott, Director of Princeton University Press, was wise enough to suggest that interpreting the *Ring* should periodically be refreshed by attendence at its performance.

Roger Parker, my collaborator in other operatic fantasies, read the entire manuscript in an early draft and helped me to hear my own voice more clearly, as did Arthur Groos and John Deathridge. Jean-Jacques Nattiez (whose command of the music-language trope is unrivaled) also read this draft, and discussed it in the course of many telephoned and polyglot conversations. Joseph Kerman, Sander Gilman, and Garrett Stewart commented on versions of what became Chapters 1, 2, 4, and 6. Since any undertaking that drifts (like this one) outside institutional boundaries means frequent demands for information and direction, I am especially indebted to those in other fields who took an interest in the project—above all Caryl Emerson, whose literary imagination meshes with devotion to music in unique ways, and with whom I have shared most of the work presented here.

Many other friends saw me through the task of writing, and I associate them fondly with different stages of the book's evolution: Mayen Würdig-Beckmann, Angelika Arnoldi-Livie, Bruce Livie, Marta Petrusewicz, Andreas Schulman, Naemi Stilman, Victoria Cooper, Rena Mueller, David Cannata, Linda Roesner, Edward Roesner, William Ashbrook, Margaret Cobb, and Robert Bailey. Lee Mitchell, who responded with extraordinary insight to odd ideas yet unformed, lightened the circumstances of their recomposition into this, their sturdier and physical incarnation.

Unsung Voices

Chapter One

MUSIC'S VOICES

WE BEGIN with a scene that explores the power of narration, by show-ing us how a certain Hindu priestess comes to tell the "Tale of the Pariah's Daughter":

> *Nilakantha* (avec beaucoup de sentiment):
> Si ce maudit s'est introduit chez moi,
> S'il a bravé la mort pour arriver à toi,
> Pardonne-moi ce blasphème,
> C'est qu'il t'aime!
> Toi, ma Lakmé, toi, la fille des dieux.
> Il va triomphant par la ville,
> Nous allons retenir cette foule mobile.
> Et s'il te voit, Lakmé, je lirai dans ses yeux!
> Affermis bien ta voix! Sois souriante,
> Chante, Lakmé! Chante! La vengeance est là!
>
> (Les Hindous se rapprochent peu à peu.)
>
> Par les dieux inspirée,
> Cette enfant vous dira
> La légende sacrée
> De la fille du Paria . . .
>
> *Tous*: Ecoutons la légende, écoutons!
>
> *Lakmé*: Où va la jeune Indoue,
> Fille des Parias? (etc.)

[*Nilakantha* (with great emotion): If this villain has penetrated my do-main, if he has defied death to come near you, forgive my blasphemy, but it is because he loves you, my Lakmé, you! You, the child of the gods! He's passing in triumph through the town, so let us gather this wander-ing crowd, and, if he sees you Lakmé, I shall read it in his eyes! Now steady your voice! Smile as you sing! Sing, Lakmé! Sing! Vengeance is near! (The crowd of Hindus gathers slowly around.) Inspired by the gods, this child will tell you the sacred legend of the pariah's daughter. *The Crowd*: Let's listen to the legend! Listen! *Lakmé*: Where does the young Hindu girl wander? This daughter of pariahs? (etc.)]

This is, of course, the setup for one of opera's most famous virtuoso numbers, the Bell Song from Delibes' *Lakmé*, which premiered—two months after Wagner died—in 1883. What happens in this scene will serve to underscore a series of distinctions critical to any interpretation of musical narration: plot and narrating, story and teller, utterance and enunciation.

Upon first being urged by Nilakantha to "steady your voice . . . sing" (the line is significant), Lakmé responds with a wash of wordless coloratura. This initial improvisatory vocalizing is what first fascinates the crowd, and, from their random wanderings (they are a "foule mobile"), strikes them into immobility as a closed circle of listeners. They hear a woman who transforms herself into a kind of musical instrument, a sonorous line without words and unsupported by any orchestral sound (Example 1.1). Pure voice commands instant attention (both ours and that of the onstage audience), in a passage that is shockingly bare of other sound. In opera, we rarely hear the voice both unaccompanied and stripped of text—and when we do (in the vocal cadenzas typical of Italian arias, for instance), the sonority is disturbing, perhaps because such vocalizing so pointedly focuses our sense of the singing voice as one that can compel *without* benefit of words. Such moments enact in pure form familiar Western tropes on the suspicious power of music and its capacity to move us without rational speech. Beyond this, however, this moment of initial vocali-

Example 1.1. Lakmé Act II: Lakmé's Introductory Vocalizing.

zation, with its strong phatic effect, prefigures the thrust of Lakmé's vocal performance as a whole.

In verse 1 of her song, Lakmé tells the tale of a poor girl who wanders in the woods, and in the course of her wandering encounters a stranger threatened by "fauves [qui] rugissent de joie" ["wild animals (who) roar with joy"]. She jumps in to save the stranger by charming the animals with a magic wand, decorated with a bell. In verse 2, the stranger, revealed as Vishnu, rewards her by transporting her to the heavens; the song ends with the narrator's address to the onstage audience, reminding them that "depuis ce jour au fond des bois, / Le voyageur entend parfois / Le bruit léger de la baguette / Où tinte la clochette / Des charmeurs" ["since that day, those who travel deep into the forest sometimes hear the gentle sound of the wand on which the enchanters' bell rings"].

Known now to most only as a coloratura showpiece (and one associated chiefly with such art-deco divas as Lily Pons), the Bell Song derives its name from the refrain that closes each of the two narrative verses, in which the soprano imitates, by vocalizing on open vowel sounds, the "magic bell" described in the story. (The coloratura passages in the refrain are similar to those initial improvisatory roulades that first pull the crowd.) Few are aware that the Bell Song is actually the "Légende de la fille du Paria," that it is a narrative, and that its fetishization of voice as pure sound is interwoven with the telling of a story. Nonetheless, the scene demonstrates the ways in which vocal performance will indeed overpower plot, for Gerald, the besotted British officer, is attracted not by the tale but by the voice that sings it. Gerald betrays himself involuntarily, and, acting equally against her will, Lakmé delivers an overtly seductive performance, and extracts one erotically fascinated listener from the crowd in which he hides. Implicit in all that has been said, of course, is the realization that the Bell Song is a scene of performance on two levels: a narrative performance, and a musical performance that the onstage audience can *hear as music*. The scene involves "phenomenal" performance, which might be loosely defined as a musical or vocal performance that declares itself openly, singing that is heard by its singer, the auditors on stage, and understood as "music that they (too) hear" by us, the theater audience.[1]

A scene of seduction, Lakmé's performance nonetheless does not seduce by means of *plot*. This by no means implies that her "tale of the pariah's daughter" is irrelevant, for in the context of the opera as a whole it might well be read as an allegory of Lakmé's own fate—eventually, she sacrifices herself to save Gerald. Nilakantha's anger at Gerald's "blasphemous pollution" of the priestess is thus assuaged by *her* death, and when at the end of the opera Nilakantha cries "Elle porte là-haut nos voeux, / Elle est dans la splendeur des cieux!" ["She brings our prayers on high, she resides in the splendours of heaven"], he associates her with the transfigured maiden of her own tale. Gerald the foreigner and imperialist is at the same moment obliquely complimented by being, with Lakmé, inserted into the tale and equated with divine Vishnu (that the compliment is put in the mouth of an enraged native is one of the opera's covert means of luxuriating in its own Orientalist romance). In this allegorical role, the Bell Song represents a common operatic type, a song whose *reflexive* narrative text prefigures the plot of the opera in which it appears. Such songs generate complicated nested reflexive spheres, and their effects are discussed at greater length in Chapter 3. Within its immediate context, however, the tale that Lakmé tells *is* insignificant, for it is not the story that acts upon its listener. The act of telling it—the act of narrating—is the point.

The crowd can be understood as naive listeners, as eavesdroppers or an excluded audience, for the real force of the performance—the seduction—is not meant for them. They are content with the story of the pariah's daughter—they will, as they say, "listen to the *tale*," perhaps as a simpler reader might "read for the plot." Gerald, to the contrary, is envisaged by Nilakantha as listening not to plot but to voice and performance. By urging Lakmé to "steady her voice," by repeating his exhortation "chante, chante," he seems to realize that she must become much more than a story telling itself; she must be a sheer source of sound, to attract—fatally—the attention of that single listener. Gerald's experience of the song is deemed by the scene's stage-manager to be an experience of a musical voice-object.[2] As if to confirm her own status as sonority rather than story, Lakmé produces music that might itself be regarded as *working against the story she narrates*, since the two musical verses, by remaining similar, by repeating, in some sense deny the progressive sequence of changing events that are recounted in Lakmé's words.[3]

Gerald, the intended listener, is in fact never conscious of the tale (Lakmé's story of Vishnu and the pariah), because he is too far away to hear her words when Lakmé delivers her formal singing performance. When the song fails to flush his prey, Nilakantha urges Lakmé to sing again, to sing until the traitor is revealed. Lakmé, exhausted by formal performance, can no longer produce either the coherent narrative, or a whole verse of the song. She merely recapitulates textual fragments and bell sounds (Example 1.2). The broken coloratura inverts the smooth virtuosity of Lakmé's improvisatory prelude (her "steadying" of the voice), and the bell-flourishes, re-

Example 1.2. After the Bell Song.

Ex. 1.2 (cont.)

peated in upward sequence as Lakmé loses control of pitch, mark the end of the performance in the face of its success (Gerald has appeared at Lakmé's side). In this epilogue, both the sequential plot described by the words of the song, and the coherent sequence of musical events in the song, have dissolved into fragments as Lakmé becomes *explicitly* a body emanating sonority. Finally, Gerald *hears*. The Bell Song's epilogue reinterprets the song, exposing plot as empty distraction, and affirming that a narrative performance can signify in ways that pass beyond the tale told. Lakmé's singing has the same perlocutionary force as a command to Gerald to reveal himself, a force not connected to the structure or the content of her story.[4]

Lakmé's performance might be conceived (though the idea deflates the scene somewhat) as transcending certain concerns of structuralist narratology and endorsing the brief of narrative pragmatics, by demonstrating how we do well to examine narrative activities rather than the events that they describe, to examine forms of enunciation rather than forms taken by utterance. Put this way, the debate sounds merely institutional. The scene is far richer, of course, but it does enact certain oppositions and above all suggests the fascinations and complexities of *voice* in the musical work.

I

Voice is a charged word within contemporary critical theory; it is less so, naturally, in music criticism. In a musical work, voices are not easily muffled. But what are the voices that sing musical compositions? *Voices* can be understood commonsensically as the human voices of opera and song: soprano, mezzo, alto, castrato, countertenor, tenor, baritone, bass. In technical terms, voices are the individual contrapuntal lines of a polyphonic composition. Any critic of opera is aware, continually, of voices in the former sense, and is sensitive as well to their role in operative performance. An attraction to opera means an attraction to singers' voices—this goes without saying. But there is also a radical autonomization of the human voice that occurs, in varying degrees, in all vocal music. The sound of the singing voice becomes, as it were, a "voice-object" and the sole center for the listener's attention. That attention is thus drawn away from words, plot, character, and even from music as it resides in the orchestra, or music as formal gestures, as abstract shape;[5] Lakmé's performance plays out precisely this radical autonomization. When opera allows itself to project this voice-object, it also runs into peril—for, according to Michel Poizat, the "presence of the performer" may well suddenly emerge to impede the listener's contemplation. We are aware at these junctures—painfully, if the high C is missed—that we witness a performance. The membrane between the pure voice-object and the voice that we assign consciously to the virtuoso, as performance, is thus thin, and permeable. In the Queen of the Night's second aria, for instance, Poizat argues that the performer is actually forced to the foreground, because the voice-object in this extraordinary piece threatens to bear *too* great an emotional charge, to become a pure unfolded "cry."[6] For Poizat, the aria shifts constantly, every time the performance (lodged in the melismatic vocalises) parts the curtains to peep out from behind the fearful voice-object that inhabits the nonmelismatic passages. I would read the aria rather as oscillating between drama—the angry tirade by the character—and voice-object that comes to the fore *precisely* in the melismatic vocalises, for the melismas, by splitting words ("nimmermehr," "Bande") and separating syllable from syllable, destroy language. So the Queen, by killing language, also kills plot, and herself as a character. She suddenly becomes not a character-presence but an irrational nonbeing, terrifying because the locus of voice is now not a character, not human, and somehow not present. This same uncanny effect, I would claim, can govern moments marked by a singing voice in instrumental (that is, nonvocal, textless) music. This fear— instilled by voice *without* a physically present human character—might well be kept in mind, as it is partly responsible for the penumbra of uneasiness that characterizes works such as Dukas's *Sorcerer's Apprentice* (discussed in Chapter 2) and Mahler's *Todtenfeier* (Chapter 4).

In making his distinctions between vocal levels in opera, Poizat attempts to define different modes appropriate to each. The first level is a rational, text-oriented one, in which the singing voice retreats before literary elements (words, poetry, character, plot). Recitative is, of course, the best representative of this mode. The second is the level of the voice-object; the third consists of moments at which either of the first two are breached by consciousness of the real performer, of witnessing a performance. Opera actually replays these three levels within itself, within a convention that will return (in Chapter 3) as one governing sign for my speculation about music and narration: narrative songs, like Lakmé's, that are "sung within the opera"; narration that is thus also self-consciously a musical performance.

Voice in music can, however, be understood in larger senses—as the source of sonority, as a presence or resonating intelligence.[7] Voice in this sense was proposed in Edward Cone's book *The Composer's Voice*, and Cone's metaphor initiated parts of my own investigation of "voices," as well as my resistance to the centering and hegemonic authorial image of "the Composer." For Cone, the "composer's voice" is an "intelligence in the act of thinking through the musical work."[8] This voice can be distinguished from the distinctive "voice" of a vocal persona in song or opera, who is the character we assume to be speaking or singing (a wandering musician, a girl about to be married, a lover in despair). In song—and much of Cone's work draws on the *Lied* repertory—the "composer's voice" may lodge itself in the piano, and may also seem to be ordering the vocal part in ways that the "vocal persona" cannot discern. Cone's vision of voice is thus one of a virtual author,[9] and he associates voice securely with a creative mind whom we assume to have made the work as a whole. The work created by the "composer's voice" is in Cone's view essentially monologic (in the Bakhtinian sense) and monophonic—not, of course, literally (as a one-line melody), but in that all its utterances are heard as emanating from a single composing subject. Cone's book is effective as an interpretative reanimation of ideas about musical composition, in insisting upon a conception of music as "sung" through time, as originating in an oscillating, sonorous body—both literally in performance, and figuratively, as music issuing from what might be called the composer's throat. Traditional musical analysis, with its orientation toward the notated score, has been relatively unconcerned with music as constituted through (literal or figural) performance. Cone presented an alternative, and one that will resist disconcerting questions. Some of the most disconcerting of these might indeed, come not from traditional musical analysis, with its straightforward formalist orientation, but rather from criticism of language and literature, from which Cone borrowed his "voice" in the first place. Voice, like the idea of presence, has suffered some battering at the hands of poststructuralists, through arguments that attempt to dislocate or disembody speaking subjects, in order to demonstrate how the subject is constituted through language, as a grammatical fiction. Voice, according to these writers, is unduly privileged in a metaphysical tradition that suppresses because it fears the contrary notion of inscription and text. But music's voices—unlike the voices assumed to reside in written texts, or voice as a metaphysical desideratum—cannot be summarily stilled in these terms. As a consequence of the inherently live and performed existence of music, its own voices are stubborn, insisting upon their privilege. They manifest themselves, in my interpretations, as different *kinds* or modes of music that inhabit a single work.[10] They are not uncovered by analyses that assume all music in a given work is stylistically or technically identical, originating from a single source in "the Composer."

One can assert the survival of music's "voices" in this blunt fashion because music (like theater) *is* live: it exists in present time, as physical and sensual force, something beating upon us. The text of music is a performance.[11] Thus music is fundamentally different from the written texts that have for the most part shaped critical theory.[12] (Poetry retains vestiges of live performance, and mediates between the extremes of live and unperformed written texts, as—in very different ways—does film.) So immediate and inescapable is music's assault upon us—as Mann implied in *Der Zauberberg*, it shouts to trap us in time—that we are inclined to assign it a source who speaks it. We tend to ask ourselves, even if only subliminally, where the music comes from.[13] Music is not merely a gaudy interruption of silence, which converges from ambient space. It is not a text writing itself, or historical events "speaking themselves."[14] Music originates from human bodies. Roland Barthes, in proposing music as "carnal stereophony," wrote that music possesses

> figures of the body (the "somathemes") whose texture forms musical *signifying* (hence, no more grammar, no more musical semiology: issuing from professional analysis—identification and arrangement of "themes," "cells," "phrases"—it risks bypassing the body; composition manuals are so many ideological objects, whose meaning is to annul the body.) These figures of the body I do not always manage to name.[15]

Barthes' hearing is sensualized by his perception of what he elsewhere calls the "grain of the voice," which he describes in one passage as "the body in the singing voice, in the writing hand, in the performing limb," that is, something *extra* in music (the grain) conceived as a body vibrating with musical sound—a speaking source—that is not the body of some actual performer.[16] In this he imagines the source of what I call "unsung voices."

To Cone's monologic and controlling "composer's voice," I prefer an aural vision of music animated by multiple, decentered voices localized in several invisible bodies. This vision proposes an interpretation of music shaped by prosopopoeia, the rhetorical figure that grants human presence to nonhuman objects or phenomena, and one that traditionally entails a strongly visual fantasy in which we imagine faces and eyes upon nonhuman forms. By speaking of music's "voices," we reconstrue the trope in an auralized form, in which imagining human faces or bodies means figuring forth sounds from those faces' lips and throats.[17] But whose are the bodies? As Barthes intimated, these bodies are not, of course, the persons of the instrumentalists and singers. The gesticulating performers are the proximate speakers of the music, as the immediate physical source of musical production. These "means of production" were, according to Adorno, what Wagner wanted to hide when he covered the orchestra pit at Bayreuth. Wagner's orchestration, "by transforming the unruly body of instruments into the docile palette of the composer, is at the same time a de-subjectification, since its tendency is to render inaudible whatever might give a clue to the origins of a particular sound."[18] For Adorno, naturally, this massing of orchestration, in which one never hears the solo instrument that points so rudely to the laboring individual, was coincident with the nineteenth century's ambitions to isolate art from the work that makes it.[19] Yet Adorno, by fixing obsessively on Wagner's orchestra, ignores the *singers*—but perhaps with reason, for the singers undo the Marxist shades of his interpretations. Wagner never swerved from operatic composition; he never "hid" the singers—so it is hard to claim that his operas (or any nineteenth-century opera) attempt to evade the spectacle of *vocal* labor. Some critics have claimed that the pleasure of opera resides mainly in gawking—from a safe and comfortable distance—at such patently dangerous work.[20]

But Adorno's claim of "de-subjectification" must be interrogated as well, by distinguishing the subjects who perform (singers or instrumentalists) from the subject or subjects who speak, or more properly, "sing" the musical work. When a late twentieth-century listener hears music, he or she may well dissociate that music from human performers: it could hardly be otherwise in an era of sound reproduction or (we could now add) electronic and computer-synthesized composition, which not only hide performers but replace them entirely. Masking the performers, however, hardly shatters the subject except in the most literal way. Masking or suppressing perception of individual performers serves, in fact, to enhance a sense of the figural subject, and in Wagner's coalesced, invisible orchestra, these figural voices may indeed sound at higher volume than they might in a visibly laboring group. Adorno himself betrayed his allegiance to the subject in his imagery, by referring to the orchestra as the composer's palette (there is still a controlling intelligence who wields the brush). In the absence of a visible orchestra (even in its presence) we do hear a subject or subjects, but not merely *the composer*: rather, we hear *singers* who sing through the bodies of the sopranos, tenors, basses, violins, horns, and all the others. Subjectivity is dispersed, relocated, and made mysterious (transcendental, Wagner might have said)—but it is by no means dissolved.

Because it exists as a living sonority, music is animated by voices, and these voices do not evaporate when music confronts the insights of contemporary literary criticism, or philosophy of language. The failure of an analogy may nonetheless serve a purpose, to nudge music critics toward less impressionistic and more skeptical stances regarding the notions that they borrow from literature. *Narrative* is one of these. My claim that *voice* cannot be suppressed in speculation on music as it can in speculation on literary texts has important consequences for thinking about the links between narrative and music. The claim stems, nonetheless, from a larger ideological conviction that critical thinking about music should consider its divergences from language and written texts, as well as differences between criticism in the two domains. Too often, writing on music and literature, or on musical and literary criticism, posits simple parallels between the two arts or the two critical discourses.

As a critical strategy, any insistence that voice and presence declare themselves in nineteenth-century music will, as we have seen, run athwart debunking moves in poststructuralist thinking, challenges to the "metaphysics of presence" as indulged in nineteenth-century philosophy and literature. Thus insistence on voice may seem mere nostalgia, reversion to old, utopian visions of music, such as that in Schopenhauer's *World as Will and Representation*, in which music was not only the single unstained language expressing the transcendent, but an unassailable sign of living presence. Most of the philosophers writing on musical metaphysics in the nineteenth century claimed that music's meaning was perfect because unmediated by corrupt and civilized verbal language (Rousseau, on the other hand, had lauded song for its inclusion of the human voice, as the highest musical genre).[21] Both Schopenhauer and Nietzsche seized upon Rousseau's first precepts (music as unstained and perfect language) rather than his second (vocal music as superior for acting as a sign of human presence). Despite radical differences in their uses of musical imagery, both treated music as primal, as irresistible, as our world's only pure representation of various transcendent realities. Both also—notoriously—privileged pure instrumental music above texted music, because texted music partook of the domesticating activities of verbal language.[22] In a famous passage in *The Birth of Tragedy*, Nietzsche imagined a *Tristan* without words:

> In giving this example, I must not appeal to those who use the images of what happens on stage, the words and emotions of the acting persons, in order to approach with their help the musical feeling; for these people do not *speak* music as their mother tongue and, in spite of this help, never get beyond the entrance halls of musical perception, without ever being able to as much as touch the inner sanctum . . . I must appeal only to those who, immediately related to music, have in it, as it were, their motherly womb, and are related to things almost exclusively through unconscious musical relations. To these genuine musicians, I direct the question whether they can imagine a human being who would be able to perceive the third act of *Tristan und Isolde*, without any aid of word or image, purely as a tremendous symphonic movement, without expiring in a spasmodic unharnessing of all the wings of the soul?[23]

The words literally prevent the death of the "truly musical" listener by bringing him to ground. This defeats the power of music. Even though Nietzsche borrowed the phrase concerning "speaking music as a mother tongue" from Wagner's "Eine Mitteilung an meine Freunde,"[24] Wagner nonetheless had no part in Nietzsche's larger claim that verbal language *handicapped* music; as a musical philosopher he anticipated Nietzsche's idea, but in inversion. Wagner claimed that verbal language was renewed, made to bear fuller meaning, by meeting music in *Musikdrama*, and that music was compelled to transcend its own absolute formal limits as a sonorous multiplication of language's rhetoric.[25]

Nietzsche's are large claims for music, typically nineteenth-century claims. Music is granted security of meaning, transcendent force, even a prelapsarian virtue. This linguistically pure object, however, must still be described *in words*. Deconstructionist critiques of *language* have fastened upon this privileging of music as symptomatic of a larger phenomenon, of Western thought governed by favor granted to speaking, to physical voice over writing, to immediate presence over distance; a central phase in Derrida's critique of Lévi-Strauss identifies the latter's stubborn (and, for Derrida, almost irrational) insistence upon music's status above literature as a repression or degradation of written forms of language in favor of the alleged living presence in voice and music.[26] Both Derrida and de Man have taken up the musical theories of Rousseau, Schopenhauer, and Nietzsche, alarmed by a central motif in the major philosophical tracts of two centuries: that they plead so warmly for one art-form's transcendent meaning.[27] De Man famously reads Rousseau's *Essay on the Origins of Language* by scrutinizing the passages on music; precisely because the claims for meaning are most grandiose in these passages, we should expect there the text's most intense work of undoing and its most central paradox.[28] While a broad interpretation of music's treatment at criticism's hands has yet to be undertaken,[29] the point is worth exploring, in order to underscore the broader issues: the complications of any conspiracy between music critics and writers on literature, and what it means to write about music.

We might consider as a brief example de Man's argument concerning the "negation of the substantiality of meaning in Rousseau." This claim is based on a reading of Rousseau's discussion of the nature of the musical sign. He points out that Rousseau distinguishes *son* (a momentary sonority) from the visual sign by suggesting that *son* is "empty." Sonority can bear no meaning, because any given instantaneous sonority (for instance, a chord in A major) could be confused with its repetition (another chord in A major), and the musical sign is therefore "never identical with itself or with prospective repetitions of itself"; as Rousseau puts it, "colors remain but sonority fades away, and we cannot be sure that the sounds that are reborn are the same as the sounds that vanish."[30] From Rousseau's characterization of the "empty" musical sign, de Man concludes that Rousseau (covertly) describes music as a "pure system of relations that at no point depends on the substantive assertions of presence, be it as sensation or consciousness. Music is a mere play of relationships . . . music becomes a mere structure because it is hollow at the core, because it means the negation of all presence. It follows that the musical structure obeys an entirely different principle from that of structures resting on a full sign."[31] Because Rousseau goes on to make the analogy between language and music, both being a "diachronic system of relationships, the successive sequence of a narrative," the emptiness of music speaks secretly for the emptiness of language. Thus when Rousseau claims music (in its form as song) as the great (and perhaps ultimate) sign of human presence, when he writes "sitot que des signes vocaux frappent votre oreille, ils vous annoncent que vous n'etes pas seul"[32]—this is no assurance, but a gesture that suggests Rousseau's self-blindness to what de Man admires as his bleak (if heroic) insight into the impossibility of signification.

What lies behind de Man's vision of Rousseauian music theory? Ideas of music as mere structure resonate less from Rousseau than from the musical aesthetics of nineteenth-century formalists such as Hanslick, whose absolutist conception of music as "sounding architecture" shapes most twentieth-century education in music appreciation. In our century, this view is the common coin of any cultured Westerner's musical knowledge.[33] Thus while de Man ascribes the description of music as a "play of relationships" to Rousseau, this concept seems to belong more to entrenched and historically limited platitudes about the purely formal or structural substance of music, projected upon the earlier text.

Rousseau makes a critical distinction, of course, between the synchronous moment in music, and its diachronous unfolding. He suggests that the *son* (sonority, and by extension any harmonic simultaneity) is meaningless. But music's peculiarity is that it becomes a sign only through time; when reduced to the single sonority, "la musique a cessé de parler."[34] A succession of empty sonorities becomes a full sign as a diachronous fabric of melody and its accompaniment; the musical sign is always made through time (put another way: *son* is not *sign*). This is also one of the givens of modern musical semiology, that simultaneity becomes a sign, and gains significance when attached to others and precipitated through time.[35] De Man, on the other hand, cannot agree that a series of meaningless moments might become meaningful; for him, music impels itself through time as if fleeing in horror from its own hollowness.[36]

Whatever immediate responses one might make to de Man's reading of Rousseau's musical philosophy—the issues raised here are the merest sketch—his exploitation of *music* marks a point of entry upon a much larger issue. De Man has, of course, replayed in inversion, as a negative to a positive, the identical strategy that he exposes in Rousseau. He can no more prove that meaning escapes than Rousseau (in his analysis) can hold meaning secure and fast. What strikes a critic of music and musical metaphysics is that both writers revert to music at a moment of crisis in the argument, a moment when proof fails and the discussion becomes a performance, and the writer a gesturing magician. Thus de Man is critically dependent on music's *not* being a language, and on the musical work's inability to speak for itself in language, since music possesses a meaning that is notoriously indefinable. In a merely linguistic universe—inhabited by writers, philosophers, critics—music is paradoxically mute, and we undertake to speak for it, to assign it meaning or the lack thereof. Music, for Rousseau, for de Man, for all writers about music, is again dealt with prosopopoeiacally, now by being made a ventriloquist's dummy, who can be made to speak any interpretation. And who would think of arguing with that terrible painted doll who sits on the magician's lap?[37]

Insisting upon the voices in a musical work may be, then, an insistence that music is radically unlike language, that the *trope* of music as a language needs to be resisted. Music may thus escape philosophical critiques of language, perhaps even escape language entirely: are verbal descriptions of music at all adequate as evocations of music, which most would prefer to adulate as an experience purified of all language? The music critic must come to terms with the fact that his or her constitution of music through words, like all verbally couched forms of explanation, has largely to do with literary and institutional traditions, with recurring tropes in writing about music, and not merely with the musical work itself.[38] Yet our experience of musical works is, of course, conditioned by verbal codes, by literary explanations, so that any attempt to separate writing about music from *music itself* is futile, because interpretive writing on a given work becomes in some sense *part* of that work as it travels through history.[39]

Music critics thus sustain a precarious balance. Music analysis, criticism, and interpretation are hindered by an assumption that its goal is the invention of words to trace some immanent feature of the musical work. But unless we ourselves are to be struck mute, we continue to talk about music, and our talk shapes our musical perceptions. Ideally, this balancing act should force us into greater self-consciousness about paradoxes inherent in arguments that liken music to language, and greater skepticism toward borrowing from literary theory to explain music. In the end, indeed, literary theory may well illuminate, if not the musical work itself, then our own writings about music; it can expose the workings of the analytical metalanguage. My insistance upon *voices* in music, we can now see, is in part a *heuristic* move that proposes a break with certain assumptions of music analysis and literary criticism as it touches upon music, and proposes that we cannot accept analogies between music and language as easily forged and straightforward. Applying linguistics, semiotics, and literary theory to music criticism, or music criticism (such as Rousseau's) to theories of language and literature, involves far more than smoothing out ragged interdisciplinary edges.

II

My claim throughout this work is that certain gestures experienced in music constitute a narrating *voice*; these gestures were historically established in opera but resonated in nineteenth-century instrumental music. Wagner's operas in particular, which I regard as pushing to their limits the possible complications of musical narration, became one source for narrating gestures of many kinds. More than this, however, Wagnerian narration raised the specter of unreliable, mendacious narrators—both human and musical—and thus called into question what is generally, in the Western tradition, taken as the moral authority of the musical voice. In Wagnerian opera, music can lie. Certain Romantic and fin-de-siècle instrumental works might be conceived as *revoicing* opera's modes of narrative speaking. The instances of instrumental narration that I discuss in Chapters 2 and 4 are, I should stress, not merely cases of vocalism in instrumental music, a phenomenon explored by (among others) Joseph Kerman. Such vocalism is essentially mimicry by instruments of musical patterns typical of vocal genres; this mimicry might take shape as a single line against an accompaniment, as certain melodic patterns or rhythms, or as certain forms (as, for instance, in Mendelssohn's *Lieder ohne Worte*). Joseph Kerman, in his "Voice" chapter in *The Beethoven Quartets*, refers to a "vocal impulse" in Beethoven's late quartets, in which melodies are shaped, as Kerman sees it, in ways reminiscent of the human voice in opera or *Lied*—for instance, with the violin pausing as if to breathe, or with a rhythmic freedom that suggests "declamatory pressures."[40] The *narrating voice*, on the other hand, is not merely an instrumental *imitation of singing*, but rather is marked by multiple disjunctions with the music surrounding it. These disjunctions, their forms and signs, are discussed throughout the following chapters—they change from work to work; they are fugitive. They exist on many levels. I propose that we understand musical narration not as an omnipresent phenomenon, not as sonorous encoding of human events or psychological states, but rather as a rare and peculiar *act*, a unique moment of performing narration within a surrounding music.

In so doing, of course, I align myself with a concern for narration as performance and enunciation, and make a heuristic move away from an earlier phase of structuralist narratology, and consequently away from conventional explanations of musical narrative.[41] Still, by adducing opera as a model, I indulge—overtly—in a form of explanation that *covertly* shapes most writing on musical narrative. Such writing is governed by one classic trope of opera analysis: that musical gestures in opera somehow represent or equal specific actions or psychological states in the accompanying staged drama.[42] Thus, in conventional narrative analyses of instrumental music, musical gestures are deemed dramatic actions or psychological events not in an accompanying stage-pageant but in the composer's scenario, which may be stated forthrightly (as with Berlioz or Mahler) or deemed occult and absent, to be discovered only by the critic (as with Beethoven or Schumann)—in which case the critic's narratively couched explanation of the piece *becomes* the absent text. Such explanations are *programmatic*.

Historically, of course, "program music" has referred not to any single musical genre but to a concept, one whose meaning shifted during the nineteenth century.[43] The eighteenth-century vogue for mimetic works that depicted plastic images, natural scenes (such as the *Pastoral Symphony*) ceded in the course of the nineteenth century to more dynamic models, to drama and plot.[44] Dahlhaus has described the history of nineteenth-century program music (in rather Foucauldian terms) as a series of schisms, first between "poetic" and "prosaic," between metaphysical descriptions of music as "suggesting the infinite," and specific literary plots hooked into specific musical works: Berlioz's program for the *Symphonie fantastique* is perhaps the most famous instance of the latter.[45] For Dahlhaus, Schopenhauer's musical metaphysics polarizes this schism by dismissing any concrete program, as indeed the text of vocal music and the staged action in opera, or the words or images that well up in the listener, or the words that the critic uses to interpret music, as secondary or imperfect impressions left by musical meaning in an imperfect material world. Music can only be corrupted by words; the *words*, whether immanent in the work (as in vocal music or opera), or accidental fantasies of the listener or critic, are once again charged with negative force.[46]

Wagner's post-Schopenhauer writings present a complicated configuration, one that has shaped our contemporary stance toward the problem, and our continued separation of music from the phenomenal world. For Wagner, a divine essence of music is distinguished from the goads to composition (scenic action or words). He seems, that is, to draw upon a hoary platonic distinction between appearance and essence, between empirical facts of his works' genesis and their aesthetic worth once the scaffolding of their actual composition was shed.[47] But things are perhaps not so tidy as this bifurcation might suggest. Wagner's public persona was, so to speak, his Schopenhauerian persona; his private persona, recorded in Cosima's diaries and practical essays such as the "Anwendung der Musik auf das Drama," tends to stick fast to a claim that both words and music are critical to understanding the meaning of his work, that words cannot fall away, and that music is changed by them.[48] Changes in philosophical fashion might cause the literary element of nonabsolute music to be viewed favorably or not; certainly Nietzsche, as we have seen, viewed the words as *grounding* music, as preventing it from becoming unbearable in its Dionysian excesses.[49] Nonetheless, composing instrumental music that claimed to represent literary plots continued to be a common practice until the end of the century.

Nineteenth- and twentieth-century analyses that describe musical works as *narrative* depend for the most part on a basic apprehension of narrative as any sequence of events (whether these are physical deeds, or changing internal emotional states). Music is *narrative*, in other words, because it mimes a drama, an assumption that is stated best and most briefly in Berlioz's lapidary comment on the *Eroica*'s Funeral March: "la marche funèbre est tout un drame."[50] Indeed, narrative accounts of the *Eroica*'s various movements (which are representative of nineteenth-century narrative analysis in general) invariably describe a *plot* or *series of actions*. A. B. Marx insisted upon this in writing that "[the symphony] is not some iconic portrait of a hero, but more, a complete drama of the life he inspired within and around himself. The *first act* represents spiritually the career of the hero, from a quiet, barely noticeable beginning, to his progress through the world."[51] Marx's analysis of the first movement identifies precise musical incidents with the hero's participation in the course of a great battle: the initial statement of the E♭ theme is his *thought* about the possibility of strife, the fortissimo restatement is the hero's decision, his *Heldenwort* determining an attack; the so-called second theme is the distant sound of martial music on the plains; subsequent sixteenth-note figures represent the assemblage of the army and their rattling of swords; the closing theme of the exposition and the final "hammer chords" a renewed call to attack. The remainder of the movement is similarly treated.

Berlioz's *Eroica* drama, typically, operates in terms similar to Marx's. He reads the second movement as a "translation of Virgil's marvelous lines about the convoy of young Pallas" in which the hero's

spoils of war are piled up by his companions, and Pallas's weeping
war-horse follows the train (*Aeneid* Book IX). The end of the movement, Berlioz writes, "is profoundly moving. The march theme recurs, but in the form of fragments broken by silences, with no accompaniment beyond three pizzicato beats in the basses; and when these
shreds of that sorrowful melody have fallen, one by one, back to the
tonic note, alone, naked, broken, and effaced, the wind instruments
cry out: the warriors' final farewell to their companion in arms. The
entire orchestra extinguishes itself on a *pianissimo* organ point."[52]
Though he does not identify many specific correspondences of musical gesture and scenario event, his connection between the march
and the Virgilian tableau presupposes that the music is isomorphous
with the sad activities surrounding Pallas's funeral. In his final para-
graph, this assumption of isomorphism is confirmed by one direct
analogy, as the final wind chord becomes the participants' *outcry* over
the scene they are witnessing. But the isomorphism of this cry is (pre-
sumably) of a different order than any connection between a musical
event and, say, the arrival of the war-horse, for here the music quotes
a sonic phenomenon in the action (the outcry), rather than formulat-
ing a translation of some nonsonorous occurrence (people assem-
bling, experiencing sadness, weapons piled high, the arrival of the
war-horse) into musical terms. In this, the *outcry* is of the same order
as the martial music that Marx imagines as part of his *Eroica* battle.

    Instead of indulging in formalist exasperation—high-handed dis-
missal of such accounts as some inadequate translation of musical
matter into drama—we do well to examine the terms of the transpositions.[53] Marx's critique in particular might fruitfully be disentan-
gled at length, for it raises a great many interpretive questions. How,
for instance, can his plot interpretation deal with repetition of the
exposition, or the altered repetition of recapitulation? Are such passages a slice of the hero's life replayed, as if a biographical film run
twice? (Possible "narrative" interpretation of such repetitions will be
proposed in Chapter 2). We can, nonetheless, begin to grasp the
moves by which both writers make their associations, by reading music as shadowing human events in another medium. Musical gestures
are conceived as *signs* for human actions or psychological states. Most
importantly, both writers generally imagine an uninterrupted inter-
face between events in the musical work heard through time, and
events in the phenomenal object (Pallas's funeral or the heroic battle),
though the music, as Marx indicates, is able "by means of an energetic
summarizing to weave the general [das Allgemeine] into a single
course of events, just as the *Iliad*, of a ten-year war, tells only the span
of a few days."[54] In this remark about the *Iliad*, Marx has drifted

closer to an idea not otherwise suggested by his interpretation—that Beethoven's music represents not a battle enacted, but rather an ex post facto *narration*, a voice telling of a battle long past: the two are of course very different. Thus, the comparison with the *Iliad* is most instructive, resonating as it does with Berlioz's comparison between the *Eroica* and another classic epic. Both play out a schism common in direct analogies between narrative music and literary narrative genres such as epic or novel. Although both Marx and Berlioz essentially read the music as enacting events (as mimesis), they compare it (in different ways) to a literary form—epic—in which a narrating voice retells or recounts events retrospectively, and at a critical distance (diegesis).

This conventional view of musical narrative—as a course of events and emotional convolutions acted out in music—has existed in two chronological phases. The first originates in the nineteenth century, with such programmatic narrative explanations of instrumental music; picaresque or dramatic interpretations of instrumental music were an important fashion in analytical writing of the nineteenth and early twentieth centuries.[55] In Germany, the tradition has continued most notably among critics writing on Mahler, who are all but universally inspired by Adorno's superb essay on Mahler's symphonic writing as *Roman* (novel) in *Mahler: Eine musikalische Physiognomik*.[56] In the Anglo-American sphere there has been a resurgence of interest in musical narrative, newly informed by structuralist models (Propp's plot archetypes, categories of story and discourse) whose conceptualizations have been applied to classic instrumental works.

A specific critique of assumptions, methods, and the results of these strategies is made in Chapter 2, but certain issues might well be signaled at this juncture. Nineteenth-century critics such as Marx and Berlioz, or musical hermeneuticists such as Schering, seldom use the word "narrative," and certainly do not dwell on the meanings that might be ascribed to it; when they invoke a literary concept, they are much more likely to refer to drama. Later writers are sensitized to "narrative" as an abstraction, as an object of extensive theoretical work. Their plotted explanations of music tend nonetheless, like those in the nineteenth century, to seek the drama in music; that is, they understand "narrative" as constituted by a plot, a progression of events in a series. For more modern writers, deciphering the musical "narrative" may thus involve neither funereal horses nor Napoleonic calls to action, but nothing more than speaking of tonal "events" or themes as "characters" in a (purely musical) drama. Indeed, the distinction between nineteenth- and later twentieth-century interpretations centers upon this one analytical point: whether the

critic proposes or avoids pronounced and specific nonmusical imagery. For nineteenth-century writers, music is conceived as vividly
representational of defined human passions and actions. For later
twentieth-century critics, it tends to be seen more calmly as sharing
certain formal or structural characteristics with verbal narrative, or as
expressing some vague, transverbal drama. These later interpretations postulate music's inability to refer concretely to the phenomenal
world—a view tacitly affirmed by the formalist color of the interpretations—yet this inability is nonetheless seen as no obstacle to viewing
music as a drama or a plot.

Much contemporary writing on musical narrative does stress its
own historical continuity with the earlier tradition, and espouses a
hopeful interpretive stance that dreams of recreating a nineteenth-
century listener's musical experience by returning to those metaphors—such as drama or narrative—that recur in both aesthetic
writing and analysis from 1800 onward. Owen Jander, adopting a
"hermeneutic" stance toward Beethoven similar to that taken at the
turn of the century by Kretschmar and Schering, has read two Bee-
thovenian works—the Kreutzer Sonata and the slow movement of the
Fourth Piano Concerto—as dramatic dialogues, arguing that early
nineteenth-century music-critical and theoretical writings affirm a
contemporary assumption that "textless instrumental music [can] 'say'
things." Leo Treitler, summarizing the Romantics' critical metaphor-
field, moves to readings of Mozartean movements as narrative.[57] Anthony Newcomb, proposing in similar fashion a restoration of plot-
explanations for instrumental music, writes:

> The conception of music as the composer's *novel* [emphasis mine], as a
> psychologically true course of ideas, was and is an important avenue to
> understanding of much nineteenth-century music: Beethoven's Fifth
> Symphony, for example, was so understood by at least some listeners
> from the outset. Thus we may find at the basis of some symphonies an
> evolving pattern of mental states, much as the Russian Formalists and
> the structuralists find one of several plot archetypes as the basis of novels
> and tales.[58]

But something like nostalgia colors all three propositions. They are
founded on a wish to recapture the agreeable charm of nineteenth-
century storytelling analyses of music, though they avoid character-
istically nineteenth-century assertions that transpose musical gestures
into concrete images. Instead, Jander's Kreutzer sonata "dialogue" is
music talking to itself about itself while Treitler's analysis of Beethoven's Ninth outlines a "tonal narrative" as an interaction between key
areas likened in turn to human individuals in a drama: "Beethoven's

manipulation of key exploits its character aspects. He composes with key as a dramatist composes with character."[59] In Newcomb's analysis of the Schumann Second Symphony, the events that the symphony enacts are seen as a *combat*—between different last-movement genres, as a *lieto fine* type that interacts with a "weighty, reflective summary" finale form.[60] But hidden away in all three is nostalgia for historical security, the second nostalgia, a belief that reduplicating the story-telling analyses of the nineteenth-century in new (rather more abstract) guises recovers nineteenth-century repertories in a perceptual form close to some historical original; as Treitler writes, "I have tried to sketch an example of the kind of understanding of a work—I would call it historical understanding—that is not likely to be caught by . . . methodologies of formalist analysis."[61] Program music—music interpreted as representation of concrete images, psychological states, or (more abstractly) as an event-series in a drama—is thus recuperated in many twentieth-century narrative interpretations.

The distinction between this modern phase (among both German and English-language writers) and the earlier custom of programmatic analysis does lie in the modern fear of excessively specific analogies between musical events and the drama that music is said to express. This fear is, itself, historically conditioned. Declarations that some musical gesture represents one phase in an ongoing Napoleonic battle have come to seem shameful and shoddy, but claims that the same gesture represents an event-sequence that can be constituted in more abstract terms—described as existing within the paramusical areas of music history, musical form, composer psychobiography—are viewed as far less objectionable. Hence Newcomb's suggestion that a musical work may be viewed as composing-out a debate between opposed musical last-movement designs ("plot archetypes"); similarly Hermann Danuser, writing on Mahler, has proposed that an "inner program" may involve conflict between two ideas about symphonic first-movement form.[62] These moves to a more abstract concept of musical drama originate as one solution to a music-historical and music-critical dilemma. We are all sufficiently intimidated by the formalist aesthetic (which dominated music analysis in the earlier twentieth century) to feel nervous about the specificity of nineteenth-century narrative analysis: above all, those weeping war-horses must be avoided. Yet as Treitler points out, various nineteenth-century writers attached certain values to music—as drama, stream of ideas, emotional flow. Thus if we aspire to historically literate criticism, we may wish to renew nineteenth-century insights. When the piece's drama becomes a conflict between musical forms or tonal "characters," the descriptions are acceptably *musical* yet still define the work in terms of an animated, quasi-literary model, and our dilemma is neatly resolved: happily we toss away our (twentieth-century formalist) cake yet consume it in full, as formalist concerns recur in softened incarnations. Many might nonetheless secretly find Berlioz's weeping war-horse more delicious, more outrageous.

Treitler, Jander, Newcomb, and, to a lesser extent, Danuser (as instances of later twentieth-century views) share certain interpretive swerves with Marx or Berlioz. For one, the question of *distance* or *disparity* between the musical fabric and the phenomenal objects it is said to express (a funeral, a battle, interactions of tonal characters, a conflict between musical forms) is rarely thematized. Nonetheless music is compared (perhaps too loosely) with a literary genre (for Newcomb and Danuser, the novel; for Marx and Berlioz, the epic) characterized *above all* by great discursive distances between a narrator's voice and the actions recounted. Adorno, on the other hand, who called Mahler's music a *Roman*, asked himself a critical question: why the music seems at times to enact, at times to *comment upon* its own enactments.[63] My question about musical narrative is similar to Adorno's: can music in fact possess *narrativity* without the *distance* engendered by discursive formulation? I would claim not, though not solely because I espouse a given position within complex literary-critical debates on what constitutes narrativity. For Genette (among others), the notion of a subject's distancing reformulation, the "voice," is the basic criteria of narrative—as the ordering and reordering discourse of a subject-voice, "a first meaning—the one nowadays most evident and most central usage in common usage—has *narrative* refer to the narrative *statement*, the oral or written discourse that undertakes to tell of an event or series of events."[64] This discourse, with its construction of a detached and ordering subject (and not mere event-series), is the *narrative*. Discursive space might be taken as one necessary mark of narrativity in all temporal genres—drama, film, dance, or music—in which mimesis at first glance seems to predominate. In coping with a genre that plays through time, film theorists typically draw attention to narrative force as residing not in some realistic depiction of the phenomenal world (the profilmic object) but rather in inserts, cuts, montages, camera angles, manipulation of soundtrack—all the things that underline arbitrary juxtaposition, that create a distance between the unscrolling film and the events that it depicts; Kaja Silverman summarized this stance by declaring that "pertinent relationships of film are discursive, not existential."[65] When music is explained as the direct *enactment* of what might be called "promusical objects" (Marx's great battle, for instance, or a drama of tonal conflict), then it is denied discursive latitude, for it is read as *being* events, and not reformulating or recounting them. Any musical-narratological analysis that assumes that the musical work is *isomorphous* with certain events will allow no divergence between these imagined phenomena and their musical analog.

In short, when such narrative descriptions attempt to describe *what* the musical narrative is, they do so in terms of what might be called a *miming model*. This model of explanation lurks beneath many narrative analyses—those discussed above as well as such classic exegetical texts as Wagner's descriptions of his own overtures, or Mahler's programs for his symphonies. The assumptions of the model might be summarized as follows: the composer invents a musical work that acts out or expresses psychological or physical events in a noisy and yet incorporeal sonic *miming*. But in this model, music is (paradoxically) mute, in that it does not *speak* of actions or emotions, does not attain a transposing power over them, and (finally) is nothing *but* the promusical objects that it echoes in sound. Like the heroine in *Und Pippa tanzt*, music dances to plots given to her from elsewhere.

Recognizing the pervasiveness of this miming model is important in that it enables us to underline the paradox in plot-analyses of music: if music mimes without distance—if it is only the composer's silhouetting of a phenomenal object—can the music itself be said to be narrative, or does the narrative quality not instead reside in what is adjunct or outside the music, the thing that the music traces? Extending this idea to its most radical end, we might think of a plastic analogy, that of a bas-relief depicting a murder. Suppose that bas-relief is subsequently covered in gold leaf, which traces its every curve without discrimination or comment. Is the gold leaf itself narrative? Can music—so long as it is understood as *tracing* a dramatic plot, a series of nonmusical actions, or a collection of psychological conditions— ever be narrative in itself? The question admits no definitive answer. But it is disturbing enough for me to believe that conclusions about *what* music expresses are irrelevant to the question of musical narration, for as soon as we decide that music *traces* those events, we make music into gold leaf, incapable of narration. To see how music might narrate, paradoxical as the formulation may seem, we must see how it does *not* enact actions from a nonmusical world, but is instead noncongruent with that world in retelling it. Music makes distinctive sounds when it is speaking (singing) *in a narrative mode*, but we do not know *what* it narrates. Adorno's claim that "music performs itself, has itself as its content" has a familiar formalist ring, but the sentence that he appends to that formulation is provocative in the extreme: *daß Musik . . . ohne Erzähltes erzähle* [that music might *narrate*, without narrative *content*].[66]

III

The most intimidating questions we can propose are those that can be phrased briefly: how does music narrate? Or, what do the voices of music—including musical narration—sound like? There is no simple answer, and the meditations provoked by that question propose throughout this book different and perhaps increasingly complex responses. In general, however, I am seeking to hear the discursive distance that is a sonorous signal for music's voices. Focusing upon the subject, the teller, and the narrative voice, and asserting that narrative always involves a storyteller and a listener, not merely a story, means adopting a specific theoretical stance toward narration. I believe this to be a fruitful position, and that study of the object (the story) stops short, for narrative is not just the structure of the object (whether we call that structure plot, action-sequences, or event-design), but a way of speaking, of manipulating time, of using figural language, of constituting events, and the *context of performance* in which narrating occurs. Exploring musical narration means thinking about voices in broader sense as well, about their marks of identity, and how such voices are projected by music.

I do not in the end see music as *narrative*. Music is easily described as a succession of events, as all of us who read either standard analytical prose, saturated with storytelling gestures ("the E♭ major key area then gives way to its dominant") or accounts of the *Eroica* as Napoleonic battle ("now the cavalry mounts, now it charges") well know. One problem involved in this conventional reading of music as plot—a problem shared by both nineteenth- and twentieth-century phases—is what might be considered its promiscuity: the entirety of any musical work, given this orientation to narrative as event-structure, can be read as narrative—which suggests an impoverishment of the interpretive strategy. The interpretive promiscuity of plot-analysis is disturbing because such analysis might easily be contrived as an industrial machine for interpretation, yet it ends (as argued in Chapter 2) in analogies without apodictic security. We might well shun any method that enables us to reach the conclusion that every piece at every moment is a *narrative*: such a method will not bring delight. But even if we accept the promiscuity, and broaden our conception of narrative to include any organized series of "purely symbolic gestures," the fact that music thus lends itself to description as such a "narrative" *does not actually constitute immanent narrativity*. Analytical prose itself may well be shaped by tropes from narrative prose genres, but dramatic or plot-biased verbal explanations are unsurprising testimonials to an impulse to emplot data that seems human and universal, that shapes historiography, philosophy, critical writing—not merely music criticism. As Jean-Jacques Nattiez puts it, music is the pretext for narrative behaviors on the part of listeners.[67]

In my own interpretations (and my own narrative behavior) I will interpret music as *narrating* only rarely. It is not narrative, but it possesses moments of narration, moments that can be identified by their bizarre and disruptive effect. Such moments seem like voices from elsewhere, speaking (singing) in a fashion we recognize precisely because it is idiosyncratic. Speaking for voice means speaking against certain poststructuralist critiques of language, and may well serve to define the ways in which arguments by analogy from literature or language to music, or from literary criticism to music criticism, are undermined by fundamental differences between music and (literary, written) text. To begin, perhaps we should end with the interpretive parable of Lakmé's performance. Delibes' scene displaces attention from the daughter of the pariahs, the wild animals, the handsome stranger, the rescue, and the transfiguration, to a woman singing to fatal purpose. At the same time, this displacement suggests a parallel removal of our aural concerns from the formal progress of her song (two verses, in which the series of events changes at the end the second time around), to other musical effects. The song, as phenomenal performance, exists separated from the musical fabric surrounding it; its recurring verses, the dead stop between them, the slight tedium of formal repetition itself all mark this aural separation, as does the autonomization of the singing voice in Lakmé's preparatory vocalizations, and her final voice-fragments. This disjunction between the phenomenal song and the opera-body is part of the musical sound made by *distance*. A musical voice sounds unlike the music that constitutes its encircling milieu. Though it does not shadow in any sense the activities of the pariah's daughter, the music of Lakmé's performance (and not her voice alone) may be understood as a narrating voice; it is defined not by *what* it narrates, but rather by its audible flight from the continuum that embeds it. That voice need not remain unheard, despite the fact that it is *unsung*.

Chapter Two

WHAT THE SORCERER SAID

Paul Dukas's symphonic scherzo *L'apprenti sorcier* (*The Sorcerer's Apprentice*, 1893) is an eventful work—so lively, in fact, that it rattles the cage constructed of assumptions about musical narration. I shall argue that *The Sorcerer's Apprentice* allows a single instance of narrating. As a way into an interpretation of that sound, however, we should remember another moment, a strange passage at the midpoint of the piece, at which its entire musical progress comes to a full stop. There is a silence, and the piece begins to regenerate itself, by repeating again and again, far too many times, first a note, then a growing fragment of the melody that is its main theme (Example 2.1). This recurring noise threatens—for a few seconds at least—infinite repetition; biologically chased fantasies of multiplying forms, cells replicating themselves, accrue to the gesture. We need know nothing of what this moment has been held to represent in order to realize that it is grotesque. Even the instruments involved are wrong. In giving a *thematic* line to the contrabassoon and the bass clarinet (that is, to instruments that are defined not as separate or autonomous but as low inflections of normal instruments), there is a false transposition of melody into a nether register—in some sense, an impossible register outside the known limits of bassoon and clarinet timbre. Melody, broken apart, descends as far into the orchestra as it can.

This central moment is a reminder that *The Sorcerer's Apprentice* is disquieting even without the title and what it conveys. We may find the piece more disturbing still when we think of that title. The name links the piece to Goethe's poem *Der Zauberlehrling* and the tale (which goes back to Lucan) of the Apprentice who uses magic to create a broom-servant who turns out to be both unstoppable and, when chopped in half by an ax, infinitely multipliable. (The contrabassoon-bass clarinet passage, of course, represents that resurrection of one broom as two). This broom that rises, doubled, to resume its task is a nightmarish figure that draws on fears of organic repetition and self-replication; observing exact duplication of a pseudo-human, we turn the process on ourselves, and the doubled broom suggests our own unimaginable Doppelgänger. In Lucan's tall tale, Eucrates, lying on his sickbed, tells of his past experiences with the Egyptian magician

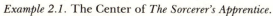

Example 2.1. The Center of *The Sorcerer's Apprentice.*

Pancrates: how Eucrates was able to overhear the trisyllabic word that has the power to animate household goods, how he himself was able to animate a broom and order it to carry water, and how he was rescued in the end by the Magician, who, after restoring order, mysteriously disappears. In Goethe's transposition, the narrative becomes a dramatic monologue, and the Apprentice *says* what happens as he is committing his foolhardy acts. The poem, in other words, transposes Lucan's past tense to become time running its present course. Time in various forms is also played out in Dukas's *The Sorcerer's Apprentice*, and if we start with the conjunction of Goethe's poem and Dukas's music, we find that the events represented by the poem, far from providing an easy explanation of the music, tend instead to underscore their disjunctions. I will, then, take the *literary* Apprentice-drama most seriously (though I will also turn the screw and read the piece as "absolute"), since *disjunction* works to unfold the question of musical narration, and provide one twist that points to the narrating voice. *The Sorcerer's Apprentice* will thus polarize an issue adumbrated (and deferred) in Chapter 1: can music establish a discursive distance, a strong signal constructing the subject's voice, and can it endow that voice with a narrative color (such as that generated in literary narrative, for instance, by the past tense)? As Ricoeur indicated in summarizing a long tradition of speculation on the linguistic signs of narrativity, tense establishes the narrating survivor, the happy man separated from events that he depicts by time (like Eucrates on his bed). Dukas's scherzo ends with this narrating voice, but the end is far from happy.

I

Ever since its premiere, *The Sorcerer's Apprentice* has been understood as enacting mimetically the actions of Goethe's Apprentice. That is to say, single musical passages are understood as *signifiers* for actions in the poetic drama, and the whole unfolding of the work, therefore, as somehow (though that *how* is left ill-defined) isomorphous with the complete action-sequence that Goethe's Apprentice describes. In this, the work is viewed basically as a semiotic encoding of a drama, in much the same way that Marx understood the first movement of the *Eroica*. (Of course, in a sense so fundamental as to be banal, all writing about music works as a semiotic system, in which musical sonority is read as a signifier for various phenomena verbally conceived.) Reading the piece as encoded drama involves the pleasant conceit explored in Chapter 1, that music duplicates the turns in a drama by musical gestures; but espousing the position also tends to imply that the music—as my radical paradox in Chapter 1 would have it—is itself not narrative, since it has been conceptualized as a film over the surface of a phenomenal object (a series of events). For the moment, however, the paradox can be set aside. Understanding *The Sorcerer's Apprentice* as a trace of the Apprentice-drama means that decoding the musical plot will be child's play.

In reading that plot, we can work initially within the limited sense of musical signifiers as what Wagnerians would call *leitmotifs*. Even so, if we read music as a series of *signifiers*, we should develop the capacity to identify different orders of signs and different forms of the relation between signifier and signified. Thus in Richard Strauss's *Tod und Verklärung*, when the gong is understood as representing death's hammer, shattering the protagonist's earthly shell to end his struggle for life,[1] the relationship might be termed iconic (in Peirce's sense), since the musical signifier refers to something sonorous (the sound of the hammer-stroke). The semiotic model that lies behind it is an elementary one: the musical moment is isosonorous with the object (the striking hammer) that it signifies. In Eco's terms, the gong hammer-stroke might be seen as a sign produced by either ostension or quotation, as a piece of aural mimicry.[2] The birdsong in the *Pastoral Symphony*'s third movement; the tolling funeral bells at the end of the Wood Dove's Song in *Gurrelieder*: all are iconic in this sense. Like all of these, the conjunction of the hammer and the gong seems unproblematic. If on the other hand we connect the so-called Transfiguration theme (which recurs throughout the piece) to the protagonist's recurring and frustrating experience of a vision of something ungraspable (so runs the scenario), we make a noniconic association between signifier (a theme) and signified (an event, the protagonist's experience of a vision). Given the many serious debates about the arbitrary nature of the linguistic sign, calling such a relationship "arbitrary" (in Saussure's sense) is a problematic move. I will keep the term, to mean that the conjunction is forcibly established and not "conventional" (it exists only within a single piece). Theme and idea are not like the two *sounds* of gong and hammer; they are not isosonorous. Most Wagnerian leitmotifs are similarly "arbitrary."[3] In conventional narrative readings of program music, the narrative is seen as a string of such signs, whether iconic (depending upon a greater or lesser degree of isosonority) or arbitrary (a given theme or musical event merely associated with a given image.) Such analyses in effect map literary moments onto musical moments, and depend upon the

making of analogy—that this musical moment resembles (by whatever means) this literary moment. We soon learn to put this kind of
understanding aside, as a game inherited from the nineteenth century and now turned trite and unprofitable.

Yet as unprofitable as such arguments might seem, they are replicated in much writing on narrative in music, which argues in essentially the same terms, forging equivalences between elements in an
event-series or psychological plot, and specific musical procedures.
One might, of course, even claim—using the same analogical
swerves—that the classic givens of traditional structuralist narratological writing (*histoire* and *récit*, actants, plot paradigms, cardinal functions and indices) have musical equivalents. In such associations, the
marriage becomes an analogy lying between the natural and the arbitrary, and what is gained by the ceremony—beyond new terminology for familiar musical procedures, or an institutional salute to the
interdisciplinary—is a critical reading whose pleasures are uncertain,
and whose simplicity is not unequivocally a virtue. Dukas's *Sorcerer*
will, however, tend to confuse straight equivalences, for despite its
apparent lack of artifice it is laboratorical, a place for experiments in
interpreting musical narration. Perceived as naive, it has become a
work of children's music, one consumed properly only by those under the age of twelve; when Jean-Jacques Nattiez carried out his psychological investigations of music's capacity to elicit narrative associations, he chose the *Sorcerer* as his text, and the population of the
Montreal elementary schools as his subjects.[4] This identification of
the work as the possession of children has, of course, determined
its popular success and its exclusion from the musical canon (which
accords status only to works by the German-speaking dead), and en-
sured that it has remained marginal in serious interpretive writing on
music. Its staging as a cartoon drama in *Fantasia* served, in America
at least, to relegate it to an ash-heap of low culture. Trivialization and
exclusion, however, may also reflect a fear of what the work suggests.
On one hand, the apparent ease with which the music can be read as
tracing a waterlogged drama may evoke generally the banality of
reading music in verbal terms. On the other, the disjunctions between
the music and that phenomenal drama can become the shadow of the
great disjunction between music and its (verbal) interpretation, which
is the shadow lying upon all linguistically couched discussion of music
(including, of course, my own). When the contrabassoon theme, in
the passage cited previously, *creates itself* (the emphasis and phrasing
are deliberate), the *Sorcerer* makes a fearful sound—but wondering
why we are made uneasy means, so to speak, asking what (at that moment) the *Sorcerer* says.

II

Initially, *The Sorcerer's Apprentice* may provide Dukasian insights into musical narrative in other works (by Debussy, or Beethoven), or may suggest the perils of the assumptions that music is narrative; it suggests, in any case, adopting without fanfare a number of pedigreed approaches to analysis of narrative. Dukas's scherzo, by means of its title, appeals overtly to its literary source. For the moment, then, we can begin as most nineteenth- and twentieth-century listeners do, by taking the drama housed in the poem as immanent (though later the piece, as indicated, will be read as if it were absolute.) Read leitmotivically *The Sorcerer's Apprentice* seems almost to decode itself.

Let us start in the middle. In stanza 6 of Goethe's ballad is a moment of forgetting. The Apprentice, having brought the broom to life with a spell ("que pour l'oeuvre l'eau bouillonne," etc.), has forgotten the word to reverse the spell: "Malheur! j'ai oublié le mot!" Without the word, he cannot make the broom inanimate, as it once was ("le mot en part de qui le rendra en fin ce qu'il était tout à l'heure"). He murders the broom with an ax ("voyez, il est en deux"). What happens next is the nightmare: both pieces rise up undeterred, and resume repetition of their task. The Apprentice is rescued in the end by the Sorcerer.

How does the music of *The Sorcerer's Apprentice* transpose into sound a moment of forgetfulness? The Apprentice's spell has from the time of the piece's premiere been identified with an idea at the end of the slow introduction, a brass fanfare of augmented chords. The chords, in being augmented, are chromatically inflected from the diatonic triad into an abnormal or ornamental form, so that the effect is one of an ordinary brass fanfare gone awry. Georges Favre referred to the chords as "musical idea, of a more ancillary nature—a kind of annunciation that is energetically rhythmicized, supported by chromatic harmony . . . called the *motif d'évocation*"[5] (Example 2.2). Favre seems to have invented the label "incantation motif," as Wolzogen did his labels for the Wagnerian leitmotifs, and in so doing postulated the augmented chords as the sign for, or the representation of, the chanting voice of the unfortunate Apprentice. The *motif d'évocation* is followed by the *creatio ex nihilo* birth of the famous bassoon theme, a representation of the broom, given animation, stepping with eerie order to its task. The augmented-chord fanfare returns at the end of the piece, followed there by *nihilo ex nihilo*: no bassoon, no theme, silence.

Any statement that the augmented-chord fanfare *represents* the incantation reflects, of course, a fundamentally leitmotivic approach:

Example 2.2. The Sorcerer's Apprentice: The *motif d'évocation*.

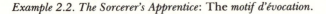

the musical element is the signifier for a dramatic idea or object. The dramatic idea is at once the words of the *évocation* ("Que pour l'oeuvre," etc.), and the word itself, *évocation*, incantation; thus the musical signifier is both quasi-iconic (musical sound as the sound of a speaking voice) and arbitrary (a theme for a word). Wagner (and his operas) played the determining role in shaping this deep-rooted assumption about how music traces events, for interpretations of Wagner's narratives have focused almost without exception on leitmotifs and their representation of the story being narrated, how a chain of symbolic motives evoke nodal points in a tale.[6] Rheingold, Ring, Giants, Valhalla, Nibelheim, Curse, and Erda, will suffice to conjure the essence of the *Rheingold* plot. This assumption is grounded in a common experience of reading literary texts: how we tend to create transitions as seams between deeds and times about which the narrator is silent. Thus the reader can generate a story from a chain of critical words, as in Humbert Humbert's miniscule story (told in the opening pages of *Lolita*) of how his pretty mother perished: "(picnic, lightning)." As the reader imagines connections and details, so the listener, knowing the associations of the motifs, might weave the links between them (Alberich steals the gold and forges a ring, the giants demand payment for Valhalla, Wotan and Loge go to Nibelheim and steal the ring, Alberich curses the ring, and Erda warns against the curse). Given any situation in which narrative is *expected*, the impulse to construct tales from a sequence of single objects is human and irresistible. It is this impulse that is both celebrated and mocked in Calvino's *The Castle of Crossed Destinies*, in which the narrator must forge mental stories to fit Tarot sequences laid by his companions. These companions (like the narrator himself) have been mysteriously struck mute; they grope for the isolated images depicted on each card, arrange those cards in lines, and in this dumb-show of narration ease "the torment of not being able to exchange the many experiences each of us had to communicate."[7]

Leitmotivic obsessions have in fact controlled interpretation of

Wagner's narratives in certain precise ways, and their role in the reception of those narratives is touched upon in Chapter 5. For the moment, however, we should stress that if leitmotivic interpretation has proven reductive, it has also, historically, been a central force in reading narrative music: Favre's leitmotivic analysis of Dukas, done so casually as to imply complete security in the method, documents how the leitmotif's hegemony extends well into the twentieth century.

But Favre's conjunction is *wrong*—or, put less brutally, his reading can be called into question by the very terms and assumptions that allow it to be made at all. In *The Sorcerer's Apprentice*, the *motif d'évocation* also recurs in the center of the piece. In the center, it precedes an important moment in the music, the rebirth and multiplication of the bassoon theme in the contrabassoon (shown in Example 2.1). Reading the work as a trace of Goethe's drama, this is (of course) the murder of the broom and its resurrection as two—two bassoon themes, played in canon. But here the assumed relationship between musical symbol and dramatic idea has broken down. Goethe's Apprentice cries of the magic word forgotten; the word is simply *not there*. If the *motif d'évocation* indeed represents the word, then Dukas has added his own musically constituted turn to the plot. Repetition of the *motif d'evocation* again and again in upward transposition is a repetition of human cries, as the Apprentice experiments with one futile spell after another before resorting to the ax.

But could we not rescue Favre's sign by arguing that the musical gesture has, in the midst of the piece, been liberated from the object in the phenomenal world (the human voice chanting a spell), and now floats without the anchor of a fixed referential meaning? Music has thus been freed for a moment from what the nineteenth-century metaphysicians would consider the accidental or corrupting association with the word. The brass fanfare, then, recurs in the middle of the piece for some other reason—some reason not having to do with Goethe's story, some wholly musical reason.[8] This interpretive escape route has become a typical strategy in Wagnerian analysis; indeed, in most analysis of texted music. The blame for contradiction (fanfare, you have appeared where there is no *évocation*) is put off on the sign. And the sign is punished. When a motif's appearance seems contradictory in terms of its symbolic force, it will be stripped of its symbolic meaning. Its recurrence is written off to the exigencies of purely musical logic.

We can, in fact, forgive the fanfare and recuperate the semiotic decoding of the work by listening more closely to the score. The word—the magic instant at which language changes the world—has not been ignored, nor has it been forgotten by the music. The symbol for forgetting is absence. Something so small and ordinary as a word is lacking in the central episode developing the augmented-chord fanfare. If we look again at the *motif d'évocation* passages at the beginning and end of *The Sorcerer's Apprentice*, we see that the exotic augmented-chord fanfare ends bluntly, in the manner of recitative, with a single, rather banal chord. This monosyllabic expletive also concludes the sorcerer's incantation at the end (Example 2.3). But the chord is missing from the middle statement. The chord, not the exotic fanfare, represents the magic word. The sign is lodged elsewhere, and the semiotic reading can be restored.[9]

III

Simple leitmotivic or semiotic readings of music usually deserve the scorn accorded them. That powerful spells might be depicted not by musical exotica but by something ordinary—a C seventh chord—is a notion that appeals to my taste for understatement. But appreciation of a fetching inversion should not blind us to the limitations of the argument by arbitrary association. Any leitmotif has more than just the two terms (musical and literary), and involves more than a simple association between musical gesture and poetic idea. This is a truism, but it needs to be stressed. The sign includes both the *sound* of the Apprentice's outcry and the word "incantation," itself signifying an idea embracing a web of potential connotations. In the same way, the musical idea refers not only to incantation, but to other musical ideas and topoi; its field of associations includes music itself.[10]

Here, we can turn to a second reading of *The Sorcerer's Apprentice* by stripping the piece of its title and hence its immanent text, and seeing it as the scherzo, as music without the extraneous literary baggage. Now, we might say, it is as absolute as a Mozart string quartet; it is no longer a prosaic work,[11] which purports to represent a concrete drama. It ceases to deal in brooms and buckets. We might see the work in Wagnerian terms as the working out of some poetic inner essence. Or, we might see it once more as dramatic—but now, as it were, as abstractly dramatic, as a plot proceeding in ways analogous to the unfolding of plot in literary dramas.

Once we begin to search for associations, we find that certain categories of structuralist analysis of narrative lend themselves easily to translation into musical terms. This ease—which is itself suspicious—is in fact a consequence of intertwined disciplinary histories; as Harold Powers has pointed out, literary structuralism in many of its phases originated as an application, to literature, of nineteenth- and

Example 2.3(a). After the first *motif d'évocation.*

Example 2.3(b). After the final *motif d'évocation.*

early twentieth-century commonplaces of *music* analysis. Thus, for instance, Lévi-Strauss derived his description of a repeated deep structure in the Theban myth-cycle directly from the visual model of the
synchronously layered musical score, but indirectly and generally
from his hypostatization of musical *structure* as a source of ultimate
beauty in all texts.[12] That Lévi-Strauss could not actually read musical
score, and that the analogy with the score is skewed (as Powers points
out) hardly reduces to insignificance his act of translation. So many
givens of classic structuralist narratology—deep or paradigmatic plot-
sequences exemplified in individual texts, the story twisted by its discursive telling—might well be translations of hallowed truisms concerning music. Traditional nineteenth-century *Formenlehre*—such as
that promulgated by A. B. Marx—analyzes individual works as re-
compositions of paradigmatic formal types (sonata, rondo, and so
forth). Schenkerian analysis—for many years the dominant mode of
technical musical analysis in England and America—provides another obvious example. The Schenker who layered the musical text
into foreground, middleground, and background, and who privileged the *Urlinie* of the background as a basic structure common to
all canonically pedigreed music, is a perfect Proppian *avant Propp*,
whose ancestry includes Hanslick's aesthetics of music as pure structure. The application of structuralist categories to music thus involves
a tautology, for if certain structuralist concepts emerged historically

from contemporary thinking on music, then rediscovering the relevance of structuralist theory to interpreting music merely closes a hermeneutic circle. Breaking out of the circle demands an exploration of its boundaries, and of how the strategy of analogy, instead of generating comfortably interchangeable objects on both sides of the language-music fence, underscores the dissimilarity of the two discourses.

Barthes' classic "Introduction to the Structural Analysis of Narrative," which synthesized and summarized an entire tradition of structuralist analysis, plays for instance upon a distinction between the "functions" of narrative—events that, enchained into a series, provide the basic unfolding of plot—and "indices," information concerning "the characters, data regarding their identity, notations of 'atmosphere,' and so on."[13] Barthes himself points out that the two exist in a hierarchical relationship (critical-ancillary, structural-ornamental) that privileges the first term. The two terms might be identified by other familiar oppositions: diachronous versus synchronous, syntagmatic versus paradigmatic, metonymic versus metaphoric. The "functions" are further ordered into a subhierarchy of "cardinal functions," which are the important turning points of plot, and "catalyzers" determining the ancillary spaces. Cardinal functions, catalyzers, indices: these ancestors of the "codes of reading" in *S/Z* are described here in stern, mock-scientific terms; in the later book, they will be constituted in language whose calorific value is somewhat higher.

How might such categories be applied to musical material? In the opening of *The Sorcerer's Apprentice* (Example 2.2), the augmented brass-chords are an atonal fanfare, exhortations to listen; the fanfare is repeated in sequence, tonal and gestural motion toward the event announced. The blunt C seventh chord—the "recitative chord"—alludes to opera, to the phatic dithering that precedes the *real* beginning, the *real* event, the number. The recitative chord is a dominant, the annunciation of an F minor tonic that has been adumbrated throughout the slow introduction. Listen: something is introduced and will now begin. What begins is the *creatio ex nihilo* of the bassoon theme. The hortatory insistence of all this suggests some "cardinal function," some unscrolled sequence that debouches in a distinct event, the bassoon solo as Main Theme of the work now in progress, and the statement of that theme in full form. In this description, the sequence is again a string of musical items, now read as executions of gestures codified by musical convention, and enclosed within a musical web. They are not arbitrarily associated with events in the Apprentice's career. But they *are* linked to verbal categories, nonetheless.

Identification of the bassoon solo as a "cardinal function" (because its musical function—something prepared by tension that operates as an obvious *beginning*—seems to coincide with Barthes' description of how cardinal functions act in literature) is of course just as "arbitrary" as identification of the brass fanfare as the Apprentice's incantatory speech. In both cases, an analogy is proposed between musical substance and a literary or linguistic concept, but one is made on the basis of an Apprentice-drama, and the other on the basis of a perceived similarity between my *verbal description* of the musical gesture on one hand, and Barthes' *verbal description* of a feature that he distinguishes as common to all narrative texts on the other. The latter case has the (seeming) advantage of bypassing silly stories about brooms and buckets, and applying itself to stern-sounding elements like *structures* or *gestures* or *functions*.

We can, of course, also locate musical versions of Barthes' synchronous and metaphoric moments—that is, the "indices" that lie on the paradigmatic axis of reading—within the music. The small units—the augmented-chord fanfare, the C seventh chord—cast above themselves paradigmatic connections to similar sonorous formulas, to all fanfares, or to opera. But so do larger sequences, creating what could plausibly be considered a musical version of intertextuality, as certain sequences refer back to specific works. A sequence composed of hortatory fanfare, blunt recitative chord, and woodwind solo cites another work whose opening events are similar (listen: annunciation of a beginning—the inanimate is animated)—the opening of Saint-Saens' *Danse macabre* (Example 2.4). An irreversible syntagmatic progress through time (the three musical gestures) brings with it potentially infinite implications, references, associations, which hover paradigmatically and timelessly above each gesture and above the sequence as a whole.

This reading could be reread by draping over it terms borrowed from any number of classic structuralist narrative tracts. But one essay, perhaps, stands out for its own reversion to a musical analogy in order to convince us of its argument and to describe most vividly the concepts purveyed: *S/Z* itself. Whatever alliterative noises may ricochet between the letters of Barthes' title, Balzac's story, the German and French titles of Dukas's work, and its generic name, these are (if delightful) merely coincidental. In *S/Z*, Barthes perceived the musical score as a symbol for his experience of narrative in two dimensions—syntactically through time, and paradigmatically in sensing at every moment resonances and associations that could flash forward or backward, out of time, out of the story (Example 2.5). This icon can be teased apart to become, in the end, another instance of ventriloquism, of

Example 2.4. Saint-Saens, *Danse macabre* (beginning).

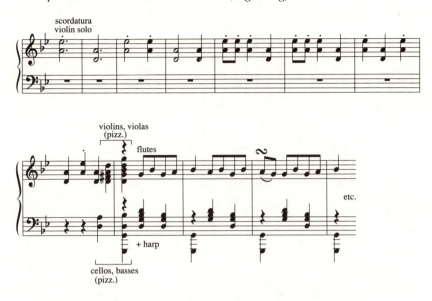

music made to speak in order to prove the truth of theory, as the opening paragraphs of *Sarrasine* are translated, through the agency of Barthes' five famous narrative "codes," into musical terms.

Dukas's triple sequence (fanfare, recitative chord, *creatio ex nihilo* of a bassoon theme)—if a function—is irreversible in time; in Barthes' terms, such sequences are governed by the proairetic code, the code of action, how events are enchained, how they begin and end. (We might say, for instance, that some musical proairetic code dictates that ascending transpositions in sequence end in stasis, in a goal.)

In Barthes' score, there are two action-sequences begun at the story's opening (the protagonist's being "deep in thought" and being "hidden behind a curtain"). They are irreversible. Each initial action brings with it a chain of gestures that end in closure (in the action of hiding oneself, one hides, one pulls the curtain shut, and one later emerges from the lair: this ends the action of hiding). An initial question later answered ("Enigma I") belongs to the hermeneutic code, equally irreversible, as a riddle is posed, false answers suggested, solutions blocked, suspense engendered, an answer given at last (the tonal choreography of a piece might be compared to the hermeneutic code: the answer comes when the tonic arrives). Both codes move in one direction only. In Barthes' score they are visualized as white notes, *cantus firmus*. They are described as embodying musical continuousness and irreversibility, and as instrumental personalities:

44

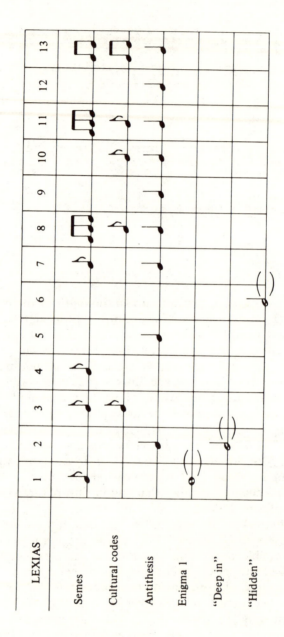

What sings, what flows smoothly, what moves by accidentals, arabesques, and controlled ritardandos through an intelligible progression (like the melody often given to the woodwinds) is the series of enigmas, their suspended disclosure, their delayed resolution . . . what sustains, what flows in a regular way, brings everything together, like the strings, are the proairetic sequences, the series of actions, the cadence of familiar gestures.[14]

The instantaneous flashes sent upward from each of Dukas's three musical gestures, the associations—like the reference to *Danse macabre*, or the connection between the blunt chord and operatic recitative—correspond, by continuing the analogy, to Barthes' semiotic and cultural codes: signs, references to history and its actors. One of the signs in *Sarrasine*'s opening pages is a recurring reference to pale trees, white ground, silver moon: color as a culturally defined sign for winter, for cold. The three paradigmatic codes (semiotic, symbolic, cultural) in Barthes' symbolic score are visualized as upward flashes above the whole- and half-note pedal points, and are described as individual instants, unconnected, not bound to the unfolding time of the story:

What stands out, what flashes forth, what emphasizes and impresses are the semes, the cultural citations and the symbols, analogous in their heavy timbre, in the value of their discontinuity, to the brass or percussion.[15]

Barthes, in short, likened the proairetic code to long pedal points and typically continuous instrumental timbres, and the paradigmatic codes to instantaneous sixteenth- or eighth-notes, flashes in the percussion or brass. My reading makes very different analogies, of course: the musical proairetic code determines the enchaining of musical events over time; the discontinuous semiotic and cultural codes are not blasts from the percussion, but something more directly analogous to their literary parallels—actual musical-historical references, citations, and symbolic conventions.

My musical analogies for Barthes' codes are, in fact, neither more nor less plausible than Barthes' own (although his, certainly, have greater verbal allure). What both sets of analogies have in common is a concealed statement about the nature of music and narrative within the structuralist world. Any music with sequences of events—thematic ideas, harmonic processes, cadences, instrumental exchanges—in short, the substance of all common-practice Western music, can be said to be narrative. A model borrowed from classic literary structuralism brings us to an interpretive promiscuity that allows musical narrative to be so broadly defined that all music is narrative, and to the proposition that it is narrative *without narrating*, and without moral or human force. Referring to Examples 2.4 and 2.5 as augmented-chord fanfare, C seventh chord, to be followed by the bassoon theme, means a reversion to (putatively) neutral terms to describe music, and with them we strike what Leonard Meyer would call an "absolutist" stance, even as we evoke language and literature to impose sense upon the musical material.

If our little structuralist analysis has demonstrated that, as an extreme case, a formalist/absolutist could analyze all music as narrative, yet still view music as void of specific expressive, cultural, or moral content, then this hints that evocation of literary structuralism is *sterile*, in the sense that it merely gives us descriptions of one set of structures that can be imperfectly transposed to match descriptions of another set of structures. What does it tell us if we speak of music with narrative metaphors (a modulation as a "departure," a harmonic period as an "action-sequence"), or catch at the skirts of literary criticism only to give us new names ("cardinal functions" and "indices," or "proairetic" and "symbolic codes")? Perhaps only, as Jean-Jacques Nattiez has intimated, that music analysis is itself born of a narrative impulse, that we create fictions about music to explain where no other form of explanation is possible, and may look to literary categories to endorse them. Nattiez makes the obvious point that music analysis and criticism tend to tell the story of a piece, as well as the less obvious one that such writing itself tends to be guided by interpretive plots (*intrigues*, in Paul Veyne's sense).[16] Berlioz's or Marx's musical analyses, as musical accounts cast as miniature Romantic dramas, are only more overtly dramatic than more technical analytical writing.[17] And these overtly dramatic forms of musical criticism, with their anthropomorphisms (themes become characters) or their picaresque trajectories, breathe human plots onto music in their retellings of pieces. Perhaps the idea of a dramatic plot is so central to human cognition, to our rationalization of experience, that we cannot resist pursuing the analogy of plot and music, even when it results in generalities, in mechanistic explanations.

Certain open questions, then, reemerge from the application of structuralist narrative theory to music. A heuristic strategy that enables us to read all musical discourse as narrative is clearly a tautological one: is there no nonnarrative music, as there are nonnarrative text genres? The juxtaposition of Barthes' musical definitions for his narrative codes with my very different definitions exposes the precariousness of the argument by analogy: my declaration that tonality is the musical "hermeneutic code" is logically no more secure than his preference for those gentle, continuous, and flowing woodwinds in that particular role.

IV

Reading musical pieces as structures made up of events that evoke generalized types—or of cardinal functions topped by indices, or proairetic sequences casting up occasional symbolic codes (as I have just done)—may have its uses, but it is important to realize that it does *not* actually identify what is *narrative* in such pieces. Many text types other than narratives are constituted of sequences that exemplify a deep structure or a paradigm (a grammatical sentence is one obvious example, a rhetorical speech another). Many inspire readerly reminiscences that pull memories of comparable gestures and texts into one's consciousness.[18] Arguing that *David Copperfield* transforms devices associated with genres such as memoir or autobiography does not identify what makes it (or a given memoir or autobiography) narrative. If we tease out this statement, we can identify the point at which critics such as Anthony Newcomb (who have reopened the question of musical narrative with all its fascinations) shift not unfruitfully from narrative to questions of genre and to a theory of reading/listening. Newcomb has assumed that if a piece or part of it exemplifies a type, and provokes a certain strategy of reading/listening, it is therefore marked as "narrative." In postulating "narrative strategies" in music, for instance, Newcomb adduces these two factors as signs that a Schumann string quartet has abstract narrativity (abstract because music can thus be regarded as narrative without reference to a specific phenomenal event-series—battle, human emotional trajectory, or the like). He suggests that listening to a work such as a Schumann string quartet, which operates by subverting expectations about formal gestures, is akin to what many literary critics identify as a common process in reading: how the reader shifts constantly between "the actions, incidents, or events that he perceives as he reckons with passing time and, on the other hand, a fund of patterns or configurations into which these events could fit."[19] Newcomb recapitulates in slightly different terms what Jakobson had earlier described as music's tendency (as an "abstract language") to inspire introversive semiosis; that is, to cause listeners to compare what they are hearing to a collection of possible musical syntaxes or types. For Jakobson, as well as countless musical semiologists, music always incites connections to other musical units that have already been heard or that are to come later.[20] While such formulations indeed seem sensible as descriptions of reading (or listening), they are not demonstrations of

music's narrativity, since (as Jakobson points out) nonnarrative genres (abstract painting or lyric poetry, for instance) are also written
and read the same way. So is a great deal of music that is not usually
qualified as "narrative." One instance of the latter is the music of Verdi's operatic ensembles, which are often interpreted in terms of how
the music tropes formal and gestural conventions of earlier Italian
opera. Such ensembles, many Verdians would argue, are best read
(heard) and understood by a listener who wavers between the ensemble and the fund of conventions that it manipulates.[21]

I depart from a more peculiar and limited point: a claim that the
signs of narrative in music include not merely an event-sequence and
a way of reading, but rather a voice with a characteristic way of speaking. Given these terms, most musical works will seem suddenly to
elude definition as narrative, and *narrative music* becomes not common coin, but a rare and potentially disruptive mode.

One approach to music's narrative mode involves, of course, invoking the familiar opposition between story and discourse (where story
essentially refers to the played-out events described by discourse),
since narrative is one special form of a discursive enunciation. Genette (among others) wrote of *histoire* and *récit*; Chatman popularized
"story" and "discourse" as English terms. While there is disagreement
about boundaries and definitions, while the opposition itself has been
cogently challenged, it has seemed a reasonable apparatus for reading.[22] More recent disquisitions on narrative have tended to undermine this dualistic model, which has in various forms nonetheless
shaped interpretation of narrative since its coinage by the Russian
Formalists.[23] In terms far more general than most *narratological* writing would allow, discourse can be taken to be the work of an ordering
intelligence—the narrator who assembles the characters and the
scenes of a play, who selects and orders events, or the critic analyzing
a text, who retells the object before him.[24] "Story" is, in the same general terms, the projection we make, from the discourse, of some a
priori and untwisted object (the whole lives of characters, of which a
novel gives us only excerpts; *Tristan und Isolde*, of which Lorenz gives
us a most idiosyncratic glimpse).

Couched in these terms, "story" is seen for what it is: a reader's or
writer's assumption, a construction spun out of discourse. This is a
subtle softening or reformulation of what Barbara Herrnstein Smith
called the "naive Platonistic dualism" that has marked dogged appli-
cations of the concept.[25] Described in this way, "story" and "discourse" are in no way sufficient as signs of *narrativity*, but simply express a more diffuse notion of arranging or interpreting objects that

may (the score of *Tristan und Isolde*, Napoleon's victory at Marengo) or may not (Emma Bovary's life) really exist. So long as the definition of "story" and "discourse" remains so general as to include almost all forms of writing or speaking, plausible musical analogies suggest themselves. Leo Treitler has read certain sections of Mozartean instrumental movements as "discourse" recounting a "story," for instance, by describing the later and varied recurrences of the G minor symphony's main theme as an "indirect presentation" (hence, equivalent to a discursive retelling) of the theme as it is heard in the opening measures.[26] Musical phenomenology has long pursued a different "story-discourse" model, though without citing the literary-theoretical concept. Jonathan Kramer's analysis of Beethoven's Opus 135 identifies the first measures as gesturally *in medias res*, as an ending that precedes the real opening measures.[27] Behind Opus 135, then, lurks an untwisted piece, some prelapsarian or *noumenal* quartet, whose normal order has been recast by Beethoven in making the *phenomenal* quartet that we know and hear. Much Romantic music, indeed, plays upon such confutations of formal gestures, of expectations: Romantic music revels in sly inversions. The first of Mendelssohn's *Venetianische Gondellieder* begins with a final cadence, goes on to an opening verse, and concludes with a reiteration of the initial "final" cadence that affirms internally, within the piece, our original sense of an inverted beginning (Example 2.6). Here, the noumenal piece that shimmers behind the phenomenal piece begins only in measure 7, and the ordering intelligence has reformed it in bringing it into our world. But is such a reformation a discursive narrating of the plot of the elusive, illusory story? Obviously not: there is more to narrating than mere reordering.

A musical work can exemplify a type—this (as we have seen) might also be interpreted as the equivalent of a discursive (that is, "narrative") recounting of a priori events. The piece invokes history by calling upon established conventions or inherited past models. A musical work may unfold in a transgression of the convention or a transformation of the model; this is a familiar and fruitful approach to analysis of nineteenth-century music.[28] Newcomb—in his association between musical form and formal gestures (such as sonata-allegro and typical phrase openings) and Propp's notion of a "paradigmatic plot"—has proposed that we understand the last movement of Schumann's String Quartet Opus 41, No. 3 as the (narrative) discourse, since the movement (which plays with rondo form—the "paradigmatic plot") can be read by measuring *its* events against formal conventions that constitute this "story":

50

Example 2.6. Mendelssohn, *Venetianisches Gondellied.*

As an introduction to the narratological approach, let me begin with a general analogy—that between paradigmatic or conventional narrative successions in literature and history on the one hand, and formal types in music on the other. This analogy makes sense, I believe, for two reasons. First, the two represent similar things, in that both can be thought of as a series of functional events in a prescribed order. Secondly, both are critically or theoretically derived in the same fashion: Seymour Chatman points out that a narrative structure is "a *construct* . . . a construct of features drawn by narratologists from texts generally agreed to be narratives." Musicologists across the ages . . . have proceeded in exactly the same way in order to arrive at theoretical formulations of such musical formal structures as ritornello, sonata, rounded binary, ternary song form, and so on.[29]

But aside from objections that might be made to Chatman's own tautologically tinged proposal—*one* reified narrative structure culled from a data-house of narrative texts—to view musical-formal conventions as a set of illusory past events (a story) and the piece at hand as a specific discursive narration, as it were, of the sonata-story, is perhaps to construe an insight about compositional process and a concept of reading (emphasizing how both composers and listeners tend to use and recognize variations upon generalized operations) as *narrativity*. Thus the essay on Schumann's "narrative strategies"—with its cogent formal analyses—proposes once again a general theory of composition and of hearing: how a work (in creation and perception) will resonate from and with its genre and established patterns of musical composition.

What are the signs of narrativity? Within the dualistic model of story and discourse, one possibility suggests itself. Ricoeur argues that much narrative discourse is set off from other discourse (which also orders and tropes) in part through its ways of manipulating time, of using tense to achieve a kind of moral distance in recasting the referential object. Past tense marks the events it represents by implying that they exist in a time closed off from us. The preterite tenses, in their instantaneous signification of this temporal-moral distance, identify narrating as a way of speaking, one way in which the peculiar and special voice of a narrator is constituted.

What now becomes of an analogy between narrating and music? Music seems not to "have a past tense." Can it express the pastness that all literary narrative accomplishes by use of past or preterite verb tenses—"it was early spring, and the second day of our journey?" To linger over "was" as opposed to "is" seems to exclude music from canons of narrative genres. Can we conceive of some musical phenomenon that has the power of a preterite tense to represent instantaneously the already happened? Put another way: Does music have a *way of speaking* that enables us to hear it constituting or projecting events as past? Or does the concept of narrative music now collapse and lie empty—in strange folds and curves?

In one respect, music's existence as a temporal art precludes its speaking "in the past tense." As Ricoeur indicated, the pastness implicit in "it was" tells us many things at once. It tells us that there is a narrator, someone who lived past the end of the story. But more important is the distance that this elicits. The past tense, as Ricoeur put it, nudges the reader into detachment:

> What is essential to the narrated world is foreign to the immediate or directly preoccupying surroundings of the speaker. The model in this regard is still the fairy tale . . . the expressions once upon a time, il était une fois, . . . serve to mark the entry into narrative. In other words, it is not just the past that is expressed by the past tense, but the attitude of relaxation, of uninvolvement.[30]

This sense of the speaker's detachment, a particular human and moral stance toward the referential object of one's speech, is one defining mark of narration: does this stance have a musical cognate?

In terms of the classical distinctions, what we call narrative—novels, stories, myths, and the like—is diegetic, epic poetry and not theater. It is a tale told later, by one who escaped to the outside of the tale, for which he builds a frame to control its dangerous energy. Music's distinction is fundamental and terrible; it is not chiefly diegetic but mimetic. Like any form of theater, any temporal art, it traps the listener in present experience and the beat of passing time, from which he or she cannot escape. No art is purely mimetic (that is, no art *is* merely the phenomenal world); rather, the mimetic genres move us by performing, they *mime* or even dance out the world in present time. They cannot disarm the action, or comfort us, by insisting upon the pastness of what they represent. Ballads are dramatic conversations or monologues that act out the story, and border on demanding live performance. When there is a framing narrator, as there is in *Erlkönig*, his presence is kept to a minimum; often (as in the *Zauberlehrling*) there *seems* to be no outside voice. Balladic subjects, and with them the listener-reader, are trapped in unfolding disaster, especially when the objective narrator is apparently absent. The *Zauberlehrling* ballad—a transposition, as we have seen, of Lucan's (diegetic) narrative into (mimetic) drama—is a present-tense monologue for the Apprentice whose voice calls out what happens ("he is already at the river," "look there—he is chopped in two!") Indeed, the ballad in

German is secretly a *performance* as well as a monologue; the Apprentice is both himself and someone who stands before an audience. An audience is requested to "look there"—"seht!" The plural imperative form ("[you all] look there—") makes it clear that this is not just the usual address to the deity (goodness, look at that!) to which all of us resort, even when alone, in times of great disaster, but an address to listeners. Thus Goethe, Hegel, and the neo-Hegelian critics of the nineteenth century saw ballad poetry—like the *Zauberlehrling* poem—as a supremely powerful genre, for it is poetry that, though written, assumes the mantle of temporal performance by lodging marks of performance within its written text.[31]

German literary theorists have tended to phrase the mimetic-diegetic distinction another way. Diegetic genres, with their surviving narrator, play both with *Erzählzeit*, the time it takes the narrator to tell, and the time of reading, and *erzählte Zeit*, the expanse of time that is told about.[32] In mimetic genres there seems to be only the time of telling. The time of telling is the time being told about; there is no teller, only time itself. This opposition has, of course, haunted theorizing about verbal narrative, taking many forms. Peter Brooks has written that with its first preterite verb, narrative "ever and inevitably presents itself as a repetition . . . of what has already happened."[33] Put another way, in the first instants of narrating, of *Erzählzeit*, all the past—*erzählte Zeit*—is immanent. A sense of the separations between story and discourse relies in great part on the separations effected by tense's action of casting into the past.

Can music, though it exists always in the present moment, create the sound of pastness? When Mahler quotes Wagner, the past is invoked. A citation is intertextual, a reference to history. It refers to an artifact from the past, but cannot create a past tense. When Goethe's Apprentice in stanza 3 cites the biblical words of John the Apostle—"habe ich doch das Wort vergessen"—history, another text, is cast up, but without forcing the catastrophe unfolding around the Apprentice—splashing, broom marching, flood—from the fatal present into the harmless past.

Can music possess—aside from discursive *space*—the human, epistemological, or moral complexities of a narrating voice? To answer that question, we might begin with those works that seem to interpret or to examine themselves through widely spaced and altered repetitions of initial musical matter. When we hear the final minutes of *Tristan*, we are reminded of something in the past, the Act II love-duet, recapitulated at the opera's end. Is Act II the played-out event, and the end of Act III the moralizing summary or epic repetition? Then *Tristan* becomes a magical literary-philosophical object, in which the *hors-texte*—the reality—is given prior to the *texte* or discursive description. (Chapters 5 and 6, on the narratives in the *Ring*, seek out the boundaries of this possibility.) This more complex understanding of musical "story" and "discourse" is one indirectly proposed by Danuser when he reads Mahler's recapitulative sections as "epic syntheses" for their specific ways of reforming previous musical materials and gestures:

> A section like the one in question [the recapitulation of the Third Symphony's first movement] attains an epic autonomy not because it detaches and isolates itself from a formal process—this in any case is merely the external indication—but rather because it consistently realizes those tendencies of form and character that were inherent in the material from its first appearance . . . now the mourning of the trombone solo [from the exposition] arrives at self-knowledge, at peaceful and satisfied fulfillment in the form of the cello melody (which goes back to a melodic turn found in the "Urlicht" movement of the Second Symphony). The autonomy of this section is, then, not immediate, but the result of a process of discovery.[34]

Predicated upon dividing the musical movement into two very different registers—as mimesis or enacted (and melancholy) reality that shifts to a mature reminiscence about that reality—Danuser's identification of an epic synthesis also identifies (though he does not state it in these terms) the detached stance of an epic voice. As Danuser has indicated, varied repetition does not, in isolation, invariably establish two such different registers (not every repetition or recapitulation is a peaceful and detached retelling). The epic quality resides in details of context, in the precise degree and force of unique transformations within unique works. (We should also recall that repetitions and transformations of sonorous formulas in verbal narrative—such as the "leitmotifs" in Thomas Mann's novels—generally belong to the diegetic voice alone; they remind us of the elapsed time of our reading or our listening, and belong to the artifice of discourse, not to the story it allegedly represents.[35] Certainly a long tradition of musical analysis rooted in Hanslick's aesthetics of form would argue that repetition actually creates structure, architecture, and hence stasis: time frozen.)

Analogies between music and a story/discourse dualism, or between music and the temporal signs of literary narrative, seem *easy*, yet end as unsatisfactory. This failure, however, is preferable to satisfying or even satiating conclusions that posit narrative as a new secret, a lift picked up on the long march to musical meaning, or a magic word (narrative) that creates a new music-critical method, the magic servant. Magic servants carry the same bucket, at first tediously, but then unstoppably; they drown us in the end. The Apprentice's animate broom is frightening precisely because it obeys mechanistically, because its work is repeated again and again. Thus, again and again might any music be dubbed "narrative." Musical works, however, rarely have the capacity to present themselves as the voice of the teller. But this cannot be said to impoverish music; rather, it lends music a terrible force to move us by catching us in played-out time. When music ends, it ends absolutely, in the cessation of passing time and movement, in death.[36]

V

In looking for the center of *The Sorcerer's Apprentice*, we will always come back to its fearful midpoint, the fragmented repetitions of the main theme in the contrabassoon and bass clarinet. Why is the passage disturbing? It is the resurrected broom, but I also suggested a more or less musical answer at the opening of this chapter. In repeating each element a few too many times, and in preparing a larger repetition—the entire piece seems to re-begin as it was beyond this point—the moment may compose out what Freud understood as uncanny repetition, recurrence (like that of the father-figure in Hoffmann's *Sandman*, on which Freud based his theory) that is threatening because it allegorizes the repetition-compulsion.[37] While the abnormal level of repetition is what first strikes the ear, however, it is one of a collection of sonorous disjunctions with the body of the piece. Another is dead silence—the one preceding the whole incident as the entire orchestra collapses out of a fortissimo atonal cluster, as well as those between the inital low Fs. Yet another is the isolation of the two bass instruments as sudden solos. The last and most complex is this painful *creatio ex nihilo* and its subsequent disappearence, the way in which the music seems suddenly to speak itself laboriously into existence, and, when the main theme returns in the bassoon in original form (see m. 34 of Example 2.1) just as suddenly *stop speaking*, giving over to some other, now-familiar musical material that is focused in that bassoon. Thus while the passage in its reversion to a solo instrument is what Kerman would call "vocalistic," it is also a *voice*. What the passage embeds within itself is not simply a repetition-compulsion, but rather the act of enunciation itself, the sound of *speaking one's art into being*. In so doing, the passage reveals in sound the otherwise silent presence of the discursive subject. It is uncanny because that subject is not a human agent, and the voice speaks from somewhere that we cannot see.

This passage establishes *distance* in certain acoustic or musical ways, and I read it as enunciation—but does either musical disjunction from the body of the piece, or existence in my reading as an uncanny subject-voice, suffice to mark this voice as narration? Not at all. Locating a narrating voice in Dukas's scherzo may also involve another return, to Goethe's poem. One way (as we have seen) of conceptualizing the association between Goethe's ballad and Dukas's scherzo is to claim that the ballad constructs certain events, and that these are traced by musical gestures. *The Sorcerer's Apprentice* is not a retelling of events, but rather a *depiction* of events, happening as we listen. The poem is like music in this respect, in being a performable drama in the form of the Apprentice's monologue. The piece might then be seen, in fact, as an extraordinarily exact or successful representation, in that at every moment it can be understood as an acting-out, with Goethe's poem, of the drama common to both. Neither narrates, neither tells a tale retrospectively, at a distance. This explanation assumes, like Berlioz's explanation for the *Eroica* funeral march, an isomorphism between actions and piece.

The poem, though bearing signs that it represents a drama and a performance, nonetheless also has one sign of nonperformance—not a word, but a black stroke, which (I would claim) is the mark of an invisible narrator. At the end of Goethe's poem, we hear the Sorcerer's voice, restoring order to the world:

> «In die Ecke,
> Besen! Besen!
> Seids gewesen.
> Denn als Geister
> Ruft euch nur, zu diesem Zwecke,
> Erst hervor der alte Meister.»

["Into the corner, Broom! Broom! Let it be finished. For the Old Master alone animates you to this purpose."]

His words are given *in quotation marks*. Who, now, is telling us what is happening by quoting the Sorcerer? We sense instantly that the poem is no longer in the Apprentice's hands, yet it is not in the Sorcerer's either—to be quoted signals another, the person quoting. A third voice enters the poem at the site of the quotation marks, and speaks a silent *"he said"* after the Sorcerer's words. So there is a third person beside the other two, a third-person narrator, to us unheard, who peers out from the quotation marks that betray his presence. This silent *"he said"* (also invisible, in that the words do not appear on the page) puts all that we have heard performed (the broom drama) into the past. The black stroke of the quotation marks therefore might also be understood as the only trace left by the historically previous version, Lucan's narrative. Goethe's reception of his antique sources thus takes visual form as these black arrows pointing back to Eucrates, the man who narrates his past to those who stand around his bed.

Dukas's scherzo can be understood at certain junctures as an event-series in which music is the transposition of the Apprentice-drama—as for example, at its center (the resurrection of the broom as twins). Long stretches of the piece, however, simply motor along without calling up any such specific associations, and the music becomes—like all music—a generalized motion through time (to connect this inevitable motion with the broom's indefatigable trotting seems so obvious as to become wholly ordinary).[38] Thus in fact there is a space between the Apprentice-drama and the piece; though they occasionally meet, they are not always isomorphous.

There is (one could argue) a great and significant disjunction between drama as constituted in Goethe's poem and in the final moments of Dukas's music, in the last ten measures of the scherzo, the slow epilogue that closes the piece (Example 2.7). Dukas's scherzo thus does not conclude with the Sorcerer's words (the chord after the *motif d'évocation*), though they are the last thing that happens in Goethe's Apprentice-drama. The slow epilogue seems to have no bearing on the drama, for it lies outside Dukas's musical representations of spells spoken, brooms in motion, water, and axes.

This epilogue is in many respects a necessary musical end, for the energy built up by the final statement of the augmented-chord fanfare demands expansiveness in closure as a counterbalance (the two tonic grunts in the low winds are hardly adequate). Many musical-formalist reasons could be adduced to explain the satisfaction inherent in such coda-gestures. They create closure by restating opening material, as in Beethoven's late piano variations, for example. In *The Sorcerer's Apprentice*, two themes (a version of the second theme, and one of the main theme) return, as does the slow tempo of the piece's opening prelude. "Version" is, however, perhaps a misleading measure of how greatly the thematic material is changed, and in the epilogue it is presented in forms distinctly *unlike* those exploited within the piece. The vocalistic solo viola singing the second theme, the quadruply-slowed and narcotic statement of the main theme, radically alter the motivic material to the extent that, while there is no actual spatial distance involved (the instruments are not literally farther away), there is an effect of filtration similar to Adorno's description of Wagnerian Phantasmagoria (music rescored and revoiced,

Example 2.7. Epilogue to *The Sorcerer's Apprentice.*

detached from its base, thus heard as if from a distance). Music is changed, moreover, in a way that does not seem developmental: the themes are not transformed as if belonging to a progressive continuity, but are so greatly reformed that they can be nothing but a new end in themselves. The epilogue possesses both the same vocalism and the same otherness against the body of the work, as the central moment of uncanny repetition. But this musically uncanny epilogue is perhaps not really disjunct with Goethe's text. If the epilogue is the sound of music's narrating voice, then it is a trace of what is constituted by the quotation marks in Goethe's poem—and, in this, a doubly mediated echo of Eucrates the narrator. The last ten measures pass over to the other world, speaking in the past tense of what has happened, in an orchestral *"he said"* that is the voice of this third man. The third man is, of course, mute during the drama, and known by the mysterious marks that appear only in the final stanza.

All three Apprentice-texts thus end with an enigma. In Lucan, the Sorcerer vanishes after speaking the counterspell, and Eucrates could never discover where he had gone. In Goethe, the black mark appears to indicate not a disappearance but the presence of an unseen and unheard man who paradoxically speaks, though he makes no sound. In Dukas, familiar music recurs oddly reformed. In Dukas's scherzo, the narrating voice (unlike that in the poem) is not silent: the epilogue is the sound of its singing. But what is this narrator telling us? Of what does he sing? In this *Erzählen ohne Erzähltes* (to evoke Adorno's phrase) we cannot know the answer, and that makes the scherzo doubly enigmatic. Given that both Goethe and Lucan break off with a trace left unpursued, we passionately wish that Dukas's narrator—who sings to finish off the enigma and close the crack— could make an end. How marvelous it is that we are presented instead with the double enigma, that we cannot understand the end this narrator makes, even though he is telling what Lucan and Goethe do not: what *did* happen?—after we heard *what the Sorcerer said*.

Chapter Three

CHERUBINO UNCOVERED: REFLEXIVITY IN
OPERATIC NARRATION

ALL OPERAS have scenes of narration, scenes in which a character tells a story. But what, meanwhile, is being done by and within the music? Put another way: what occurs at this juncture that brings music together with a representation of the scene of narration? Operatic narration must lie at the heart of any speculation about the "voice" of musical narration, yet is often perceived as dull, and literally goes unheard.

Is operatic narration in fact an interlude of tedium, and, as such, a time during which one's thoughts are free to depart elsewhere? If so, perhaps this is not all bad: wandering from the music can have its advantages. We tend to assume that performed art must engage us at every second, that a capacity to exact this state of enthrallment is a sign of its greatness, for distraction (according to Tolstoy) "hinders the infection" that great musical art (the most direct of all arts) will produce.[1] Nonetheless, most performed art casts up passages during which the listener's attention is no longer captured by either the material or the performance; in a real sense, such passages give it shape. They are phases in a rhetorical flux that allows important moments to emerge by contrast. When music commands complete attention for more than a few minutes, it does so to self-consciously dramatic effect. Such is the force, for instance, of the penultimate B♭ section in the Act II finale of Mozart's *Figaro*, which sustains a sense of irresolution (despite its conventional harmonic closure) in order that Figaro's fumblings toward explanation (why does he have Cherubino's commission?) be drawn out to an exquisite pitch of nervousness.

Moments of operatic narration, by contrast, generate for most listener-spectators some sense of deflation, of having been abandoned by *action* on one hand and *music* on the other (the pairing is significant, and its implications are discussed presently). Joseph Kerman, with typical grace, captured this sense in writing of the opening of *Tristan* Act III, of a moment at which some narrating appears inevitable:

Two other notorious Wagnerian techniques are especially well-handled
in the "Delirium" scene . . . the first is the long passage of plot résumé,
during which some major character relates the course of previous action,
with the liberal assistance of leitmotivs. Most opera-goers suffer plot résumé for the purpose of initial exposition (Isolde's long "Narration" in
Act I), barely tolerate it in the *Ring* (they may not have been there the
previous evening), but strongly object when Wagner reviews in leisurely
fashion action that they have actually just seen on stage. This he does
often enough—and what aware listener has not quailed at the beginning
of Act III when that disingenuous Shepherd asks Kurwenal to explain
Tristan's illness? But the principle behind such résumés is a genuinely
dramatic one: to reinterpret past action in a new synthesis, determined
by fresh experience.[2]

What is most telling is Kerman's sense that in opera narrating is experienced as a species of pain, to be borne for the sake of a psychological revelation attendant on the narrator's new synthesis of troubling actions from the past. The pain is both epistemological (we have
already witnessed the events being described and we will be bored)
and musical (the passage will be a kind of half-music, a loose, declamatory assemblage of leitmotifs judiciously mixed). Two assumptions
lie behind this double distress. First, leitmotivic quotation, that least
of musical procedures, is assumed to be the means by which the music can shadow narration: a familiar claim, as we have seen. Second,
operatic narrators are assumed to be *reliable*, neither lying nor dis-
torting, but presenting a greater truth. Put another way: narrating is
not itself seen as an *act* within *action*.

But is this always the case? Or should we ask with narrative prag-
matists whether narrators *use* narrating to seduce or otherwise mis-
lead an interlocutor, thereby underscoring the *scene of narrating* as an
allegory of art's power over its listeners?[3] More radically still, do
scenes of narrating constitute an interlude of reflexivity, at which the
narrative performance reflects upon the greater performance in
which it is embedded? Lucien Dällenbach describes such reflexivity in
written or visual art forms in terms of an "internal mirror that reflects
the whole of the narrative in simple, repeated, or 'specious' (or paradoxical) duplication," distinguishing between such reflexivity and
other layered utterances (symbol, allegory) by pointing precisely to
what might be considered the reflexive moment's reluctance to sit still
and be decoded: "it alone is neither opaque nor transparent, it exists
in a form of double meaning, whose identification and deciphering
presupposes a knowledge of the text . . . consequently the hermeneutic key can never open up the reflexion until the narrative has re-

vealed the existence and location of the reflexion."[4] Reflexive narrative scenes are far from tedious, for at such dizzying junctures, one must continually waver between the two spheres.

I would claim that both possibilities—that narrators may exploit narration, and that narrative moments may be *reflexive*—are raised in any operatic narration, and raised moreover in two domains: textual *and musical*. This is not to say that all operatic narratives do assume a reflexive function or underscore the performance of narrating; indeed, a poetic and musical distinction is generally maintained between what might be called "monaural" and "reflexive" narrating. But to understand the distinction is also to identify the many situations in which it collapses, in which musical modes associated with monaural narration are crossed with those associated with the reflexive. This conjunction characterizes Wagner's narrative scenes, but is not limited to them; indeed, the great moments of operatic narrating are those that waver as it were in another domain, adding to the oscillation inherent in the reflexive moment a shift between reflexive and monaural modes.

By "monaural," I mean operatic narration designed to convey concisely an accurate and unfictionalized report of real events. This information is necessary for either the audience or one of the characters on stage. The *Mauerschau* (in which someone standing on a wall shouts information about what we cannot see) is one typical example; another is the messenger who brings unexpected news (Spoletta rushing in to tell Scarpia, in Act II of *Tosca*, that Napoleon has won at Marengo). In pre-Wagnerian opera, these are occasions for recitative, and as such, so limited musically as to be only half-music. The *secco* recitative preceding Don Giovanni's famous aria in Act I of Mozart's *Don Giovanni* is classic, for the damping down of music to strummed harpsichord allows the sung word to be maximally clear, and hence the narrative information (that Donna Elvira is out of the way, that Leporello has been at mischief among the peasants) to be grasped by both Don Giovanni and the audience. The relationship between the two interlocutors—here, as immoral twins, both aroused, both complicit—as well as the brevity of the exchange precludes any sense that Leporello is *exploiting* narrative to some larger purpose involving his listener (indeed, Don Giovanni is able to anticipate most of what Leporello will recount). But above all, the music, by withholding most of its own substance, by being *secco* recitative, tends to pragmatize the exchange and suggest the improbability of any reflexive turn at this particular point.

Mozart consistently sets narration without obvious mythic resonance or reflexive purpose as recitative. So strong is the association between the two that a set piece can be interrupted *in medias res* when narration begins. This is what happens in the trio in Act I of *Figaro*, at that famous juncture where the Count is asked to reveal what he knows about Cherubino's misbehavior, and does so in an embedded recitative[5] (Example 3.1). At first hearing, we are aware only that narrating has brought with it the utter cessation of the trio's forward motion, a radical and shocking jump into another musical mode. At first, the narration *seems* straightforward. We are given a report—accompanied by illustrative pantomime—of yesterday's incident: how Cherubino hid under the table at Barberina's house. But when the Count in demonstrating his actions ("tiptoing forward very quietly, I lifted up the tablecloth, and discovered the page") lifts the dress off the chair, when Cherubino is exposed again at the very moment at which the Count narrates yesterday's discomfiture, two *times* are brought together. Cherubino's half-terrified face expresses the onset of vertigo that all—the Count, Basilio, Susanna, and we—must feel at this conflation.

The coincidence of narrating and enactment has, in fact, created a reflexive moment of peculiar force, for the Count's act of narrating seems to engender the disaster of which it tells. That is, beyond reporting events past, the narration conjures up its own content, demonstrating that while it enables us to *imagine* events, it can also *produce* them as the narrator speaks. The act of narrating has a protean power; something of the magical—not merely of prestidigitation, but of the divine—therefore adheres to this familiar comic moment. Significantly, enactment and narrative retelling face each other here across an expanse of music that has changed with their confrontation, for as soon as the Count begins to reenact, he shifts from recitative and takes up, with the orchestra, music from the body of the trio. That he sings the same descending motif originally sung by Basilio (when the latter speaks of Cherubino) has been taken as a leitmotivic gesture (that is, the Count sings a manner of Cherubino motif at the moment that he is speaking of, and unveiling, the page). This is a leitmotivic interpretation that seems limited at best.[6] The immediate effect of a return to the musical discourse of the set piece is of a return to musical action out of recitative. In some sense, *music itself* thus returns precisely at the reflexive moment in the narration, as if to underscore a conjunction both rich and unstable. It is only in retrospect that we hear how the entire recitative whispers sounds from the number, as in the first measures: chords interspersed with talk, but cast into a timbral and gestural recollection of the trio's opening *Tosto andate* (low strings, rumbling with B♭ third figures). Musically, the narration becomes an attenuated quotation, a fragmented résumé of

Example 3.1. Cherubino's Uncovering in *Le Nozze di Figaro* Act I (trio).

Ex. 3.1 (cont.)

u - so,   io, dal mu-so in - so - spet - ti - to,

a tempo

guar-do, cer-co in o-gni si - to.   Ed al - zan-do,   pian, pia -

ni - no,   il tap - pe - to   al ta - vo - li - no,

(Showing how he found the page, he lifts the dressing-gown from the chair and discovers Cherubino.)

(astonished)

ve - do il   pag - gio.   Ah! co - sa veg- gio!

music that otherwise exists as a coherent whole. Thus the narration in the *Figaro* trio dissembles; it plays at monaural narration (straight information, straight recitative) as it builds to a moment at which its reflexivity is revealed as if by magic, and the Count's narrating produces Cherubino out of a chair.

Reflexive narrating within opera or theater has a certain vibrancy; the time it occupies hums—not least with the listener's mental movements between the small narrative performance and the events (the greater performance, as it were; the enacted drama) in which it has been set. This view of reflexivity is critical to my interpretation of musical narration, and will recur leitmotivically; this is one of the reasons I use an aurally charged language to describe it. But the aural imagery is also meant to underscore differences between reflexivity in performed art, and the similar phenomenon—*mise en abyme* (a modish term now exhausted by repetition)—in written texts. Dällenbach (who writes chiefly about nonperformed texts) expresses the in-

terrelationship between events and their reflexion both in terms of
his controlling visual metaphor, the mirror within the painting, and
in plastic, almost architectural terms, speaking of a "semantic compression and dilation" in which "the transition from the story being
told to its reflexion implies two different operations . . . a *reduction* (or
structuring by embedding), and an *elaboration* of the referential paradigm (or structuring by projecting a metaphorical 'equivalent' onto
the syntagmatic axis)."[7] In the case of performed arts, we need to
stress the *oscillation* involved in understanding such moments. One
moves between comprehending the reflexion (the "story within the
story") as a miniature résumé of the whole, and the whole as a projection through greater expanses of time of a pregnant microcosm.
Acknowledging this restlessness will remind us of opera's temporality
and aurality. The *Figaro* trio, by invoking sheer resonance—the in-
fusion of richer music from the number—at the reflexive moment
becomes in my view axiomatic for operatic narrating in the nineteenth century. In the earlier (pre-Wagnerian) tradition there is, on
the whole, a consistent dualism, one both cited and dissolved in the
Count's narration: on one side, ordinary, brief, and realistic narrating, factual reportage, and the half-music of recitative; on the other,
narrative reflexivity accompanied by musical transformations of
many sorts.

Operatic narrating is admittedly *relatively* rare, for practical reasons
(including those adduced by Kerman) that are not hard to understand. First of all, as Kerman suggests, narration stops dramatic action. This is hardly uncommon in opera, of course, in which action
frequently comes to a halt during a contemplative number; Dahlhaus
and Gossett (among many) have attempted to define levels of time
and action in traditional scores.[8] But such contemplative pauses invariably involve lyric meditation whose poetic texts are better suited
to operatic arias for one practical reason: lyric text in opera arias
must be denatured by fragmentation and nonsensical repetition, and
it is calculated precisely to bear such distortions, to be expanded or
compressed as needed to fill up aria's musical volume. Few of us care
how often the Queen of the Night says, "So sei sie dann auf ewig
dein," or how she mangles the words and their syntax. As she sings,
we are listening for musical sense and structure, and though her
avowal is passionate, it enunciates no critical dramatic action, no important clue to understanding.

Narrative text cannot (or, at least, ideally should not) be twisted
into a verbal mass and spread indiscriminately under a musical structure. Narrative exists to tell its story, in the proper order, in a form
audible to interested listeners: hence the *secco* recitative that accom-

panies Leporello's reports, a half-music that allows comprehension of the sung word. The inviolability of narrative text places heavy restraints on any accompanying music; for operatic composers it was easier to avoid the occasion of sin by avoiding narrative exposition. Indeed, both types of narrating—monaural and reflexive—share this basic technical problem, that the words are not to be treated as mere acoustic roughage. In monaural narrating, the solution is the half-music of recitative, itself barely musical—Edward Cone called writing recitative a "surrender of the musician's function."[9] Reflexive narrating demands, as it were, greater musical courage, precisely because the presence of more elaborate music at the reflexive node has the capacity (as in the *Figaro* trio) both to underscore narrative reflexivity by sheer sound, and to *enact reflexivity in music*. Music's capacities for enacting reflexivity are my central concern. But there is no single way that music is reflexive; rather, the nineteenth century saw multiple forms of reflexivity, many of which lay on a spectrum between recitative and number. Put another way, they lie everywhere between an amorphousness that seems barely musical, and the most self-contained and rich of musical forms.

I

Historically, narration in Classical and nineteenth-century opera had two traditional and musically dissimilar modes of presentation: recitative and inserted storytelling song, a song in repeated verses usually called a "Ballade," "Romanze," "Lied," or "canzone."[10] Narrative song appeared in opera in many languages, from Pedrillo's Romanze in *Die Entführung* to the Veil Song in *Don Carlos*, or the Bell Song in *Lakmé* and beyond. Between these extremes, however, existed alternative modes. The narrative moment in the *Figaro* trio was one, but there were others in operas of the next generation, such as the dramatic narrative dialogue sung in Rossini's *Ermione*, or the *Melodram* liberally supplied with symbolic musical gestures in Schubert's *Fierabras*; in the latter, a spoken text is declaimed over music that draws attention (by means of sudden contrasts, dissonant sonorities, and a familiar arsenal of emphatic sounds) to certain phrases. The reflexive capacity of narrative song (which often tells the opera's own story in compressed or disguised form) was exploited from the beginning, yet the conventional musical design of narrative song (the repeated verses)—as in Lakmé's Bell Song—sets up interference with the very idea of progressive musical narration. Narrative song, despite its apparent musical simplicity, thus represents one of opera's most elaborate points of tension.

Wagner's *Der fliegende Holländer* contains what is probably the most famous of operatic narrative songs (Senta's Ballad); similar strophic narrative songs also appear in Marschner's *Der Vampyr*, Meyerbeer's *Robert le Diable*, and Boieldieu's *La Dame blanche*. This particular group is special, for these four operas share a dramaturgical conceit. All invoke a familiar Romantic trope: a representative of the supernatural intrudes upon humanity. Nineteenth-century librettists and dramatists cast the myth in many forms; if it was debased by being taken literally in Marschner's *Vampyr* (whose protagonist seems more at home in the penny dreadful than in the unseen realm), it was elevated and recomposed in works such as *The Lady from the Sea*. Meyerbeer's *Robert* is the half-human child of a demon, bent on contracting his own earthly marriage; the white lady is a betrayed female ghost, an ectoplasmic Donna Elvira, who returns to earth to stalk philandering baritones. The four narrative songs within these operas are, however, also special in being textually reflexive in Dällenbach's sense. The myth in all four operas is both played out on stage and narrated at a critical juncture by one of the characters, who sings the narrative song not knowing that he will be an actor in the tale that he tells. The songs, unlike many narrative songs in opera, narrate the action that surrounds them.

The narrative song, which became a familiar operatic topos of the early nineteenth century, had its roots in Romantic ballad poetry and in musical settings of that poetry as *Lieder*. ("Ballad" is used here loosely to refer to the brief, strictly strophic narrative art-poetry typical of the German Romantic tradition.[11]) Narrative in the ballad unwinds over multiple verses of identical prosodic and structural design, whose identity is often reinforced by a refrain that is repeated at the close of each verse. The epic formula, or repeated refrain, was typical of the poetry that art-ballad contrived to evoke; that is, of traditional folk-ballad. In folk-ballad, of course, the repeated formula had a critical mnemonic function in the composition, performance, and transmission of an orally constituted repertory. Yet the refrain was more than this. The repeated text also presages and continually reinterprets the events narrated, its recurring sound an ominous beat that articulates the story's progress.[12]

As we saw, however, in Lakmé's Bell Song (in Chapter 1), the repetitive structure of strophic song is (apparently) at war with the events that its words describe. Narration, Goethe's poetic "Ur-Ei" with its mixture of dialogue, epic (objective) description, and lyric, represents the passage of time, represents history both played out and commented upon.[13] But this forward-moving pageant is realized within an eternally repeating sonorous structure, and is trapped in the unvarying strophic beat. The dialectical tension between narrative metamorphosis and structural repetition is itself a poetic device, for the monotony of rhyme, meter, and strophe forces the reader-listener to fix on the meaning of the words and not their sound: to listen to the story. In poetry whose sonorities are more elaborate, whose syntax and strophic design are more baroque, we begin to hear the music of the words above their discursive meaning.

Beyond this, the monotony of balladic poetry is used to heighten the unpredictability of balladic drama. Goethe's *Zauberlehrling*—the ballad already encountered in Chapter 2—is typical in this. We are lulled by the pattern established in the first two stanzas, as the plot unfolds in the long strophes (the wizard has gone away, the broom sprouts arms and legs and marches off with the bucket) while, in the shorter sestets, descriptions of events give way to a narcotic, hieratic spell ("Walle! walle / Manche Strecke"), the refrain text. But the poem thwarts complacency; magical actions begin to seep into the refrain position. The broom is set in motion, it fetches water, it fetches too much water, the Apprentice cannot remember the counterspell, and in desperation he chops the broom into pieces. Within the *sestet* the broom rises from the dead, and the description is devised to echo the sound of the nonnarrative refrain: "Walle! walle" becomes "Wehe! wehe"; "Zwecke" and "Strecke" resound in assonant rhyme with "Knechte" and "Mächte"; "reiche" is linked to "beide" and "Eile." Expectations of a pattern repeated (actions in the long strophe, spells or outcries in the sestet) are thwarted to dramatic effect, and we, tripped up by verse, experience as surprising a mutation as that observed by the Apprentice.

Goethe preferred strictly strophic settings of his ballads, in which the single musical unit was repeated without variation for the singing of all verses.[14] His stance is not surprising. If the same music runs under each verse of text, then the music merely echoes the repeated phonetic and prosodic cycle of meter, rhyme, and verse-length; it effaces itself to become the patterned sonority of words made louder. Music neither interprets the poem nor introduces an alien element—its own sonic reemphasis—but instead collaborates with the poem, helps the words to shout out their own sounds. Artful collisions of formal structure and actions described (like those in the *Zauberlehrling*) can survive the addition of such music. Goethe's notorious distaste for Schubert's *Erlkönig* setting (and his preference for the original setting by Corona Schröter) is thus not simply a mark of musical philistinism. Schröter's setting was hardly more than a bit of patterned melody for the recitation of each verse.[15] In Schubert's setting, music reacts to an action-progression constituted within the poem, for each verse is set to different music as projection of the unwinding plot. But by turning its eyes to dramatic activities, the music obscures the strophic structure, and so overwhelms and destroys the tension between dramatic progression and formal design. What one might call a "ballad phenomenology" thus might well stress how the monotonous poetic and musical sound pushes the mutating plot into the foreground, as the listener's attention is drawn from predictable repeating sonority to unpredictable dramatic mystery. Simple strophic music is in reality reverent to dramatic plot, but this reverence takes the form of ignorance, and so-called "through-composed" settings of narrative ballads, by breaking free of repetition in order to create musical representations of action-sequences, overwhelm their texts by burying them in musical matter with its own fascinations.

Erlkönig itself was written as part of the libretto for an opera, *Die Fischerin*, a *Singspiel* first performed in 1782 with music by Schröter. The heroine sings the ballad as a curtain-opener. When she has finished, she announces that she has now sung all the songs she knows; the action begins. Ballad and Romanze settings in early nineteenth-century opera were (like most inserted songs) invariably strophic, and, like Schröter's *Erlkönig* music, calculated as artful imitations of folksong's simplicity. In this way, narrative song also addresses the one technical demand of operatic narrative: that the sung word be comprehensible. Emmy's strophic song from *Der Vampyr* (Example 3.2) is typical. The soprano tells her listeners that she knows a fairy story about a vampire; would they like to hear it? She describes in her Romanze how the "sad glance" of a mysterious stranger lures a young girl to her unfortunate end. The repeated refrain, "Denn still und heimlich sag ich's dir, / der bleiche Mann ist ein Vampyr! / Bewahr' uns Gott auf Erden / ihm jemals gleich zu werden" ["For I whisper to you in secret / the pale man is a vampire! / may God be by your side / that you never become his like"], is echoed by the chorus at the close of each parallel verse.

What might be called the paradox of narration in song—that the repeated music seems to speak across the progressive action narrated—is a paradox that serves to expose the assumptions lying not only behind operatic criticism, but behind most writing on music and narrative. Put another way: The paradox reveals the degree to which musical *development*—whether we call it sequence of events, expectation aroused and fulfilled (on Leonard Meyer's model), or merely progress—is simply equated with the notion of an enacted plot. Kerman, for instance, echoing countless operatic critics, privileges the "interplay between . . . action and music" as elevating Mozart above his Baroque predecessors, and stresses how "action and musical *con-*

tinuity" (emphasis mine) are made one in Mozartean and later opera.[16] The equation—plot events and musical events—is, as we have seen, one a priori of most ascriptions of narrative qualities to *instrumental* music. This assumption is, then, profoundly shaped by a secret operatic model, a vision, as it were, of Mozart's finales as a compositional factory in which *real* events, events palpably present in the bodies and movements and words of singer-actors, are shadowed by an enacting music.

II

Reflecting on reflexivity in sung narration may serve to untwist the paradox. In *Der Vampyr* the song is, as Dällenbach describes the type, "programmatic" in that it occurs near the opening of the opera, and "provides a 'double' for the fiction in order to 'overtake' it and to leave it with only a past for its future."[17] The rest of the opera is fated to follow its directive, potentially to struggle against its directive (as the heroine resists or is rescued from her fate). The same is true of *Robert le Diable*. In *Robert* the ballad is sung by the bard Rimbaud, who has traveled south from Normandy, entertains a group of Sicilian knights by telling how the Norman princess Berthe was won in marriage by an unknown prince, that she bore him a son, Robert, and how this stranger turned out to be demonic as well as Byronic. The Sicilian knights, understanding the conventions of balladry, take the tale to be fiction, but the grown-up Robert is also in the audience, and his furious reaction to the song is found suggestive. This song (Example 3.3) is slightly more complex musically than Emmy's Romanze, since the third verse involves rhythmic compression and harmonic shifts in the accompaniment. In general, however, Rimbaud's Ballad exemplifies the antagonistic tension between musical plot and textual plot that is characteristic of all ballads. The plot narrated defines passing time, from Berthe's disdain for marriage to the arrival of the stranger, his (pur)suit, the marriage, Robert's birth; the enchaining of events is an enchaining of changes, of unfolding, continual development, irreversible over time. This small history is contained within three parallel verses, prosodically identical, each concluding with a repeated refrain. As in the *Zauberlehrling* poem, or Emmy's Romanze, the history is thus *told*, out loud, in a sonorous envelope of rhyme, meter, assonance, that is repetitive, and returns always to its initial noises, to play the pattern over and over again. The musical setting, with its repeated single unit for strophes 1 and 2 and a slightly varied version for strophe 3, is no more than the repeating cycle of the words-as-sound, shouted louder, or pushed

Example 3.2. Der Vampyr Act II: Emmy's Romanza.

from the sonority of spoken poetry to the more elaborate sonority of music.

The contradictions inherent in narrative song resonate in this instance more elaborately in other domains. For one: thesis and antithesis (sequential plot versus unvaried repetition of sonority) are subsumed in classic dialectical fashion by a broader concept that unites what might be called the small history told in "Jadis régnait" with a larger history invariably implied by reflexive sung narration. In ballads telling of numinous intruders such as the vampire, the events related are always abstract or antique, lodged in an absolute past. (Rimbaud recounts not his own experience, but events from a time sealed off from him.) Decoding the operatic convention, one knows that this fictional ballad adumbrates the drama to be played out, that the intruder will reappear, and that the fictional can thus break into a real world. This recurrence, inevitable, unvaried, charges the figure with his uncanniness. So the small history—Berthe, the suitor, the marriage, the child—seems to trace a unique, linear path through time, but the greater history knows better, that each new beginning is a replaying of the same sequence, ending in the same disastrous closure: time marked by the dull beat of repetition. This greater history is seldom incorporated explicitly into ballad texts (no hint of it is given in "Jadis régnait"); yet it is nonetheless pressed into the ballad, encoded in the prosody of the verse and in the music, both of which have bypassed the small history of the "plot" altogether. What is articulated are two images of history—one marked by Hegelian romances of progress, the other bleaker, of history as repetition, as abrupt reversion to flawed origins.[18]

Narrative song, then, may be seen as a locus of *intrusion*, at which myth writes itself into the continuity of the present, and ensures that the future either enacts myth or struggles against it, being in either case determined by it. The generative power of narrating, symbolized by the *Figaro* trio, is exercised in narrative song to encompass the whole of the surrounding opera. As with *Figaro* this locus is marked musically, here in two different ways. First, the music of the song enters *into the body of the opera* when the song is cited in fragmentary form at Bertram's first appearance (Example 3.4). This might seem no more than anticipation of Wagnerian leitmotivery, yet it exists within a more complex system in which the relation between a generative-predictive song and future action becomes a relation between composition and auto-citation. Second, the song marks its reflexivity by a symbolic musical simplicity. Where the Count's narration in *Figaro* wavers from recitative to a richer music, an evocation of a surrounding number (the trio), Bertram's song is characterized by

Example 3.3. Robert Le Diable Act I: Rimbaud's Ballad (Verse 1).

Ex. 3.3 (cont.)

R. dé-daig-nait tous les a-mour-eux: quand vint à la cour de son

R. pè - re un guer - rier, un prince in-con - nu, et Ber - the, jus - qu'a-lors si

R. fière, d'a mour sen - tit son cœur é - mu, son cœur é - mu!

cre - scen - do

(avec mystère)

R. Fun-este er - reur, fun-este er-reur, fa-tal dé-

R. li - re! car ce guer - rier, car ce guer - rier é - tait, dit-

R. on, Un ha - bi - tant, un ha - bi - tant, du som - bre

T. E - tait, dit - on?

B. E - tait, dit - on?

cresc.

R. empi - re, foi de Nor - mand, foi de Nor - mand, c'est un dé-

p

Ex. 3.3 (cont.)

Example 3.4. Later citation of Rimbaud's Ballad.

Ex. 3.4 (cont.)

che - va - lier Ber - tram, mon plus fi - dèle a - mi; pour

quoi d'un air d'ef - froi le re - gar-der ain -si?

Alice *(trembling)*

C'est... qu'il est... en no-tre vil - la - ge... un

(almost spoken)

beau ta- bleau re - pré - sen-tant l'ar-chan - ge Saint Mi-chel qui ter-

ras - se Sa - tan...   *(hesitating)*   et je trou - ve.

Robert

A che- vez! quel

Alice

Qu'il res - sem - ble

trouble est le vô - tre?

Robert

A l'ar -

Alice *(excitedly)*   *(whispers)*

Non vrai - ment!   à l'au - tre!

pressez.

chan - ge?

cresc.

pressez.

repetitive formality, signifying a critical fact: the song's status as a *musical performance*. Reflexivity is marked the second time, as it were, by *singing*—in such a way that every character on stage hears the song *as sung*. *Being a musical performance*, the song is a sonorous mirror of the greater performance, the arias, ensembles, orchestral flourishes, preening singers, and appreciative applause that is an operatic performance, Meyerbeer's *Robert le Diable*, to which we are witness. The song, foregrounding the process of performance, also makes musical improvisation and composition palpable; it forces us to deal explicitly with ourselves as listening subjects, for we—the audience—are mirrored by the rapt listeners on stage.

III

Senta's Ballad in *Der fliegende Holländer* has always seemed a close relative of Emmy's song. Wagner had intimate ties to Marschner's opera; he conducted *Der Vampyr* in Würzburg in 1833, and for that occasion revised (and partly retexted) Aubry's aria in Act II.[19] In *Der Vampyr*, Emmy's Romanza seems to conjure up the vampire himself, who makes his entrance a few moments later; this dramatic conceit was echoed by Wagner in *Holländer*.[20] Fragments of text, familiar Romantic formulas—the "bleicher Mann" and the "bleicher Seemann," the "trauriger Blick" and (in Eric's Dream) the "düsterer Blick"—appear in both texts. The two numbers are similar formally, for Senta's Ballad is, of course, also strophic, with a nonnarrative refrain doubled by the chorus. Senta's Ballad is, however, a "pivotal" rather than a "programmatic" node, occurring in the center of the work and thus exemplifying what Dällenbach termed the "predilection of the narrative for *retro-prospective mise en abyme*," which "provides a fulcrum between the 'already' and the 'not yet,'" making it more enigmatic, less prescriptive of the future: for the listener, more open.[21] Senta's song is, moreover, forever set apart from any of its predecessors by what happens in its final seconds, an explosion in which Senta interrupts and usurps the third choral refrain and identifies herself with the redeeming heroine: "Ich sei's, die dich durch ihre Treu' erlöse" ["I am the one whose faith shall redeem you"]. Thus she brushes aside all pretenses that such songs are antique and irrelevant by confirming in explicit terms the song's reflexivity. She personifies, at this moment, Hegel's definition of balladic "content and coherence . . . born by the subject himself."[22]

Senta's Ballad, like Rimbaud's song, is more than a number existing in isolation from the opera around it. Wagner's famous comments in "Eine Mitteilung an meine Freunde" (1851) make this clear; he reported in the essay that in writing the music for *Der fliegende Hol-länder* he had begun with Senta's Ballad, and when setting the rest of the libretto, he found that "the thematic image I had created [in the ballad] spread itself out involuntarily over the entire drama like a continuous web; without further effort on my part, I had only to con-tinue with and complete the development of the various motivic cells contained in the ballad."[23] This characterization of *Holländer* as an interrelated "web of themes" was an exaggeration, and reflects a vi-sion in 1851 of yet-uncomposed music for the *Ring*; a vision pro-jected in retrospective interpretation of the earlier work.[24] *Holländer*, like *Robert*, is of course a rather conventional score: separate numbers strung together, each with its own thematic identity and (despite the patina of musical transition that connects one number to the next) with its own tonal and gestural closure. The *Holländer* numbers are beads jostling one another on a string, not the net of interwoven threads that Wagner would place before our eyes. Yet his description was not entirely specious; certain beads are streaked with spots of identical color. No listener can possibly miss the auto-citation of Sen-ta's Ballad in the body of the opera. Several times a strongly marked family of musical motives is quoted within some individual number; the family includes the main thematic ideas used in Senta's Ballad. In evoking the motivic signs for enactments of the legend in the human world, and for the narrations of legend as fiction, in devising a mu-sical metaphor for the link between the two levels, Wagner re-sponded to reflexivity in a way that sets *Holländer* (like *Robert*) apart from *Der Vampyr*, in which there are no such musical symbols for the dramatic device. The text's reflexivity—its function as both summariz-ing and creating (through a synchronic projection of its content) the opera itself—is, as in *Robert*, associated with this tenuous musical re-flexivity. Unlike *Robert*, however, the citations both follow and pre-cede Senta's ballad, whose pivotal position—its capacity to resonate in two directions—thus allows a more elaborate musical interpenetra-tion of song and opera.

In creating these thematic cross-references, Wagner exploited mu-sic's most familiar and least interesting narrative competence: the leit-motif, with its association of musical motive with a specific phenome-nal image or event. In *Der fliegende Holländer*, the recurrences of the motivic family are tied to both onstage enactments of the legend (such as the appearance of the Dutchman's ship "with blood-red sails" in scene 1), and the legend's retellings from the mouths of the many participants in that enactment—in Senta's Ballad, or Eric's Dream, or the Dutchman's own confession in the final scene of the opera. The musical motives, then, are defined from the outset as signifiers for certain elements in the story. The famous association between the open fifths of the Horncall motif (the first motif in Senta's Ballad) and the physical presence of the Dutchman is only the most familiar of these signs. Senta's Ballad in isolation, considered formally, is a three-verse song whose repeating musical verse cannot read or react to the changing images of an unfolding story. The ballad's music reacts to the poetic text in another way, by leitmotivic saturation of its monotonous, and repeated musical verse.

IV

Singing a strophic narrative song invokes convention and a historically established operatic archetype. Most narrative songs are not reflexive (the *Erlkönig* itself and the ballad in *Hans Heiling* are two examples). Indeed, narrative song's overt meaning is that the story is irrelevant (mere entertainment); only certain songs harbor a second (hidden) meaning, that the song is reflexive. Narrative song can, occasionally, trump its own second meaning, by frustrating the secret expectation that the song reflects the opera; this is what happens in the comic ballad about the dog in the nighttime in *Der Freischütz*. Senta's Ballad is not merely reflexive, however, for it transcends the reflexive moments in *Vampyr* or *Robert le Diable*—it is *metareflexive*. In its immediate context (scene 2 of the opera), it is one voice (with the Eric-Senta dialogue, Eric's Dream, and the Dutchman-Senta duet) in an ongoing debate, held within the text itself, about the epistemological status of reflexive narration in opera. The opening move in this conversation occurs when Senta's story is cast as narrative song, told in a formal and historically distanced tongue. Senta's words are thereby interpreted; she denies their verisimilitude. They are a fairy tale, meant to divert, without the power to determine human fate. The legend is only *at first* represented as fiction, so that its fictional status might be denied, when Senta cries out "*ich sei's*, die dich durch ihre Treu' erlöse." In confirming her identity as the song's subject—saying that legend will come true—she identifies myth as prescriptive, denying the first meaning of narrative song in a triumphant recognition of its reflexivity. Yet only a few moments later, she denies her denial, telling Eric, "ich bin ein Kind, und weiß nicht, was ich singe" ["I am a child, and do not know what I sing about"]—comforting words designed to allay his fears for her sanity. The ballad is now a fairy tale, "sung by a child." "*Are you afraid of a song, of a picture*," Senta asks Eric (but her song, as it turns out, is fearful indeed). In this series of moves—a ballad, an identification of its reflexivity, and a retraction of the identification—Senta's hysteria and spiritual chaos are depicted, as she wavers between belief and disbelief, and between human and transcendent destiny. Equally vertiginous is the epistemological spin that allows no rest—is the ballad's story fiction, or does it *predestine* Senta's life and the outcome of the plot? Two elements signal the truth of the matter, and the outcome of the debate. One is sheerly sonorous. The ballad exists at a violent musical contrast from its surroundings; though formally simple it is sonically charged, its opening a terrifying calculated plunge from the Spinning Song's girlish idiocies to the empty fifths of the Horncall motif. This move across such a vast musical-stylistic distance hints at reflexivity. The second is Eric's Dream Narration, which also denies the ballad as fiction in confirming Senta's momentary identification of herself with the ballad's heroine. The dream narrative is a passage unique in *Holländer*, one in which reflexivity exists outside narrative song, and thus within a setting that establishes no mythic distance between teller and tale. As in the Count's narration in *Figaro*, the reflexive moment is therefore all the more powerful.

Eric rushes onstage in time to hear Senta's great outburst at the ballad's close, and a few moments later he retells her story in a new guise. The ballad and the dream are two focal points in the long second scene, different versions of the same story.[25] Eric's Dream (Example 3.5) is meant to be a warning but, as the stage directions indicate, Senta falls into a "magnetic slumber" as Eric speaks and "appears to be dreaming the very dream he is relating to her."[26] At times, Senta's foreknowledge of the dream narration enables her to anticipate Eric's words; he allows her to usurp small fragments of the unfolding story, and the verse lines are split between them:

> *Erik*: Du stürzest zu des Fremden Füßen,
> Ich sah dich seine Knie umfangen,
> *Senta*: Er hub mich auf . . .
> *Erik*: . . . an seine Brust.

[*Eric*: You threw yourself at the stranger's feet; I saw you clasp his knee . . . *Senta*: He raised me up . . . *Eric*: . . . into his arms.]

But her prescience fails: she cannot see how the dream ended. Eric's reply to her last "und dann?"—"sah ich aufs Meer euch flieh'n" ["I saw you depart over the sea"]—is ambiguous. He seems not to say what he really saw after Senta embraced the stranger. What follows is an outburst by Senta, set to the music that had accompanied her explosive line at the close of the ballad ("ich sei's, die dich durch ihre Treu' erlöse"). And Senta's outburst here—"er sucht mich auf" ["he is searching for me"]—opens the opera to the *intrusion* that is its

Example 3.5. Der fliegende Holländer: Eric's Dream.

Sen- ta, lass dir ver- trau'n: ein Traum ist's!— Hör' ihn zur War- nung an!

(Senta sits down exhausted in the arm-chair; at the beginning of Erik's recital she sinks into a kind of magnetic slumber, so that she appears to be dreaming the very dream he is relating to her. Erik stands leaning on the arm-chair beside her.)

ERIK (in a stifled voice)

Auf ho- hem Fel- sen lag' ich träu- mend, sah un- ter mir des Mee- res

Ex. 3.5 (cont.)

Fluth; die Brandung hört' ich, wie sich schäumend am U- fer brach der Wo- gen

Wuth: ein fremdes Schiff am na- hen Stran- de er- blickt' ich,—

selt- sam, wun- der- bar: zwei Män- ner nah- ten sich dem

SENTA (her eyes closed)

Der And're?

Lan- de, der Ein',— ich sah's,— dein Va- ter war.

30

(as before)

der düst're

Wohl er- kannt' ich ihn; mit schwarzem Wams, die blei- che Mien'—

35

Blick — Und ich?

(pointing to the picture)

der See- mann, Er. Du kamst vom

Ex. 3.5 (cont.)

Hau- se her, du flogst den Va- ter zu be- grü- ssen;

doch kaum noch sah' ich an dich lan- gen, du

stürz- test zu des Frem- den Fü- ssen, ich sah_____ dich sei- ne

Er hub mich auf —
Knie' um-fan-gen — An sei- ne Brust; — voll

Inn- brunst hingst du dich an ihn, — du küss- test ihn mit hei- sser

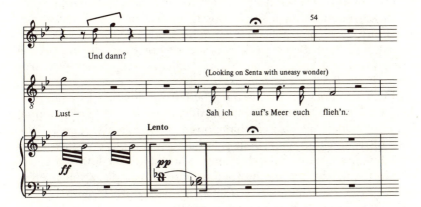

Und dann?
Lust — Sah ich auf's Meer euch flieh'n.
(Looking on Senta with uneasy wonder)

central theme. She envisages the unreal, the fictional, searching for her and, in her, seeks its portal into the human world.

Despite Senta's prescience, her hysterical "magnetic slumber" and its intimations of medical pathology, Eric is the key to the dream's meanings. In weaving the dream, the Hegelian Wagner whispers to us to distrust Senta for her prim operatic narrative, for her selection of a historically pedigreed archetype, to distrust its implications of the legend's fictionality. When Eric is granted his dream, the legend draws ominously closer to its enactment in the real world. Senta's Ballad tells a story in general terms and at a distance, while Eric's version of the same story is peopled not with abstractions like the "true woman," but with characters from the opera: Daland, Senta, himself. Dreaming, which can foreshadow reality, has a privileged status far more secure than that of ballad poetry, mere exposition of supernatural events. Eric's own banality only enhances the force invested in the intruder that he describes, whose shadow, seemingly, can touch anyone. When Eric declares at the end of his scene that his dream has come true, the legend is at last dislodged from fiction, and Eric's line "Sie ist dahin! Mein Traum sprach wahr!" ["She is gone! my dream spoke the truth!"] lays a bridge over which the Dutchman can walk, to appear at last before Senta a few moments later.

In the debate concerning reflexivity, Senta narrates conventionally, denies the implications of that conventionality, retracts her denial. But Eric's narrative is the turning point, after which both Senta and the audience understand that the legend *will* become real. In this ironic reversal of nineteenth-century stereotypes, access to the magical tale's reality is transmitted by a bourgeois character to a hysterical genius, and this reversal has musical presence. Senta's Ballad, with its threefold repetition of a single closed musical unit, is rigidly structured into music's most elementary and predictable formal type. The formality of the balladic mode is challenged by Eric as he makes the music for his dream; where Senta's Ballad is representative of a genre, Eric's Dream is *sui generis*.

This is the story of the dream. The last sounds that Eric hears in the waking world are a pair of B♭–D♭ thirds falling to D♭–G♭ (Example 3.5, mm. 2–6), scored for combinations of woodwinds. Over this, Eric sings his prefacing recitative line, "I had a dream; listen to its warning." The first sound in the dream world is that of the low bass F, the A–C in the winds, and the muffled hunting-horn calls, a sonic reference to Eric-as-hunter, as a man set apart by this profession from the briny individuals that otherwise populate the opera. The hunting horns define the narrator's presence at the opening of the dream, which begins with Eric himself, watching and hearing the sea, the world set apart, from the high cliff that is his own domain. For these first four lines, Eric intones his words over a two-note horn figure repeated monotonously in the bass registers as one element in the motivic wallpaper backing his words. In this limited sonic world, the musical turns at "a strange ship . . ." (m. 21 onward)—marking Eric's first glimpse of the Dutchman—have tremendous force. The initial tonal realm of Bb minor is abandoned, as is the original accompanimental figure. Indeed, the two-note horncall that had rumbled under the first four lines (bracketed in the example) is transformed into the iconic three-pitch horncall (mm. 24–26) that is associated with the visual presence of the Dutchman; thus Eric's presence as narrator recedes and we are transported from his cliff to the drama below. From this moment on, the musical substance of the narrative will be spun out of ascending sequential repetitions of the Dutchman's horncall, through the pitch areas Gb, Ab, A, C, Db, D, Eb, E, F, Gb, G: a juggernaut that could continue infinitely, and that defines no harmonic center.

Eric and Senta do not so much sing as intone; the open fourths and fifths of the Dutchman's horncall infiltrate and come to dominate their vocal idioms as both are drawn into the vision. At the end, when Senta sings, "und ich" (m. 35), "er hub mich auf" (m. 45), "und dann" (m. 52), she merely drones the open fourth, the opening interval of the motive, as if the musical icon has robbed her of any other melodic tongue. There is no musical closure to the dream, for Senta's last question, "und dann," is answered not by music but by silence: the ascending harmonic series simply stops. Eric's ambiguous reply, "sah ich aufs Meer euch flieh'n," is set to the peculiar falling thirds, Bb–Db to Bb–Gb, the last music heard outside the dream, before we fell into Eric's narrative landscape. The *sound* calls Eric out of the dream and back into real time; we hear it as the resumption of a Db–Bb–Bb–Gb oscillation that had been ringing out, and that was interrupted for a few instants by a dream, a state of unconsciousness. But while the sound signals the dream's end, Eric's words apparently contradict the signal: he tells the end of his dream, "sah ich aufs Meer euch flieh'n." The sound interprets Eric's enigmatic reply by revealing that this vision did not lie within the dream. We cannot know what—if anything—he really saw.

Eric's Dream is a continuous musical web that links musical transformations with events narrated, in a way impossible in strophic narrative song. The Dutchman's horncall is drawn from the two-note motive that anticipates it: a musical process of motivic transformation, but it happens at the moment that Eric spots the Dutchman's ship. The vocal lines are progressively saturated with the intervals of the Dutchman's horncall: a musical dynamic that also acts as metaphor for the dream's waxing power over the dreamers, the ascending harmonic sequence has the same force. Finally: the dream has no formal shape, no structural repetition of thematic periods, no harmonic closure. Its beginning and end are marked off by the odd D♭–B♭–B♭–G♭ thirds that define no single key. We cannot understand it as a musical object (like a ballad, a song, an aria), for it is an assemblage of musical impulses that underline the narrative's progress, and that, in so doing, also undermine music's very fabric, undermine formal coherence.

The ironic reversal, granting Eric a dream of the legend's real power over the human actors, is thus given its musical presence in the contrast between the dream and the ballad. Senta's musical narrative invokes a balladic aesthetic wherein structured music is merely a prosodic background for words. Eric's musical narrative addresses the content of his text, and in so doing relinquishes its purely musical continuity, becoming unstructured and vagrant. Indeed, the myth of intrusion, the archetype behind the drama, is played out in the musical aesthetic of Wagner's setting: into the ordered world of number-opera and its historically entrenched formal types comes a musically enigmatic language that is born of narrative exposition, and that is a musically anarchic principle. Wagner's willingness to devise music that in some sense narrates the actions that his narrator recounts also proved to be a means of liberation from a historical imperative.

V

Eric's Dream Narration and Senta's Ballad are quite different, in that one is an act of narrating, while the other is both an act of narrating *and* a musical performance. Their other dissimilarities fall out of this first distinction. Eric's is a verbal *performance*—for the ordinary man or woman, telling one's dreams is an amateur's simulation of more formal narrative performances. But Eric does not self-consciously perform *music*, is not a singer singing within the opera. Musically, the dream narration seems much like Kerman's idea of a typical Wagnerian narrative, a discursive, declamatory collection of leitmotifs loosely organized. But this conventional notion that such Wagnerian discourse is recitative to a higher power is an incomplete explanation in this case. Recitative would suggest merely *monaural* narrating, non-mythic events straightforwardly represented. Eric's Dream Narration is rather a mixed or independent solution, a new narrating aesthetic (as unique as that in *Figaro*), devised for a reflexive moment.

Eric's Dream Narration differs, as well, in possessing a pragmatic function. Eric admonishes Senta to "hear it as a warning" ["hör ihn zur Warnung an"]; his narrating becomes a blatant attempt to control the listener through fear, for Eric hopes to win Senta back with his story. As usual, the attempt to exploit narrative toward seduction backfires: "one does not," as Chambers points out, "narrate with impunity . . . to tell a story is an act, an event, one that has the power to produce change, and first and foremost to change the relationship between the narrator and the narratee."[27] To frighten a woman is to woo her, but to risk defeat, and the dream narration merely *assures* Senta—and in the end Eric—that the dream spoke the truth, "mein Traum sprach wahr." Performed narration (that is, narrating within drama or opera) may seem to end by underscoring the *truth* of what occurs in the stage-world, in that the play-within-the-play creates a kind of double negative (performance within performance) that becomes a positive, affirming what we see.[28] Eric's entire Dream Narration, indeed, might well be a *lie*—the possibility is raised both by that framing sonority, and Senta's apparent anticipation of his words, which could instead imply that Eric, with his eye to Senta's fantasy, shapes the narration as he goes along. Even so, it proves itself *true*.

Senta is different. Her ballad is doubly reflexive, both narratively and musically. Put otherwise: it is reflexive not only of an utterance, structure, or text-object (the plot of the opera), but also of acts of enunciation, structuring, and making—the acts of singer, composer, and, not least, the listener, whose role in constituting structure is as active as the performer's or the composer's.[29] These *acts*, which are in ordinary terms secret and inaudible (we do not hear Wagner composing, only the product of his labor), are thus made audible through the artifice of onstage performance.

To understand the *artifice* of performance, we must understand that characters in Romantic opera, while they can hear performed song, do not otherwise hear their musical milieu. For now, that statement can be taken at face value; the issue of this odd deafness is taken up at greater length in Chapter 4. The leap from normal operatic music to phenomenal song should not be erased by an embracing vision such as Edward Cone's (he argues that operatic characters hear all of the music all of the time, a claim that imaginatively inscribes the figure of the Composer into every operatic being), lest we lose our awareness of reflexivity as a charged and far from ubiquitous operatic phenomenon.[30] This distinction has musical, aural presence (as we have seen), and I shall argue that it is a gesture transposed from opera to instrumental music, where it can be heard as a moment of narrative performance in Mahler's *Todtenfeier* (discussed in Chapter 4). Wagner's later operas, however, collapse this distinction (so carefully maintained in *Holländer*) between phenomenal song or performed sung narration and the music otherwise outside and unheard by the subjects in the stage world. The later Wagnerian operas represent *narrating uncovered*. Put another way: they involve moments when phenomenal musical performance seeps into the body of the opera, when a concealing fabric is therefore drawn from the opera-body, revealing its metamorphosis into musically reflexive sound. The body of the opera, that is, echoes those acts of enunciation, structuring, and making, once only replicated in performed song.

VI

This unveiling occurs in Wagner's Orpheus opera, *Tannhäuser* (1845, revised throughout the 1840s, and again in 1860–1861).[31] Tannhäuser, as a character who is a singer-composer, has been acknowledged as one of Wagner's autobiographical self-portraits (in this, a relative of Walther von Stolzing, Hans Sachs, or the musician Tristan). Of all these characters, it is Tannhäuser whose musical presence is most distinctly marked as that of a composer through the agency of single device, one that Wagner never again exploited with such obsessive consistency: musical (leitmotivic) recurrences in the opera are represented as the sound, in our world, of music inhabiting Tannhäuser's mind.[32] Tannhäuser, of course, is directly identified as musician when he sings phenomenally in the Act I Hymn to Venus, and in that pageant of onstage performance, the Act II Song Contest. But it is his single act of narrating, the Rome Narrative, that *uncovers narration* and, in this, anticipates Wagner's later operas. In the Rome Narrative, a statement that is not (at first) textually reflexive mutates into reflexion, and a performed (musically reflexive) song becomes the body of the opera.

Eric's Dream, an obviously reflexive juncture, tells a story heard before, and a story soon to be enacted on stage. Tannhäuser's Rome Narrative is different. It is neither programmatic nor pivotal (to return to Dällenbach's categories) but simply a *coda*, coming at the end of a long evening. Tannhäuser recounts events not presented on stage, narrating the story of his pilgrimage from Thuringia to Rome in a time between spring, at the end of Act II, and fall, in Act III. This fact (that Tannhäuser narrates what is otherwise neither seen nor heard) initially marks the narrative content as nonreflexive, though the described pilgrimage to Rome in some sense mirrors in inversion the enacted pilgrimage back to Venus, played out from the moment that Tannhäuser walks onstage. Whereas Eric's Dream could draw upon motives previously established as symbols in creating analogies for narrative, Tannhäuser's Rome Narrative, in dealing with events unrepresented within the opera, on the whole cannot. The world that Tannhäuser describes has been given no previous musical identity, only the one that he creates for it from moment to moment.[33]

The Rome Narrative begins like any number: self-sufficient, with its proper thematic ideas and harmonic design. The strophic narrative song broods over it, but delinquently; the Rome Narrative begins as a distortion of performed narrative song. The text preserves remnants of strophic structure; lines 3–8, alluding to Tannhäuser's wish to atone for the "angel's sweet tears," are echoed in lines 21-22:

> Inbrunst im Herzen, wie kein Büßer noch
> sie je gefühlt, sucht' ich den Weg nach Rom.
> > Ein Engel hatte, ach! der Sünde Stolz
> > dem Übermütigen entwunden;
> > für ihn wollt' ich in Demut büßen, (5)
> > das Heil erfleh'n das mir verneint,
> > um ihm die Träne zu versüßen,
> > die er mir Sünder einst geweint!
> Wie neben mir der schwerstbedrückte Pilger
> die Strasse wallt', erschien mir allzu leicht. (10)
> Betrat sein Fuß den weichen Grund der Wiesen,
> der nackten Sohle sucht' ich Dorn und Stein;
> ließ Labung er am Quell den Mund genießen,
> sog' ich der Sonne heißes Glühen ein;
> wenn fromm zum Himmel er Gebete schickte, (15)
> vergoß mein Blut ich zu des Himmels höchsten Preis;
> als im Hospiz der Müde sich erquickte,
> die Glieder bettet' ich auf Schnee und Eis.
> Verschloss'nen Aug's, ihr Wunder nicht zu schauen,
> durchzog ich blind Italiens holde Auen. (20)
> > Ich tat's, denn in Zerknirschung wollt' ich büßen,
> > um meines Engels Tränen zu versüßen.

[With burning heart, more penitent than all, I sought the way to Rome. An angel had driven out the pride that used to rule me; for her I wished to do penance, to pray for salvation denied me, to dry the tears she wept because of me, a sinful man. The most heavily burdened pilgrim seemed to me to carry little. If he walked on soft meadows, I trod barefoot on thorn and rock. If he drank to quench his thirst, I sought the sun's hot glow. If he sent prayers to heaven, I offered up my blood; when he rested in the inn, I made my bed in snow and ice. Eyes closed, ignoring their beauty, I went blind in Italy's meadows. I did this, for in contrition I wished to atone, to sweeten my angel's tears.]

This seems to be a gesture toward the imperative of refrain. Lines 11–20 are a second verse that parallels a first verse in lines 1–2, but the huge second verse, with its long litany of antithetical juxtapositions, dwarfs the first verse, just as the first refrain in lines 3–8 outweighs its less loquacious relative in lines 21–22. The cyclic verse-refrain-verse-refrain design remains, but its proportions have gone awry.

The memory of recurring musical verse is present alongside the remnants of the balladic verse structure. Both text "verses" begin with the identical eight-measure phrase (an ostinato theme; see Example 3.6, following mm. 1 and 22), both end similarly with a cadence to F major cast in the ecclesiastical sounds of sustained woodwind chords (following mm. 17 and 52). The interior expansion in the second verse (mm. 30–51) is a tonal and motivic digression between these two pillars of the ostinato phrase and the F major cadence. The strophic song still haunts this passage (up to line 22), but imperfectly.[34] Formality is used self-consciously and mockingly. When Tannhäuser narrates with a faint balladic accent, he is condescending to a bourgeois listener (Wolfram) by speaking in that listener's own conventional operatic tongue. A terrible history is thus made palatable to ears easily outraged. In this, Tannhäuser's balladicisms are like his sneer in the preceding dialogue, "sei außer Sorg', mein guter Sänger! Nicht such' ich dich, noch deiner Sippschaft Einen" ["have no fear, my dear Singer! I seek neither you nor one of your company"], a lash at the self-righteous society that exiled him. At the same time, however, Tannhäuser serves himself, cloaking his tragedy in artifice in order to keep it at a distance, starting with this limping ballad to brush his tale with fictitiousness. In this way, he can confront it.

But the pretense of strophic order and balladic distance begins to crumble after his cry, "nach Rom," a quotation from the end of Act II and the words that sent him into exile:

> Nach Rom gelangt' ich so zur heil'gen Stelle,
> lag betend auf des Heiligtumes Schwelle.
> Der Tag brach an: da läuteten die Glocken,   (25)
> hernieder tönten himmlische Gesänge;
> da jauchzt' es auf in brünstigem Frohlocken,
> denn Gnad' und Heil verhießen sie der Menge.
> Da sah' ich ihn, durch den sich Gott verkündigt,
> vor ihm all' Volk im Staub sich niederließ.   (30)
> Und Tausenden er Gnade gab, entsündigt,
> er Tausende sich froh erheben hieß.

Example 3.6. Tannhäuser Act III: the Rome Narrative, opening section.

102

Ex. 3.6 (cont.)

Rom. Ein En- gel hat- te, ach! der Sün- de Stolz dem

Ue- ber- mü- thi- gen ent- wun- den; für ihn wollt' ich in

De- muth bü- ssen, das Heil er- fleh'n, das mir ver- neint, um ihm die

Thrä- ne zu ver- sü- ssen, die er mir Sün- der einst ge- weint!

Wie ne- ben mir der schwerst- be-drück-te Pil- ger die Stra- sse

wallt', er-schien mir all- zu leicht: be-trat sein Fuss den wei- chen Grund der

Wie- sen, der nack-ten Soh- le sucht' ich Dorn und Stein; liess

Ex. 3.6 (cont.)

-schloss'- nen Aug's, ihr Wun- der nicht zu schau- en, durch-zog ich blind I- ta-

- liens hol- de Au- en. Ich that's, denn in Zer- knir- schung wollt' ich

poco riten. *dim.* *p*

bü- ssen, um mei- nes En- gel's Thrä- nen zu ver- sü- ssen!

[I came to Rome, the holy city, lay praying at salvation's gate. Dawn came: the bells rang, heavenly songs rang from above; a cry of pious joy broke forth, for the songs told of mercy and grace. Then I saw him, through whom God speaks, in dust the throng fell prostrate before him. And to thousands he gave mercy, he pardoned them, bid them rise joyfully.]

The words "nach Rom" represent instantaneous motion, a swift departure from the countryside of the first part. The narrator, "eyes shut fast, blind" through Italy's meadows, first perceives Rome as sound: bells, anthems, shouts of joy. His blind eyes open upon a divine figure who is only "him," "da sah ich ihn, durch den sich Gott verkündigt." The moment of the journey's completion, "nach Rom," breaks the imperfect formality of the opening, with an odd effect of tonal transportation from the F major woodwind cadence of the refrain to a distant D♭ (Example 3.7, mm. 59–63). Tannhäuser abandons the thematic and tonal realm of the initial verses. Lines 23–28 (mm. 62–85) and 31–32 (mm. 97–105) are set similarly to music derived from the "Dresden-Amen" tune. The music for the two passages is parallel; only scoring and key are changed in the second passage, and the effect of a cleared sonic palette at "nach Rom" is repeated at "da sah ich ihn" (compare mm. 59–63 with 88–91).

The music's own tongue and the story told in the narration now intersect on many levels, and uneasily. The broad—musically illogical—tonal shifts for "nach Rom" and "da sah ich ihn" are certainly metaphorical, calculated in the first instance to represent the sudden transportation of the narrator's presence to a distant scene, as Tannhäuser compresses his weeks of wandering into a moment of arrival, and in the second instance to underline a different motion: the motion of the mind when a blind eye opens to a single image. The "Dresden-Amen" tune is a sonic icon whose meaning is defined outside *Tannhäuser*; its associations with sanctity and Catholicism could be taken for granted. Here, the "Dresden-Amen" tune is also used in a piece of musical mimesis, depicting bells, hymns, and anthems so that we can hear them with Tannhäuser. The basic parallelism of the two passages (mm. 59–87 and 88–105) is a piece of musical-formal structuralism that disregards the changing events depicted by the continuing narrative. Yet even while the thematic formal parallelism is at odds with the narrative's progress, a critical rescoring (from winds to brass) and the tonal change (from D♭ to E♭) take account of this progress. Narrative's demand that it be symbolized, a demand for musical unrelatedness, affects tonality and scoring, and yet is contradicted by the musical coherence and relatedness that find their expression in

Example 3.7. The Rome Narrative, central section.

Ex. 3.7 (cont.)

be- tend auf des Hei- lig-thu- mes Schwel-le.

Der Tag brach an, da läu- te-ten die Glo-cken, her- nie- der tön-ten

himm- li-sche Ge- sän- ge: da jauchzt' es auf in

brün- sti- gem Froh-lock- en, denn Gnad' und Heil ver-

-hie- ssen sie der Men- ge.

Da sah ich

ihn, durch den sich

110

Ex. 3.7 (cont.)

-liess. Und Tau- sen-den er

Gna- de gab, ent- sün- - digt er

Tau- sen- de sich froh____ er- he- ben hiess.

the thematic-formal repetition. Music half-listens to the story being told.

In the final part of the Rome Narrative, there is a fundamental change in the music's stance toward the narrative. This marks the moment of *uncovering narration*, and a final move from song into the opera-body. Tannhäuser has been motionless since his cry "nach Rom"; now he once again begins a physical journey. Duplicating in microcosm his entire pilgrimage, he approaches the Pope, and begins his confession. In accompaniment, the ostinato theme of the narrative's first verses returns, but now its function has been transformed. There, it was semantically neutral, a thematic item used as the building material for a neat eight-measure phrase. Here, it is given a completely different musical presence (Example 3.8). The motive is stated; there is a pause; Tannhäuser says, "da naht' auch ich"; the motive is stated again, dissonant, presented as a hesitant fragment punctuated by long silences. When Tannhäuser calls again on the ostinato, presents it as a fragment, and pauses to say, "then I too drew near," he makes a musical symbol out of that ostinato motive: the ostinato motive mimics the halting recommencement of motion as Tannhäuser takes his first steps toward the Pope. This is an extraordinary moment. A symbolic meaning is given to us, and at once we rehear and reinterpret the Rome-Narrative's opening verses. What was pure theme, a recurring ostinato motive, is reinterpreted as a secret sign, with a secret meaning retrospectively appropriate to those first verses. The motive is an audible metaphor of physical motion, of the progess of a journey.

In transforming the ostinato motive from purely musical idea to musical sign, Tannhäuser arrives at the threshold of a new musical aesthetic that will govern the Rome Narrative's final moments. Now, as in Eric's Dream, all formality is abandoned, and the music is created from an assemblage of unrelated, fragmentary moments that react to the events in the narrative. The diminished sevenths associated with Venus are cited at Tannhäuser's confession of his liaison (mm. 106–12). The diminished fifth A–E♭, scored for brass and low strings, the chromatic bass motive that accompanies the pope's curse (mm. 129–43) also has a previous association, with Tannhäuser's ominous entrance, following Wolfram's aria. Several seconds of silence mark Tannhäuser's loss of consciousness (m. 149); an iconic quotation of the "Dresden-Amen" music (m. 150) sounds at his "von fern tönten frohe Gnadenlieder"—once more, he hears the music of the hymn, now far away.

The journey to this musical world from the strophic feint of the Rome Narrative's initial moments has been as long as Tannhäuser's

Example 3.8. The Rome Narrative, final section.

Ex. 3.8 (cont.)

- theilt, dich an der Höl- le Gluth ent- flammt,

hast du im Ve-nus-berg ge- weilt, so bist nun e- wig du ver-

-dammt! Wie die- ser Stab in mei- ner Hand nie mehr sich

schmückt mit frisch- em Grün, kann aus der Höl- le hei-ssen Brand Er- lö- sung

116

Ex. 3.8 (cont.)

pilgimage, and is a metaphorical journey as well. In contemplating his past, in approaching his memory of the pope's words, the singer cannot maintain his ironic pose; he becomes entangled in his tragedy and abandons the artifice of convention. Tannhäuser in effect *begins to make music* as a translation for the events that he narrates, and, in so doing, his singing voice is altered to *become* the discursive and leit-motivically active voice that otherwise speaks through the remainder of Act III.

VII

"Tannhäuser makes music": the phrase is deliberately artificial. It res-onates from others that have occurred before. Emmy asks her on-stage listeners whether they would like to "hear" her fairy tale; Senta announces that she will "sing a song"; Eric admonishes Senta to "hear" the dream; Tannhäuser sings, "hör an, Wolfram, hör an" ["lis-ten, Wolfram, listen"]. Formal operatic narration begins with an ex-hortation, an invitation to listen, at times merely to the words of a narrator, at times to a musical performance. When a character in opera sings "hör an," and launches into a narrative song, the listeners know that music is sounding around them. By performing narrative in song, he or she underscores doubly two acts of making—enunci-ating words in narrative, and producing music. For a few moments, he or she is both a poet and a composer, whether sea captain's child, or hunter, or, like Tannhäuser, in truth a maker of songs.

This scene of *creating narration* evokes variable musical responses, from the formal rigidity of Emmy's Romanza, the varied strophic bal-lads in *Holländer* and *Robert,* to the collapsed music of the Rome Nar-rative, where the scene of performance intrudes into the opera. In the Rome Narrative, in other words, we do not lose our sense of Tannhäuser as both narrator and composer when the strophic open-ing begins to dissolve. Tannhäuser is no longer singing a narrative song, and yet he still *sings*; the sounding world of the opera comes from him, he hears the music that he creates. A border that is usually clearly marked—the border between music that the characters do not hear and are not aware of singing, and songs they can hear—has been dissolved. Wagner's dissolution of this border created opera in which the characters live in a realm animated by music that they at times seem to hear, at times to invent. Of course Wagner thereby in-sinuated himself into his imaginary realms, for these listening and composing characters with their various professions—knights, prin-cesses, courtiers, valkyries, gods, shoemakers—stand for the poet-composer behind them all. Elusive as it is, the illusion of the character who *hears* is a characteristic element of Wagner's language. Act III of *Tristan* is born of this illusion; when the "Alte Weise" passes into the orchestra during the second part of Tristan's narrative, we are aware that the music we hear comes from Tristan, that we are hearing what he hears as he lingers at the edge of our world. And this illusion was one element of Wagner's language that (unlike leitmotifs) few other later composers could mimic. Perhaps only a very few recognized it for what it was: the capacity of the characters to hear every sound around them is the truly Wagnerian aspect of *Pelléas*.

But in the case of *Tannhäuser*, the illusion of the composing singer carries with it some irony. The purely musical sense of the Rome Narrative, the more periodic and tonally closed structure of its beginning, begins to dissolve at the very moment that the music begins to *represent* the story that Tannhäuser's words describe. If Tannhäuser has composed the Rome Narrative, if Wagner presents himself, through Tannhäuser, as the composer, then the Rome Narrative itself becomes a warning. This is the story that it tells: should music begin to reflect the narrator's words, then music welcomes a dangerous and seductive intruder—incoherence—into an ordered musical world. *Tannhäuser* completes a process adumbrated in Eric's Dream (equally disordered from a formal point of view) by staging music's disorder under the pressure of narration as an authorial enunciation, at the reflexive moment at which performing singing becomes the opera, and the opera becomes singing on another level. *Tannhäuser*'s music thus also allegorizes within itself the myth of intrusion that informs its own supernatural plot.

The association between the myth of the numinous intruder and music's scenes of narration became a trope of nineteenth-century music, both operatic and instrumental. Thus before turning to a new problem—how the musically radical and "formless" operas of the *Ring* embody acts of narration and performance—we should turn to opera's scenes of narration as they resonate in an instrumental work: Mahler's *Todtenfeier*.

Chapter Four

MAHLER'S DEAFNESS: OPERA AND THE SCENE
OF NARRATION IN *TODTENFEIER*

IN OPERA, the characters pacing the stage often suffer from deafness; they do not *hear* the music that is the ambient fluid of their music-drowned world. This is one of the genre's most fundamental illusions: we see before us something whose fantastic aspect is obvious, since the scenes we witness pass to music. At the same time, however, opera stages recognizably human situations, and these possess an inherent "realism" that demands a special and complex understanding of the music we hear. We must generally assume, in short, that this music is not produced by or within the stage-world, but emanates from other loci as secret commentaries for our ears alone, and that characters are generally unaware that they are singing. When they can hear ambient stage music (as in the ballads reviewed in Chapter 3), their cognizance is made perfectly clear. This assumption—one that, I would claim, constitutes a basic perceptual code in hearing and viewing opera—of course enables its own fabulous contradiction. Put another way, the assumption, as ground, allows as figure those moments whose effects were described at the end of the preceding chapter—the moment at which a character, like Tannhäuser, appears to pass across the boundary between the phenomenal and the noumenal, and to hear beyond realistic song to that other music surrounding him. This effect allegorizes the experience of the opera-spectator (who "hears the music"), and at the same time splits the authorial-compositional voice (who "creates the music") by relocating that voice in a character newly aware that he or she is a performer (who by singing is also "making music"). Like phenomenal song, such moments are the means by which opera flaunts itself, representing within itself those who watch and hear it, who write it, and who perform it, even as it blurs the distinction between the three functions. The same appetite for self-referentiality, of course, inspires all those operatic plots that explore the power of music (*Orfeo, Tannhäuser, Die Meistersinger*), or that deal in the lives of singers or the production of opera (*Tosca, Der Schauspieldirektor*).[1] Strauss and Hofmannsthal, with the prologue to *Ariadne auf Naxos* (or Strauss alone with *Cappriccio*), have perhaps the heaviest of hands with operatic self-referentiality, which in earlier generations does not so wholly upstage other concerns. Wagner's self-quotation of *Tristan* in *Meistersinger*—to say nothing of *Meistersinger* itself—marks a way-station in the turn toward such later extremes of referential self-consciousness.

What one might (if whimsically) call the "deafness" of operatic characters is thus prerequisite to instants of hearing whose force is symbolic. Yet not all operatic eras are alike, and some characters seem hard of hearing where others do not. Certain Baroque operas, as well as Mozartean and the later Wagnerian works in particular, more often mix noumenal and phenomenal music; when Don Giovanni, in the middle of the Act II trio, sings the melody of his mandolin serenade (a phenomenal song) to woo Elvira, for instance, he appears suddenly aware that he is exploiting music, and thus that he inhabits, as a singer, a musical number. Yet in early Romantic opera, the noumenal music seldom breaks through to the stage-world, remaining most often strictly unheard; the phenomenal music (songs, stage-band marches, fanfares, and the like) seems more precisely isolated. This more careful separation probably reflects Romantic concerns with the notion of "unheard music," and a view of music (alone among the arts) as a higher form that originates in a transcendental and inaccessible space. The Romantic operatic characters who do not "hear the music" thus may reproduce what early nineteenth-century aesthetic culture would see as the condition of ordinary mankind, and the exclusion of bourgeois individuals from an artistic and specifically sonorous vision. Beyond this, the Romantic fascination with supernatural librettos may (as hinted at the end of Chapter 3) mark a complex and inverted double projection of the two opposed musics into a plot of opposition between humans and supernatural intruder. On one hand, opera by its nature always in effect proposes these two musics; one is worldly and audible, the other otherwordly, silent, and (like most supernatural figures) perceptible only to individuals coded as hysterical or artistic. On the other hand, it is precisely phenomenal ballads whose subject is the supernatural—that is, songs that constitute "worldly and audible" music—that are heard as an acoustic and textural intrusion upon the "normal" discourse of opera. This double projection proposes any mingling of the two musics as a transfiguring moment at which the mundane and transcendental cross, in an operatic-metaphysical dance that desires neither resolution nor end.

To argue (as some have) that operatic characters are constantly aware of their musical medium is to erase the figure-ground structure; that is, to collapse precisely that distinction that allows moments of hearing to attain their compact allegorical force. In *The Composer's Voice*, Edward Cone postulated some degree of separation, writing that while "from a realistic point of view . . . a character is unaware of singing," we must "accept the music" as a subconscious presence in that character's mind. But in a later essay, he retreats even from this degree of separation, writing that "when characters subsist by virtue of the operatic medium, the musically communicable aspects of their personalities have been brought to full consciousness, so that the characters naturally express themselves in song—song of which, in the peculiar operatic world they inhabit, they are fully aware."[2] While Cone's vision of aural awareness is particularly relevant to Mozartean opera, and Wagner's later works and certain post-Wagnerian operas, it is perhaps too broadly cast. The passages that are adduced as reflecting characters' awareness of surrounding music are precisely moments of phenomenal song, like Senta's Ballad, or the songs by numerous Orpheus figures through operatic history (like Monteverdi's and Gluck's Orfeo, as well as that disguised Orfeo, Tannhäuser). At such moments, however, the leap from the normal operatic world (often also the leap *to* a reflexive moment) is huge, and this very leap—the degree to which song is set apart as performance—is a means of artistic complexity and tension. The example that Cone sees as most "beautifully illustrat[ing]" his general point serves rather to call it back into question:

> As for the Seguedilla in Act I . . . for dramatic purposes [it] must be considered realistic. Yet how does Don José react to the Seguedilla? "Tais-toi! je t'avais dit de ne pas me parler!" ["Be quiet! I had told you not to speak!"] To which Carmen replies, pointing up exactly the ambivalence that interests us, "Je ne te parle pas, je chante pour moi-même." ["I'm not talking to you, I'm singing—for myself."] One of the great attractions of Carmen—who from this point of view might be considered the ideal operatic heroine—is her overt realization and enjoyment of the medium in which she moves, the medium that makes it possible for the Seguedilla to function simultaneously as speech and song.[3]

The scene from *Carmen* leads to Cone's conclusion that "Orpheus is not the prototypical operatic hero for historical reasons only: his role as composer-singer symbolizes what it means to be an operatic character"; that is, that operatic characters *hear* (in some sense create) the music that is their continual accompaniment and only voice.[4] Cone would eliminate the polarity between phenomenal and noumenal music, and, in arguing that all operatic characters *hear* their musical environment most of the time, propose that operatic characters invariably allegorize the master-figure of the Composer. Carmen's Seguedilla, in a greater context, however, seems to speak for the separation between opera and phenomenal song. José's prohibition (the line is significant—"*I had told* you not to speak"), though it interrupts the song, is first of all a repetition of an earlier line, in the spoken dialogue preceding the song:

> *José*: Ne me parle plus, je le défends!
> *Carmen*: C'est très bien, seigneur officier. Vous me défendez de parler, je ne parlerai plus. (Elle chant)

> [*José*: Don't speak to me any more! I forbid it! *Carmen*: All right, my dear officer; you forbid me to speak, so I won't speak any more. (She sings)]

When Carmen breaks into song, José knows perfectly well that she is *singing*, executing an overt musical performance; yet his sexual panic compels him to stammer out something *illogical*: of course Carmen is, while singing the Seguedilla, "not [just] speaking." When she replies, "I'm not talking to you, I'm singing—for myself," the line is an elaborate tease: clearly she is not singing "for herself," and just as clearly she conveys her awareness of José's confusion. It is a brilliant piece of characterization. And far from demonstrating that the Seguedilla is *not* phenomenal song (but nonetheless musically audible to Carmen), the line proves the very distinction Cone would deny. Carmen's predilection for phenomenal song can be seen as a badge of her scandalous femininity (when she performs by singing, she attracts and terrifies José), and her rejection of an order that galls her (performing a song in response to arrest, she sings, "coupe-moi, brûle-moi, je ne vous dis rien" ["torture me, burn me, I will not *say* anything to you"]).[5] This urge to perform sets her apart from others in the opera (only Escamillo, the other "wolf" character, has similar tendencies).[6] It sets her apart from countless more passive female operatic characters. No model for the aurality of all operatic characters, Carmen (with Orpheus) is instead a unique being whose singularity coalesces most strongly in opera's reflexive moments.

In Romantic opera, that distinction between phenomenal song and "unheard" music is thus maintained—to marvelous effect, to heighten those rare moments when the two embrace. After Wagner, the situation is much more diffuse. Wagner's force as operatic revolutionary resides in part in his dissolution of barriers between music heard and unheard. In *Tannhäuser* (as we saw), what was unheard music may seem to wash into the protagonist's consciousness, creating the illusion that we now hear music that is resonating inside that character's mind. Traditional explanations of Wagner's pivotal role in operatic history—that he liberated the dissonance, that he loosened formal structures into "unending melody"—need to acknowledge this other (unheard) element of his musico-dramatic thought.

Throughout this chapter—which is concerned ultimately with resonance from the Romantic operatic milieu—I will frame operatic
characters' alternation between "hearing" and "not hearing" their
musical milieu as one between hearing and deafness. The shift can
be conceived in other ways as well, and we should begin by thinking
about them. It is an oscillation between phenomenal and noumenal,
thus a vibration between two very different orders of temporally juxtaposed music—an animating one. I shall argue that this oscillation is
a projection or doubling of oscillation in another realm: a shift between performing narration on one hand and enacting dramatic
events on the other, defining a move across a discursive space. Phenomenal narrative song in opera is a (heard) musical performance set
against the unheard operatic music that functions (in part) as accompaniment to action, to the unwinding of a simpler form of time. Senta's Ballad, in halting action, also renders forward time past, epic
time. Any operatic narrative—whether in *Trovatore*, *La Nonne san-
glante*, or *Pique-Dame*—creates such a node, a layering of time, in
which real elapsed time, the time it takes the performer to perform,
is laid over the time represented by the narrative. The musical consequences of these layerings are deep. In what follows, I shall link the
musical and temporal penumbra that accumulates at such moments
to readings not only of opera, but of an instrumental work, Mahler's
Todtenfeier—considering its musical text, but also its context as a work
associated with Adam Mickiewicz's play *Dziady*, and its interpretive
reception. I shall argue that the movement enfolds within itself an
oscillation present not only in scenes of operatic narration, (and, significantly, in Mickiewicz's play) but in the Romantics' artistic obsession with the figure of the numinous intruder, itself, as we have seen,
a librettistic emplotting of the collision between music that can be
heard, and music apart and transcendent.

I

Deafness and music seem antithetical. Putting operatic music in terms
of characters' deafness to it may thus be a perverse move, but it is
deliberate; it underlines a fear that opera buries within itself. The
"deafness" that might coexist with the tremendous musical activity of
opera is one of the secret terrors of the genre. (Suppose that while
attending a performance of *Tosca* you are suddenly transformed,
given the musical ears of an operatic character. You are struck deaf
to most of the singing; everyone merely speaks—except at certain
moments, during the offstage cantata in Act II, when you are able to
hear the phenomenal performance. Though many might gladly do

without much of Puccini's music in that particular work, this experience would nonetheless be nightmarish.) Deafness is an unthinkable destiny for any musical individual, and thus Beethoven's biography has been dominated both openly and secretly by the single fact of his loss of hearing. Beethoven, reified as the human form of genius and indominability, above all serves as a figure of tragedy: the deaf composer. His fate haunted Wagner, who, like many others, preferred to heroicize this fate and wax lyrical over Beethoven's consignment to a silent world—because in Wagner's view, the musical works themselves would not otherwise have been possible:[7]

> But never and in nothing had he pleasure, save in what henceforth engrossed him: the play of the magician with the figures of his inner world. For the outer now had faded out completely, not because its sight was reft from him by blindness, but since *deafness* held it finally far off from his ear . . . what saw the spellbound dreamer when he wandered through Vienna's bustling streets, with open eye fixed on the distance, and animated solely by the waking of his inner tone-world? . . . so is genius freed from all outside it, at home forever with and in itself. Whosoever could then have seen Beethoven as Tiresias, what a wonder must have opened to him: a world walking among men,—the In-Itself of the world as a living, mortal man.[8]

Beethoven's affliction is deemed enviable, yet the passage carries no conviction, and seems to exist to stave off fear of deafness with its sound. *With its sound*: that is the point. In the *Beethoven* essay, Wagner's own prose style, with its accretion of adjectives and its length—with its musical repetitions—becomes pure sound that must ward off the silence of deafness. This fear—veiled in this passage—will be exposed violently at the end of the essay, in Wagner's account of a terrible scream, with which a musician-dreamer awakes from sleep. Not remembered upon wakening, the nightmare is a dream of silence.[9]

Against Wagner's prose, calculated as a defense against deafness, we can set Gustav Mahler's undisguised terror:

> When you wake out of this sad dream, and must re-enter life, confused as it is, it happens easily that this always-stirring, never-resting, never-comprehensible pushing that is life becomes horrible to you, like the motion of dancing figures in a brightly-lit ballroom, into which you are peering from outside, in the dark night—from such a distance that you *can't hear the music they dance to!* Then life seems meaningless to you, like a horrible chimera, that you wrench yourself out of with a horrible cry of disgust [emphasis mine].[10]

The musician's despair at his apparent deafness is agony over the *affliction* and at the same time agony over life *as if* one were struck deaf. Yet deafness (now not any real organic deafness, but an *effect* of deafness) becomes greater than itself as a metaphor for loss of understanding and the experience of observing moving forms with a sense of their emptiness. In a grotesque transition, the figures spinning to the mute waltz ("life . . . like the motion of dancing figures") become life as the "horrible chimera," the monster whose limbs are illogically assembled from many species, thrashing its serpent's tail in eerie silence. The chimera can also be a stuffed animal assembled of disparate parts such as owl's head, fox's body, and boar's feet—a baroque fancy typical of Germanic hunting culture. In both mythic and comic form, it is an object congealed out of false metonymic juxtapositions, and, as such, a physical tribute to the failure of logic. Its appearance in Mahler's text serves to project his despair at "meaninglessness" in another form. Mahler conscripts this "meaninglessness" to a point about music itself, for in writing that one can sense rhythmic motion without hearing it, and in construing this as the tormenting inability to find "meaning," Mahler finally reconstrues his "deafness" as the impossibility of locating meaning *within music*. Deafness is an inability to interpret the sounds that thrash the air, or the black notes that wind across the pages of score. The text—Mahler's (interpretation of) deafness—becomes a bleak vision of incomprehension.

Mahler's text was a program note, written in March 1896 in a letter to Max Marschalk, providing a conceptualization of the third movement of his Second Symphony as a route to understanding the piece.[11] Ironically, the program note, with its key to interpretation, attempts to ward off the possibility that listeners might hear the movement as Mahler's protagonist sees the dance—as incomprehensible sonic contortions and a random choreography of notes; in providing this reading of the movement's meaning, Mahler wishes to rescue his listeners from the very incomprehension (deafness) that the explanatory text describes. Taking the note's suggestions at face value, we might ask what parallels exist between Mahler's note and the *music* of the symphonic third movement. Or rather: how has the Second Symphony's third movement been received in accounts that seek to define its meaning? We can detect a recurring strategy through several readings, a strategy directed (of course) first toward accounting for the music in terms of the program note. We see in certain cases interpretations that avoid taking the music as a transposition of the little drama described in the program note; in others, we find accounts of a precise relation between events in (or suggested by) the note and events in Mahler's movement. In all cases, however, the apparent deafness of Mahler's protagonist must be transformed. An image of "not being able to hear"—heavily charged with aurality as it is—must be suppressed even in dramatic or plot-oriented readings that attempt to take account of the program note's image field. "Deafness" becomes the enharmonic comma that is caused when we try to combine the program note and the music into a whole.

The third movement of the Second Symphony is a scherzo conceived as triple-meter *perpetuum mobile*, a recomposition of an earlier *Wunderhorn* song, "Des Antonius von Padua Fischpredigt" ("St. Anthony of Padua's Sermon to the Fish"). The meter plays a role in certain interpretations; Constantin Floros saw a reference to the "brightly lit ballroom" described in Mahler's program note in the movement's waltz topos.[12] Floros's reading thus neatly inverted Mahler's text by spatially reforming the experience that Mahler's note describes. Where the subject in Mahler's version is far away from the music, Floros—by identifying the movement as *being* the waltz in the ballroom—lodged his subject with the dancers, inside, warm, and listening to the music. From where the subject stands in Floros's reading, he or she might well look through the window from the other side, to see that hungry figure out there in the dark. He or she is *not* participating empathetically in the emotion of Mahler's excluded protagonist, not hearing what he hears—silence.

Any reading that lodges us with the subjective consciousness of the protagonist must, however, take greater pains to *account* for what he *does not hear*. What, now, is the waltz? Suzanne Vill begins from the similarity between Mahler's program note and Heine's poem "Das ist ein Flöten und Geigen," concerned also with an observer outside a ballroom. The poem was set by Schumann in *Dichterliebe*—as a song that Mahler knew well:[13]

> Das ist ein Flöten und Geigen,
> Trompeten schmettern darein,
> Da tanzt wohl den Hochzeitreigen
> Die Herzallerliebste mein,
> Das ist ein Klingen und Dröhnen,
> Ein Pauken und ein Schalmei'n;
> Dazwischen schluchzen und stöhnen,
> Die lieblichen Engelein.

[Such playing of flutes and fiddles, trumpets come crashing in; my beloved must be dancing a festive wedding-round. Such humming and

such ringing, such drumming with English horn; and in between the
sobbing and groaning, of angels sweet and small.]

Both Heine and Mahler postulate what Vill terms a "discrepancy between outer and inner reality," expressed by Heine in the final ironic
couplet concerning the "sobbing and groaning" that exist, secretly
and inaudibly, "between" the music of the celebration. For Vill, the
music of the Schumann song, like the music of Mahler's symphonic
movement, represents not the outer phenomenal reality of fluted and
fiddled dance tunes at the wedding, but a secret noumenal sonority
heard only by a despairing observer—the secret "music between."[14]
Significantly, this gap between appearance and reality, which is filled
in Heine's poem with the secret groans of angels, is both spatialized
and emptied out in Mahler's program note. Spatially, it becomes
physical distance—the protagonist is far away. Emptied out of all
sound, it becomes his deafness.

Hans-Heinrich Eggebrecht, by returning to "Des Antonius von
Padua Fischpredigt" (the song that was the musical model for the
symphonic scherzo) also reads beyond Floros's direct linking of dance
image and waltz time. The mock-naive text of the Fish Sermon is seen
as an allegory of listeners' incomprehension of artistic utterence, of
the despair of the speaker before his audience.[15] Mere *attention* (of
the fish to the sermon) does not prevent failure to grasp a message.
Eggebrecht argued that in recomposing the song as a symphonic
movement, Mahler composed out the allegorical subtext of the poem.
For Eggebrecht, the scherzo traces a fundamental plot structure, an
inner subjective stream, whose trajectory is similar to that ascribed to
the protagonist in Mahler's program note. A composer, misunderstood, bored by the inevitability of being misunderstood, falls into
anomie, and experiences a moment of despair that explodes into
what Eggebrecht terms an orchestral "scream" 465 measures into the
scherzo.[16] In making his plot of anomie and despair, Eggebrecht has
constructed—in much the same semiotic terms as A. B. Marx on Beethoven—an eventful drama mimicking the psychodrama within the
subject, and hence a reading unlike Floros's, and differing from Vill's
in that it views the music not as a secret but vague inner sound of
sobbing and groaning, but as the more precise trace of a well-shaped
psychological flow. Eggebrecht is thus (of these three) the only critic
to make specific connections between music and event. Musical analogies for the interior drama of suffering include, for instance, the
perpetuum mobile rhythm that becomes a recurring sense of futility—
as Eggebrecht translates it, a sighing and Nietzschean thought that
"oh, everything is always the same [immer das Gleiche]." Yet like Vill

and Floros, he has squeezed out the deafness—"you can't hear the music they dance to"—that Mahler makes central in his reading. Eggebrecht accomplishes this shutout by dislodging deafness from the subject and moving it to his audience. The listeners who misunderstand the speaker—fish who "stay as they were"—are figuratively deaf. The deafness that (in Mahler's note) sets off the subject's scream of despair now afflicts someone else. All three—Floros, Vill, and Eggebrecht—are, in short, forced (each in his or her way) to press away Mahler's unhearing man.

Vill and Eggebrecht, in transmuting the programmatic subject's experience of silence to experience of an inner sonic world, in fact retrace (if unconsciously) Wagner's Beethoven fantasy. Like Wagner, they take the man who screams because he "hears no music" and create a doubled figure, the Romantic hero and the Composer. If this figure is alienated and unhappy, he nonetheless hears that "play of the magician with the figures of his inner world." This hero's consciousness speaks itself in music (thus identifying him as the Composer), and we hear this consciousness in the form of the symphonic movement. Both in other words perpetuate a strategy that defends against the silent void by postulating the existence of some secret internal music subsequently projected outward as the work. But to identify the similarities of their interpretive moves is not to break out of their impasse, for escaping this strategy seems unimaginable: how can music coexist with deafness, with not hearing?

Rather than attempt to solve the riddle right off, we might turn back to Mahler's own obsession. He marked the image of deafness by repeating it in two versions of the program, suggesting that it not be so easily laid aside.[17] This *repetition* plays out the origins of the program note itself, as a repetition from other sources. The program note was, in fact, more than an explanation for the symphonic movement: the man who peers into the ballroom was borrowed, and the note remakes other literary texts. Three are well known and fairly frequently cited in critical interpretations of the movement: a scene from *Werther*, Heine's "Das ist ein Flöten und Geigen" (cited previously), and a scene from Chapter 6 of Eichendorff's *Ahnung und Gegenwart*, in which Leontin and Friedrich observe a waltz party through brightly lit windows.[18] Another is Adam Mickiewicz's play *Dziady*, translated into German as *Todtenfeier* (1887) by Mahler's friend Siegfried Lipiner. Mickiewicz's play is, of course, entangled with the composition of the Second Symphony, though with the *first* movement rather than the *third*. The history of this entanglement goes back to 1888: in that year, Mahler wrote a symphonic movement entitled *Todtenfeier*, evoking with this title Mickiewicz's play; in 1894, the piece was reused in slightly altered form (without its literary title) as the first movement of the Second Symphony. This symphonic poem *Todtenfeier* (later the first movement) has long been associated with the play—a natural conclusion, given Mahler's original title. There is, however, a more covert link, since Mahler's later programmatic fantasy for the *third* movement itself rewrites an incident from *Todtenfeier*, a moment at which the play's Wertherish protagonist, Gustav, tells how he crept silently as a thief to spy on his beloved's wedding to a rival suitor:

> Die Mitternacht erhellen tausend Flammen,
> Man hört Karossen tosen, Kutscher schrei'n,
> Schon bin ich nah' der Mauer, schleiche vorwärts,
> Zwänge den Blick durch die krystall'ne Thür.
> Die Tische all gedeckt, die Thüren offen—
> Musik, Gesang—ein Festtag wird begangen.
> Ein Toast, ein Name—wessen? Nein, ich sag's nicht—
> «Sie lebe!» tönt's—die Stimme kannt' ich nicht—
> «Sie lebe!» schallt's aus tausend Kehlen, «ja,
> Sie lebe!»—Still fügt' ich hinzu: «Leb wohl!»
> Da ruft—o die Errin'rung schon ist Tod!—
> Da ruft der Priester
> Noch einen zweiten Namen—und: «Sie leben!»
> (Wie auf die Thür starrend)
> Wer dankt dort lächelnd? diese Stimme kenn' ich:
> Wohl sie.—Ist es gewiß? das Spiegelglas
> Läßt mich nicht seh'n,—ich werde blind vor Wuth,
> Ich dränge an die Scheiben, will sie sprengen:
> Da stürzt' ich hin,—mein Leben brach zusammen![19]

[Midnight is brightened by a thousand torches, you can hear the coaches clattering, the coachmen yelling; soon I am close to the wall, I creep forward, force myself to look through crystalline windows; the table is set, the doors open, music, song—a festive day being celebrated, a toast, a name—whose? No, I can't say—"Long may she live" sounds—I knew not the voice, "Long may she live" echoes from a thousand throats, "Yes, long may she live." I whisper in reply: farewell. Then—the memory itself is death—then the Priest calls out a second name—and: "Long may *they* live!" (As if staring at the door) Who is it who, smiling, thanks him? I know this voice: it is hers. —Is it? The mirror does not let me see,—I am blinded by anger, I press up to the glass, I want to burst it asunder: then I fled away—my life came to an end.]

Gustav's narration gives us a miniature drama, in which the rejected lover skulks unseen and excluded. Mahler's protagonist also sees a festive celebration—the dance in the ballroom—from outside. Yet Mickiewicz's man in the shadows experiences (like Heine's) the horror of his beloved's wedding solely in terms of sound—as a din, shouting, crying, music, singing. His loss of sense is a loss of sight; the mirror in the room frustratingly refuses to reflect his beloved's face and he ends blinded both by the misplaced mirror and his rage.[20] In Mahler's transmutation, sight is restored. But silence has replaced the music, and the horror is not the frustration of vision and the pain of thwarted love, but rather horror that music is there but inaudible, and that the meaning it bears is lost. Deafness (for Mahler) signals an inability to read and decipher the meaning of the dance, with the deaf man like one struck into idiocy. Mickiewicz's Gustav crushes his body against the glass to reach futilely toward the ballroom. But Mahler's protagonist is so far away from the center, so wholly outside, that he can no longer hear the meaning made by the world.

II

I have lingered on the provocations of deafness, and its presence-in-absence in the critical texts tied to Mahler's Second Symphony, in part because deafness has the capacity to deny music. *Deafness* is also the place where one special interpretation of musical voices can begin—paradoxically, of course, because deafness is the deepest imaginable antithesis to music, the one thing that a deaf person can never possess, a form of discourse unthinkable and unattainable. The deaf learn language, learn to read lips, but can never experience music. Thus musical performances—in concert halls, opera houses, and salons—are sites for various epiphanies of self-knowledge throughout fictions about the deaf. In Musset's sentimental story "Pierre et Camille," the deaf heroine's first experience of grief and exclusion is at a children's dance-party; the score is evened, though, when she meets her future husband at the Opéra. Music, the occasion of two critical incidents in her life, nonetheless remains inexplicable to her, irrelevant except as defining a place of social intercourse. Nabokov's short story "Music" makes of music the same silence. A piano recital brings together a long-estranged couple; he—struck deaf to the music—only sees the gesticulations of the performer, while his memory, released by the sight of his ex-wife, recalls the past to him. Music is not sound, but a bell jar that has trapped the two estranged lovers together for the silent space of an hour.

For the deaf man, all voices are unsung, not in one sense of the word—being unpraised or unrecognized—but in that they are undone, silenced, and dead: deafness means the end of music. Deafness acts like the Curse motif in the *Ring*, which (as I argue in Chapter 5) kills narrating and silences the voices of narrators. But where, in the *Ring*'s world, the Curse is in some sense a mysterious external agency that strikes at narrators and ends their performances, deafness strikes internally, as an affliction continually borne, ending our ability to hear voices that may well still be singing. In opera, nonetheless, the unthinkable is possible: deafness-in-music. Deafness exists as a virtual idea, exists "between" opera's music, just as the silent groaning and sobbing exists "between" the wedding music in Heine's poem.

III

Wagnerian opera breaks the barriers between phenomenal and noumenal music and does so in complex ways. *Tristan* is charged with signals for hearing; its world resounds with phenomenal singing and playing. In Act I, the young sailor sings from the masts; Act II opens with Isolde's and Brangäne's argument about what each hears—Brangäne insisting that King Marke's horns still sound, Isolde hearing the sounds of rustling trees, of water in the brook. Yet phenomenal sounds, like the Rome Narrative in *Tannhäuser*, can infiltrate the opera-body to the extent that the two are entirely commingled. In the Isolde-Brangäne scene, Wagner represents their two forms of hearing in a justly famed orchestration game, one of the great instrumental transformations of the nineteenth-century repertory.[21] Brangäne's hearing of the real horns is projected by the choir of backstage horns, with their pantonal wash of horncall intervals. As Isolde tells of *her* experience—what she hears—the intervallic cloud of the backstage horns passes to the pit orchestra, where, revoiced and reorchestrated, it is recognizably the same tonal collection, the same music, but as if heard (understood, interpreted) by another mind, by hopeful Isolde (Example 4.1). We hear—with Isolde. The music emanating from the orchestra at this moment seems to be a trace of sound inside her mind, this sound pushed outward, sung to us. She is no longer deaf to music that *we* can hear, for *she* has imagined it and created it, and in this is momentarily celebrated as the locus of authorial discourse.[22] In Act III, it will be Tristan's turn to hear and re-create music, when the melody of the "Alte Weise," initially a phenomenal tune performed by the Shepherd onstage, passes into the pit orchestra. We experience once more the effect of eavesdropping inside the consciousness of another, an effect that inscribes the au-

Example 4.1. Hearing horncalls in *Tristan* Act II.

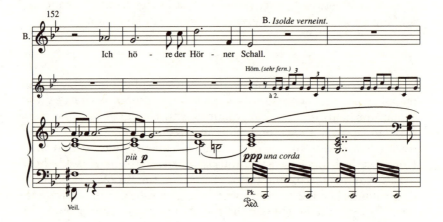

thor into the music. Tristan, dying and delirious, hears what we heard—the "Alte Weise" of the Shepherd's horn—but he hears (interprets, remakes) it to recreate it as his own in an act of creative recasting that we *overhear*.[23]

Such moments collapse opera's conventional barrier between heard and unheard. Thus while exhilirating, they are also frightening. By collapsing the barrier, they assail us with the potential for deafness, in inverting our usual privilege of hearing what the characters cannot: suppose, such moments may say, that the operatic characters now hear music that *we* cannot? Isolde's question at the moment of her transfiguration—"don't you hear? hört ihr nicht?"—might be addressed not to her stage audience but to us, suggesting the existence of a secret music beyond the "Liebestod" that we *can* hear. Are we, now, the deaf ones? The thought is disquieting. The phenomenal music of opera—the songs, performances, shepherd's melodies, and dance orchestras—are intrusions from outside to be properly kept separate from the normal musical discourse of opera, but Wagner permits this outside music to usurp opera's normal sounds. Wagner's intercalation of the two worlds is thus also frightening for its gesture of a violated border or invasion. In *Tannhäuser*, performed narrative song—as well as the narrative passages in general—allegorizes, as we have seen, the numinous intruders of German Romantic opera's archetypical and xenophobic supernatural plot by entering into and becoming the opera-body. When the Rome Narrative is invaded by musical incoherence, when as performed song it usurps and becomes the fabric of operatic music, the music writes upon itself the unsettling image of Tannhäuser's seduction by the underworld's forces.

Strauss's *Elektra* rivals *Tristan* in one respect—that precise musical means are employed to project a drama of hearing. *Elektra*'s music, like *Tristan*'s, is polyphonic not in the usual musical sense, but in the sense of possessing different languages or musical registers, many of which serve to set off heard from unheard music.[24] The musical voice that is most direct, more marked than the others, is Elektra's voice, precisely because it is she who lays claim to the exalted power of hearing the music that surrounds her. Near the end of the play, Chrysothemis asks Elektra a question that recurs frequently in Hofmannsthal's play and Strauss's libretto: "don't you hear?" Elektra, solipsistic in general, ever ready to shout that she "does not want to hear," replies quite differently here:

Chrysothemis: alle umarmen sich, und jauchzen, tausend
Fackeln sind angezündet. Hörst du nicht, so hörst du
denn nicht?

Elektra: Ob ich nicht höre? ob ich die Musik nicht
höre? sie kommt doch aus mir.

[*Chrysothemis*: everyone is embracing, and rejoicing, a thousand torches
have been set alight. Don't you hear? Don't you hear? *Elektra*: As if I
don't hear? As if I don't hear the music—the music comes from me.]

This exchange foregrounds a drama of hearing that is played out
through the opera, one whose central musical focus is Elektra's narrative monologue in scene 2. That monologue is self-consciously a
musical performance, though it has few indices of phenomenal song
characteristic of eighteenth- or early nineteenth-century opera: Elektra does not seize a lyre and admonish her audience to listen to her
song. Her identity as singer, and the monologue's status as a performance, is suggested both intrinsically, within the monologue, and extrinsically, in the surrounding opera's text and music, even by aspects
of her Sophoclean prototype. Sophocles' Elektra, for instance, claims
that only one way of speaking remains open to her: singing epice-
diums and "sorrowful laments." She has been not reduced but transformed by her sorrow, into a being whose only tongue is musical—
and in that final exchange with Chrysothemis she identifies herself as
cognizant of the music that surrounds her, but more than this, as its
source.

IV

Elektra epitomizes a final opera-historical turn in the mingling of
heard and unheard, which is at the same time a mingling of music
for performed narrating with music of enactment and real passing
time. Strauss liberates Elektra from deafness; Wagner whispers in
Tristan that operatic characters' deafness may now have become our
affliction—by means of textual and musical gestures that project a
sense of a music beyond what we can hear. Both, however, have done
so by contriving musical modulations between opera's two distinct
modes of noumenal and phenomenal music. Mahler's vision of deafness seems to speak rather for a violent separation between the state
of hearing/understanding and that of deafness/incomprehension.
Transferred to operatic terms, *Mahler's deafness* (his program note)
evokes an earlier state of opera, a state in which the barrier is still
intact and its breach or collapse a shock. Interpreting Mahler's music
thus depends upon returning to operas that foreground three oscillations: that between narrating and enacting, between heard and unheard, and between an intruder and an imperiled terrain. Meyerbeer's *Robert le Diable* whose characteristic phenomenal ballad was

cited in Chapter 3 (as Example 3.3), perhaps most forcefully exemplifies this type. The opera was savaged by Wagner in polemical attacks upon his early rival, but (as we have seen) resembles his *Der fliegende Holländer* in certain respects. These resemblences include the reflexive ballad, that device also exploited in *Der Vampyr*.

Rimbaud's Ballad can serve to remind us of the plot of *Robert le Diable*, since the ballad, like those in *Der Vampyr* or *Der fliegende Holländer*, reflects that plot in mythic form. Just as an unknown prince long ago seduced the princess Berthe, so has he now returned to seduce his own son Robert to devilish ways; Robert's seduction constitutes the chief action of the opera. *Robert le Diable* thus involves the familiar gothic conceit—the demonic figure (the unknown prince, who takes the name Bertram) comes disguised to the human world, seeking a particular individual whose soul is therefore in peril.

This states the plot-type baldly, as baldly as its earlier description in Chapter 3. But to focus upon a model plot as if it were one of Souriau's dramatic archetypes is to evade the historical issues raised by the nineteenth-century texts that unfold along these lines, and it is these historical issues that should now be broached. What happens to the net of aggression and pursuit when the intruder is male and the object female (that is, when supernatural intrusion becomes more openly a sexual threat, as in *Der fliegende Holländer*, or *Der Vampyr*), as opposed to a male pair (*Robert le Diable*, or "The Sandman") or a numinous woman and a human man (Hoffmann's *Undine*, or *La Dame blanche*)? Why is the two-woman story so rare (*Lohengrin* and *Die Frau ohne Schatten* come to mind), and so inclined to embed the central pair within rival relationships that draw force from their confrontation? What significance does the popularity of the type have in terms of a historical and cultural milieu, the xenophobic Germany of the post-Napoleonic era, in which Heine could easily identify these numinous intruders as Jews? Sander Gilman has argued that German and Jew alike read the Jew into this German Romantic figure of the otherworldly outsider. His language is marked (Bertram speaks cabbalistic words that the other characters find disquieting; the Dutchman's conversational style is deliberately bizarre and baroque). He can be "heard" as otherworldly by a sensitive listener, while his appearance may be unremarkable. Gilman considers this outsider wholly negative, a projection of hatred that becomes, for Jewish writers, self-loathing.[25] But is the outsider as black as he or she seems? While these numinous intruders must be suppressed by the plots they inhabit—driven back to Hell, killed by silver bullets—they also elude their suppression. And in theater, in opera in particular, it is less their *end* that defines them than their vocal presence. Bertram the character may dissolve like the Wicked Witch of the West, but can Bertram's *basso nero* voice possibly be killed by mere plot? Operatic intruders are thus empowered by both their physical voices and their status, as those who challenge bourgeois order and secure Christian ontologies, as bearers of foreign languages, mysteries, and art itself. Dr. Miracolo, in Offenbach's *Tales of Hoffmann*, is crooked and bald; he speaks jargon, he preys on young ladies. Yet Antonia sings for the first time as an artist (not as polite bourgeois female) when, in the famous trio, he literally gives music to her, and drives her to transcend an ordinary destiny.

Rimbaud's Ballad mimics folk song (as described in Chapter 3) yet it also mythicizes Bertram, in that Bertram's story—which draws strength from the richness of this historical context—is recounted within the formal and hieratic mode of phenomenal narrative song. That mythicization depends not merely on the details of the story recounted, but on the mode of its balladic presentation. The social surroundings of narration and the act of narrating—occult in written balladic texts—multiply their force in becoming live in opera; once again, the act of narrating comes to take on a force rivaling that of the plot being narrated. Rimbaud's act of narrating—executed as a song—also raises the point of resistance that we encounter in all strophic narrative songs: where the text narrates, does the music also narrate? But beyond this, does the music, by charging itself, mythicize Bertram? The music for Rimbaud's song charges itself by existing, like all narrative song, as a profound local shift in musical register. The domains in which this shift occurs are not all present in actual sounds; indeed, some exist as it were "between" those sounds. We might put this shift in the following terms: when the narrative song is performed within an already sung medium, this performance twists the musical fabric as if to underline the distinction between performance unheard and heard, and to mark the song's reflexivity. This means that the song is the locus for a buildup of excitements: an epic moment of absolute past time comes into the present drama, the reflexive "mirror in the text" is suddenly uncovered, and the operatic characters suddenly become aware of their musical voices.

Music (as argued in Chapter 3) has the power to signal these metaphysical explosions at the reflexive moment in various concrete ways (as in the Count's narration in the *Figaro* trio). What happens in the case of narrative song is peculiar. The musical transposition of these displacements is not some rich confusion or elaborate musical symbolization of depth and layering. Music acknowledges the explosion by imploding. The music in "Jadis régnait" has become markedly simple, as if a mass of musical substance had been suddenly deleted or leached out. In "Jadis régnait" (as in all narrative song) the music is drawn back to an elementary formal pattern of repetition; but, more than this, to a monotonous microrhythm that recurs throughout the entire verse, to an almost absolute harmonic stasis (there is not a single sustained modulation away from the key of C). Set apart as a musical drone, this music is radically *unlike* the normal musical discourse of the surrounding opera. The complex node that exists at the performance of narrative song, in short, produces exaggerated musical simplicity. This formal repetition and reduction of means, is, however, not a musical failure, but a musical gesture whose meaning must extend beyond the notes of the song itself to the song as performance (heard by the operatic characters) and narration. More than this: as a sudden musical break, the song recomposes (in an alternative way) the plot of the opera that it inhabits. This musical act of narrating—with all those sudden diminishments—is as much an intruder in the musically richer normal discourse of opera as the numinous outsider is within the bourgeois societies depicted in the Romantic libretto. Meyerbeer's opera, and all those like it, has found a way of embedding the Other within its own way of speaking. This is not to say that Bertram does not have his own proper musical voice— Meyerbeer gives him a particular timbral color, motivic and harmonic habits, and a fondness for the diminished seventh and minor keys, and these are, in a sense, musical forms of his corrupt and occult speech. But the twisting of opera into performed song, the shift to the embedded act of narrating, are all displacements of the intruder into the voices of opera itself, and the opera-body thus becomes the breached and "imperiled terrain" menaced by such intruders.

Action shifts to narrating, and normal operatic music shifts to phenomenal song: these are oppositions that have spilled out of Rimbaud's song. Opera will always give rise to two terms—whether "speech versus music" or "operatic music versus phenomenal performance." This set of oppositions can be extended (through the mediation of the latter pair) to "representing enactment versus representing narrating." Only the theater audience at an opera is endowed with perception of the entire spectrum. Rimbaud's Ballad as a type defines a ragged oscillation in pre-Wagnerian opera, with narrative song always marking a leap to the second term, to music, performance, and narrating. The song exemplifies the move from enactment to narrating and performance, a shift as violent as Mahler's imagined breach between deafness and hearing.

V

Meyerbeer's ballad can be heard as projecting an oscillation typical of Romantic opera, as defining a narrating register of music as a gesture of intrusion—music contextually detached from the music that embeds it. While not all intrusive gestures thus constitute *narration*, a particular kind of oscillation can mark a narrating voice in one particular instrumental case: Mahler's *Todtenfeier* (the first movement of the Second Symphony). Perception of this "voice" is grounded not wholly in an abstract analysis of the music, but also in speculation about the movement in terms of the *plots* that have been told about it—from Mickiewicz's *Todtenfeier* to the present.

The symphony's *Todtenfeier* movement has been, like the third movement, long considered a "narrative" and as such has been the object of efforts to decode its musicodramatic sense; indeed, Mahler's music in general (like much of the late nineteenth-century symphonic repertory) provokes a great deal of such narrativizing behavior. Eggebrecht thematizes this behavior, and asks what it is within Mahler's work that acts as the irritant that releases such activity. Literary titles are one provocation, and Mickiewicz's *Todtenfeier* (known to be the inspiration for Mahler's movement in its original 1888 incarnation) is the obvious point of departure for its interpretation.[26] One explanation for the association between the play and Mahler's music is merely vague and topical; Vill, Floros, de la Grange, and others have proposed it. *Todtenfeier*'s opening sections (the beginning of Part II in Lipiner's translation) depict a Polish-Lithuanian folk ritual invoking and celebrating the dead. Mahler's symphonic movement is obviously a funeral march; it has all the conventional musical topoi of the genre (C minor tonality, march rhythms, scoring, and so forth).

Alternative explanations appeal to more specific details. Hefling, for instance, reads the symphonic movement in part as encoding the second section of Part II of Mickiewicz's play, and so in analyzing the piece paraphrases in English the immense monologue that closes Part II.[27] This monologue is delivered by Gustav (the protagonist) to a rustic hermit, and we discover in its course (though without surprise, given his ghastly pallor and his sinister effect upon small children) that Gustav is a ghost. He has killed himself, and returns to warn mortals of his fate. Gustav's monologue, an uncontrolled mosaic of religious, literary, and philosophical meditations on assorted Romantic tropes (love, madness, suicide), is articulated into three large spans by mysterious happenings in the hermit's house. After the first part of his monologue, a clock chimes three times. After the second part, a cock crows (three times, of course). After the third part, three candles are extinguished as if by ghostly hands. The monologue is not generally "narrative" (to call it so, as Hefling does, means conflating its many modes—lyric, narrative, philosophical), but at least one coherent story is recounted, when Gustav recalls his tragic romance, confesses to spying upon his beloved's wedding (in the passage cited previously), and hints at subsequent suicide. Later in the monologue, to the horror of his confessor, he will reenact that moment of suicide, affirming its reality.

Hefling suggests that various musical events in the symphonic movement may straightforwardly be aligned with elements from Mickiewicz's scene (though he leaves aside a distinction that I consider significant, between the course of events that Gustav *narrates* on one hand, and events that happen in the hermit's cottage during that narration on the other). A clock tolls three times; a tam-tam strikes three times in the movement's course. Measures 324–29 (dissonant chords cast in percussive hammer-strokes that immediately precede the so-called recapitulation) become "Gustav's raging [that] builds to the dissonant dénouement of his reenacted suicide." Cello and bass sixteenth-notes opening the movement represent Gustav the vampire, knocking at the priest's door. That this cello-bass material is realized into a sort of main theme during the course of the movement is viewed as a musical parallel to Gustav's gradual revelation of his own identity. Similar correspondences are multiplied over the course of Hefling's analysis.[28]

Taking an ironic tone with such analogies comes easily, and does not do justice to critics' sensitivity to the problems of their own plotted analyses. Potential absurdity is one of these problems, for there is a moment in many programmatic analyses at which the analytic performance seems simply to fail, to falter on the faint ridiculousness of having to associate sixteenth-note figures with vampires come to call. As Dahlhaus wrote of Adorno's sociological decodings of Mahlerian gesture, "these are merely verbal analogies which have no basis in fact," which "appear suggestive but are rarely capable of being demonstrated conclusively."[29] Dahlhaus himself might well be reproached for suggesting that sonata form is a "fact" in Mahler's music while plots (whether sociological or gothic) are not. Both are tropes that precondition the work of composition and of interpretation, and neither is immanent in the musical text. "Sonata form," because it is an abstraction with musical pedigree, a commonplace and apparently cool or neutral idea, will appear to provide a more solid (if also less toothsome) explanation of the music than Gustav's volley of knocks, so concrete, so histrionic.

Hefling's emplotting of Mahler's movement as a Romantic mono-drama—arrival, reminiscence about past hopes and tragedies, philosophizing, rage building to a suicidal crisis, moralizing dénouement—attempts to account for a sense of an emotional-rhetorical shape to the music. So long as plot may be expressed in such vague terms—similar to Eggebrecht's plot for the "Fish Sermon" movement—programmatic interpretations slide down easily enough. Only the attempt to identify specific musical moments as precise dramatic moments in Mickiewicz's monologue for Gustav frustrates us for its combination of specificity and arbitrariness (though there is a certain appeal in its extravagance), as with the inevitability of the straight semiotic swerve, the claim that *this* event in the music stands for *that* event in the text. Significantly, such specificity always seems to be a goad to proposing rival marriages of textual and musical event. Measures 223–43 might plausibly be read as the "celebratory music" that Gustav says he heard while spying upon his beloved's wedding, the subsequent fortissimo interruption by the movement's opening material in E♭ minor as the subsequent moment of suicide[30] (Example 4.2). This "celebratory music" (as Eggebrecht and Floros noted) exemplifies a particular Mahlerian trope, "Musik aus der Ferne"—passages whose instrumentation produces the effect of music heard from a distance, as if played by some other, tramontane orchestra. Such moments are acoustically deracinated, and thus spatially deluding. This music might well be conceptualized as a *specific* representation of an event, a composing-out of "Gustav strains against the glass and hears toasts, songs, music from afar." What seems significant about the passage, however, is nothing so concrete, but rather its dispersed intimation of *otherness*. Reading such an effect in *operatic* terms, it becomes the intruding phenomenal music that breaks the body of the piece. In its effect as music "heard from outside" this moment draws to itself associations that resonate from Mickiewicz's image of the spy outside the wedding, from Mahler's recreation of that image in his program note for the third movement, to phenomenal song's intrusion as a site of narration.

VI

There is no direct, specific link between Mahler's music and Mickiewicz's text; there is no one-for-one mapping of plot events (Gustav, spying, hears music) into symbolic musical choreographies (mm. 223–43). There are, instead, certain *oscillations* that the symphony shares with the play. These oscillations in both texts evoke opera. Reading Mahler's symphony must thus collide with Mickiewicz's

142

Example 4.2. "Musik aus der Ferne" in the *Todtenfeier* movement.

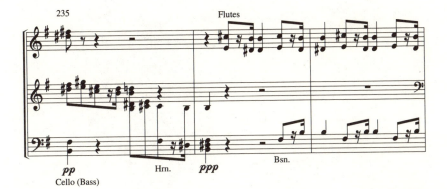

Ex. 4.2 (cont.)

textual manipulations of narration in various forms, and the initial trope of deafness—deafness as a symbol of opera's musical leaps between action and narration, between music unheard and heard—rebounds upon narration in Mahler's instrumental movement.

Mickiewicz's *Todtenfeier* Parts I and II might, to be sure, be seen either as frustratingly ordinary or shamefully derivative.[31] Parts I and II are a compendium in dramatic form of standard German Romantic tropes. They bring the following to the stage (not necessarily in this order): funeral rites, Bürger's Black Hunter, *Waldesgrauen*, the hero Gustav as a Werther doomed to suicide, clocks that strike midnight, and a vampire. Such lavishness attests mainly to the pressure of the Germanic education that Mickiewicz (well-nigh besotted with German Romantic culture) had absorbed; the play's scrupulous footnotes to its own allusions to Goethe, Schiller, Eichendorff, and Heine speak of this thoroughgoing *Bildung*.[32] It also attests, significantly, to specifically *operatic* imaginings—for otherworldly figures, common in German stories and poetry, appeared in theatrical form not chiefly in spoken drama but in opera libretti of the Romantic tradition. *Todten-*

feier is, in this respect, much more an opera libretto than a play, and can indeed be aligned with the type represented by *Robert*, or *Holländer* or *Der Vampyr*: the libretto dealing with the supernatural intruder. Mickiewicz's play is an extravagant multiplication of that plot, in which the intruder is written and rewritten into the drama, taking alternative forms as if the shape-shifting ascribed to him in folklore were reenacted as literary proliferation. For example: The final scene-fragment of Part I presents Gustav as a hunter, separated from his companions and lost in the forest. He lights a fire, meditates on his condition, and sings two songs. From offstage, another song is heard—one sung by "der schwarze Jäger" (the Black Hunter). This satanic figure was popularized in Bürger's ballad of hunting hubris, "Der wilde Jäger" (in which the figure appears as the "black fist" that rises from the earth to grab the protagonist), and in Weber's *Freischütz* (as Samiel, who stretches out his "black hand" to seize his victims). The Black Hunter approaches Gustav as if to claim him, and Part I breaks off with Gustav's stammered pleas for mercy. Part II begins with an autobiographical verse monologue recited by a vampire who begs his listener, "[du] hörst geduldig, was er dir spricht, / Der Gast aus dem Todtenreiche" ["hear with patience what he has to say to you / This guest from the realm of the dead"] (26)—thus also asking for the audience's attention on behalf of the various spirits who appear during the rites of conjuration. Gustav's own intrusion upon the rustic priest (as another "guest from the realm of the dead") is the last and loudest of these apparitions. Gustav thus plays a double role; as mortal he experiences the invasion in Part I, and as intruder he menaces those still living in Part II.

Multiplication of the numinous intruder makes *Todtenfeier* a German Romantic libretto in excess, yet the text is operatic in a more critical sense: in exploiting the same kind of reflexive pairing as *Robert* or *Der fliegende Holländer*, and using the characteristic operatic strategy of formal *narration* as pre-text, pivot, or coda encapsulating and reflecting its own dramatic plot. As in operas of the Romantic tradition, the myth of the numinous intruder is both narrated to us and enacted before us, but again *Todtenfeier* enhances the process. In Part I, the encounter between human protagonist and numinous intruder is enacted (Gustav and the Black Hunter), only to be narrated in another form as the Vampire's ballad. Part II's central monologic scene—Gustav's arrival at the old man's house, and the narrative phase of his monologue—works on both levels. Gustav narrates an autobiographical tale involving indirectly an encounter with a "black intruder" while, at the same time, he has left his life's narrative (suicide) in order to enact before his confessor (and before us) the intrusion upon human spheres that he describes in his act of narrating.

These nested reduplications constitute one form of *Todtenfeier*'s textual oscillations—that between enactment and narration. Yet *Todtenfeier* oscillates in two other realms. For one, speaking is interspersed, in mimicry of Goethe's dramas, with *singing*. Finally, oscillation in this mode is reflected by a third form. Whispering its own operatic concerns (and testifying again to Mickiewicz's obsessions with German Romantic art), the play also alternates between spoken-theater and libretto *text*. One leap from play to libretto occurs during the conjuration ritual in Part II, at the appearance of a beautiful maiden-ghost. Marked explicitly, with the usual verbal cues for libretto text ("recitativ," "duo"), the operatic mode can be seen in the maiden-ghost's recitative and aria:

> Recitativ.
>
> Ihr kennt mich: Röschen,—ich lebte ja hier,
> Und heute noch singet und sagt ihr von mir:
> Vom Mägdelein, das schön war und hold.
> Und doch keinen Freier gewollt;
> Nach neunzehr Maien voll Spiel und Tand
> Starb's hin in der Blüthe der Tage,—
> Und hat nicht Sorge noch Klage,
> Noch wahres Glück gekannt.
>
>   .   .   .
>
> Ewig schweb ich auf der Welle,
> Fühl den Boden ewig weichen:
> Kann des Himmelreiches Schwelle,
> Kann die Erde nie erreichen!   (42–43)

[You know me: a young rose,—once I lived here, and even today you sang, and you said of me, said of this girl who was young and beautiful, yet whom no suitor desired; after nineteen May-times, filled with games and playthings, she died, in the fullness of her days. She knew not care, nor complaint, nor true happiness. (. . .) Forever I float on the wave, feel how the ground forever yields, never can I reach heaven's threshhold, never can I touch the earth again.]

This sung recitative, with its concluding rhymed four-line aria text, is a fragment of libretto preceded by an equally operatic duet between the maiden-ghost and the Guslar, the priest who has conjured her. Less sudden is opera's moment of departure from the text. The maiden delivers her long recitative, follows with the brief aria, but the choral reply afterward is generically ambiguous. They repeat the words of the ghost-maiden's aria, but it remains unclear whether they sing or speak. Between the merely spoken, and operatic singing, is a separation that is set out quickly and clearly, but dissipates slowly.

Todtenfeier produces oscillations in many domains, yet one could argue (if somewhat perversely) that all of them fall back to a single opposition: not hearing music, hearing music. The most straightforward in this respect is the juxtaposition (à la Goethe) of the spoken-theater text with inserted songs. The opposition is exemplified in a more complicated way by the shift between enacting events (Gustav and the Black Hunter) and (re)narrating them (Gustav's monologic narration), a shift that in its resonance with the operatic device of the reflexive ballad also evokes the leap from operatic music to phenomenal song, from music that characters cannot hear to music that they perceive. In a final turn, this opposition is writ larger, in the hypotyposis of an overarching modulation between spoken-theater and opera itself. The mutations into operatic text are junctures at which opera intrudes upon the base material of the spoken drama, and when the word "recitativ" appears on the page it is as if (during a performance of the play in the theater) an opera had absurdly and instantly begun to be performed. These mutations are then, themselves, a hypertrophic node of phenomenal music, an acoustic explosion into music. As the performance of opera within spoken theater, they parallel the performance of song within opera.

Dwelling on Mickiewicz's *Todtenfeier* refreshes a vision of this schism or change in register that delineates the narrating voice. In its imagery, the play is ordinary, an encyclopedia of the folk-gothic in forms now all too familiar. If its imagery is paltry, however, one aspect of the text's presentation is not, this vibration between two ways of speaking (merely speaking and singing), two modes of representation (enactment and narrating), and two forms of theater (spoken play and opera libretto). Thus Mickiewicz's text embeds within itself the critical oscillation between noumenal and phenomenal music, between a corresponding *enacting* and *narrating*, that inhabits all opera and that is particularly violent in pre-Wagnerian works like *Robert le Diable*.

All these forms of oscillation are in the end synthesized, allegorized with explicit references to music, in Mahler's misreading of Gustav's confession of spying. Mickiewicz's Gustav describes how he witnessed the wedding of his beloved from outside the ballroom, his face pressed against the glass, *hearing the music*. For Mahler, this became a man far away from the dance, and *unable to hear*. This deafness, we now see, is an operatic affliction. At this instant, what is Mahler's transmuted protagonist but an operatic character who discovers what no other operatic character will ever know—that he is deaf to the music that surrounds him? Mahler's rereading of Mickiewicz's image thus holds within itself this secret operatic terror. His protagonist, pressed to the margins of his world, is an operatic character banished from the stage and freed from the operatic illusion, but the escape brings no solace. The escape suggests a metaphysical barrier crossed or collapsed, while the protagonist's inability to "hear the music" affirms that the fissure between the sung (the music we hear, but he cannot) and phenomenal song (the only music he can possess) cannot be bridged.

VII

This fissure, as we have seen, has a direct musical presence in opera, as an unmediated juxtaposition of two unrelated musics, and the musical reductions that mark phenomenal song. *Juxtaposition*: this is the critical word. The gesure of performed narration sounds itself in *Todtenfeier* not merely as the effect of a *song* in general (a *Lied*).[33] Rather, the movement creates a deliberate disjunction, in which an evocation of song specifically creates a breach with its larger surroundings—the effect not of *Lied*, but of inserted operatic song, and of operatic narrative.

Readings of Mahler's *Todtenfeier* movement (following a long music-analytical tradition) have preferred to search for coherence, for a single form or structure, rather than phenomena as troubling as disjunction, oscillation, or intrusion. To define the latter, however, one might well begin with points of agreement about the former. There have been minor disagreements about the musical structure of the movement, but at first glance it seems straightforward; Vill explains that structure as follows. First, we hear an exposition of the main thematic group in C minor (mm. 1–47), a contrasting theme in E major, a retransition to some sort of varied second exposition of the main material and the contrasting theme (mm. 64–116). The development section has two main spans, one beginning at measure 117 with a play upon the contrasting theme, and the other at measure 244, with the violent fortissimo reprise of the movement's opening measures in E♭ minor. The recapitulation is prepared with the usual buildup, and enters at measure 331. Everything after the decisive C minor cadence, the structural cadence in measure 391, is an epilogue, based upon another repetition of the main thematic group.[34]

Other critics who have read the first movement's structure do not notably disagree with Vill's parsing-out. Such a clean consensus seem to speak generally for the justness of this (sonata)-formal view of the movement's trajectory, as well as for the pervasiveness of a common music-analytical assumption that sonata form is a fact of symphonic first movements. Formal description may serve as a predicate to consideration of how the movement blurs or plays upon formal gesture.[35] Such choices, or manipulations, of formal shape can be seen as expressing a dramatic plot themselves. As Hefling puts it, "musical process projecting cogent form *is* the drama."[36]

Vill, however, shifts from formal description to a different sort of conclusion. Beginning from Adorno's vision of "epic" qualities in Mahler's writing, qualities that generate a sense of detachment, she makes an intriguing sociological comment on the sonata pattern and the Funeral March topoi in the movement:

> Mahler combines the basic tragic mood with the element of impetus in march, a combination, however, that symbolizes at once a collective motion, and that motion's effect of "gathering together" . . . the Funeral March is used like a kind of membrane [eine Folie],[37] an element of form and expression, which encloses an individual, subjective grief in the expression of general grief over a trans-individual threshhold situation [death]. That is, the grief of the individual is converted into assuagement, by means of objectification, by its communalization into a familiar form.[38]

For Vill, the various programs that Mahler wrote over the course of time for the first movement (most of which describe "observing" the funeral of a hero, and none of which resemble Mickiewicz's drama) covertly propose a similar agenda. The observer is distanced; he constructs the funeral through his observation. The same effect of distance is attained within the music for the movement. *Language*, as a bearer of subjective impressions, capitulates before *music* as a force of objectification and hence greater power of expression. Like others, she experiences the movement's unfolding of a dramatic conflict (its element of "language") as musically constituted in a struggle between various distinctive thematic-harmonic ideas. This dramatic sense of sonata trajectories is a familiar one. Her hearing of the movement, however, is also doubly exposed. The "membrane" of Funeral March and sonata tropes, which seals the work into itself, generates a sheen of distance from any raw drama, from a sense of enactment by a suffering, living persona. Though Vill does not put it in these terms, she senses the entire movement as the enunciation of an epic voice that objectifies individual tragedy by respeaking it in a communal and distancing mode.

Vill's reading is beyond formalism since it views *form*, in effect, as manifesting *voice*, or at least as an "objective" way of telling a mood (tragic) and a drama. This, not the particular formal analysis itself, is what seems most fertile in her interpretation. Indeed, one could take issue with her (and most critics') assumption that the movement is "in sonata form" at all.

For one thing, the "main thematic group" recurs, as it were, too many times, each time as a rebeginning, asserting itself repeatedly against a radically *different* musical gesture (Example 4.3). The "contrasting theme" (usually called the "Gesang" or "Song" theme, after Mahler's name for it in his musical sketches) comes as an interruption, though putting it in such relatively neutral terms is somewhat misleading. The metaphorical language employed in verbalizations of this moment itself speaks for a deep sonic break; Richard Specht wrote of a "plötzliche Wendung," as did Paul Bekker; Reilly of the "emotional distance from the previous Funeral March, accomplished through inversions in almost every musical parameter," Floros of the

Example 4.3. The first "Gesang" interruption.

"intense contrast in character," Vill of a differentiation so sharp that the juxtaposition engendered the basic drama of the symphonic movement: "the renunciation of any idea of compromise or communication between opposites."[39] More violent than the *contrast* or *irreconcilability* of the two ideas, however, is the convulsive reentry of the Funeral March ideas *against* the single tremolo note that makes a sudden end of the "Gesang" in measure 64. This paroxysm, a huge sonic stagger from one sound to another, is replayed like an obsession through the movement, at measure 244 (cf. Example 4.2) and again, its sharpness muted or dampened, in measure 391. Against these recurrences, two more gradually prepared repetitions of the Funeral March opening (one beginning in m. 147, and one at the recapitulation in m. 329) are less ragged. The recapitulation reentry *is* signaled by conventional musical means (buildup on the dominant, "demanding resolution"), and is not a tonally disjunct intrusion upon the decaying "Gesang."

In evoking the formal choreography of the movement, we might best speak of cycles, of digressions that congeal into these points of repetition and articulation.[40] Quibbles over the movement's form are, however, an interpretive red herring. What seems significant is not the pattern itself, but these various sites of hyperbolic musical disjunction. Cracks fissure the music at the entry of the "Gesang" and at certain reentries of the Funeral March. They mark the boundaries of a membrane laid down by an outside "voice." They mark the entry of a song suddenly performed.

With the "Gesang" there is not merely a musical *contrast*, but a registral shift to musical discourse that signals a *singer* and a *song*. The third and most complicated "Gesang" episode, in measures 208–43 (cf. Example 2.4), contains a range of mutations. Registral shift into singing is first made instrumentally—made, that is, in a realm where Mahler typically indulged his taste for eccentric and fantastic extremes. There is a double explosion of harp activity (mm. 208 and 226), where the harps had been almost mute before. In this context, the explosions have Orphic force; these are not just the usual symphonic harp *passagi*. The harp is foregrounded in such an extreme, baroque manner that its intrusion is like an alarm or declaration, as if the instrument is reclaiming its pagan meaning as lyre and accompaniment to epic singing (in this, it is similar to the sudden and loquatious harp that ends Stravinsky's *Orpheus*). Mahler's sudden switch to the tramontane orchestra "aus der Ferne"—his bleaching back of orchestral timbre—is a doubling of an acoustic otherness begun by the suddenly excited harps. The second "Gesang," (starting at m. 117) and the last (starting at m. 362) speak themselves as phenomenal song in other ways. They also foreground the harps. But they are also marked by musical *blankness*, by a sense of substance that is leached away (Example 4.4). Melody is diminished and simplified, gently repetitive. Harmony is drawn back to a drone, a circling plagal bass figure that loses even this minimal motion to become the sustained tonic E♮. When we sense an allusion to *Die Walküre* (the "Magic Fire" music in the English horn at the end), we read the allusion not as symbol but as self-reflexive statement. *Walküre*'s plot and author are irrelevant, neither a clue to decoding yet another *Todtenfeier* "plot" (is it really a story about Brünnhilde?) nor a piece of evidence for Mahler's psychobiography. *Walküre* as opera is critical. By enfolding *Walküre*, the "Gesang" tells itself extrinsically as operatic. By means of its peculiar and marked musical diminishment, it tells itself intrinsically as phenomenal song, and as a voice from outside.

VIII

Mahler's "deafness," Mickiewicz's man in the shadows—are fragments, isolated images with a certain resonance. These fragments have suggested a means of hearing a gesture of musical narration in music without a referential object—but the suggestion, like all verbal interpretations of music, remains itself a performance and not a masterplot. But perhaps it can serve to suggest that moments of musical narrating involve rending the fabric of music (whether in *The Sorcerer's Apprentice*, *Der fliegende Holländer*, or *Todtenfeier*): thus they create interpretive dilemmas. Such moments (and their sonic textures) are often pushed aside by traditional musical analysis with its bias toward marks of "coherence" and its reversion to normalizing terms ("organized," "unified," "structured") that have one unfortunate critical effect: they emphasize how self-questioning, richer music (like Mahler's, like all opera) resembles music more ordinary. Awareness of the "narrating voice" draws our attention from places that house coherence to places where such displacements occur, and thus may well encourage us to find critical means to hear and interpret otherwise marginalized gestures. But defining such moments involves more than a move toward music-critical or music-analytical revisionism. The narrating voice imperils, as does the numinous intruder, with his effect of disruption and the otherworldliness he imports into bourgeois society. Thus this musical gesture of intrusion, as I have intimated, can be interpreted culturally, as a trace of nineteenth-century fears (and obsessions) with the notion of otherness. One must, however, also read beyond this first and plausible musicosociological equation. Nineteenth-century culture saw this numinous intruder in

Example 4.4. The last "Gesang" interruption.

Ex. 4.4 (cont.)

many guises—as despicable outsider, as revolutionary, as ironic voice, as a carrier from the site of an "unheard" sound. Narrating voices within music, like these strangers who haunt the Romantic tradition, create their own dissonant moments, interrupting the spaces surrounding them. Thus in a final interpretive turn (and recalling that strange double projection elaborated at the opening of this chapter) we can align this voice with those central operatic moments that assuage their characters' deafness, by breaching the separation of noumenal and phenomenal and bringing "unheard" sound into the human world on stage. Moments of musical narration enact this quintessentially Romantic vision: the transfiguring confluence of music heard and unheard, of singing sung and unsung.

Chapter Five

WOTAN'S MONOLOGUE AND THE MORALITY OF
MUSICAL NARRATION

HUMAN NARRATORS come in many forms. Some are completely reliable: most epic narrators speak with detachment, and thus with authority. They elicit trust. But human narrators may also be revealed as immoral by giving tongue to lies, by speaking themselves buffoons, unreliable, or dubious. Then their stories will *ring false*, for while we may not *know* that the story is a lie, something about its presentation betrays its teller. When narration is allied to music, sensing truth demands doubly acute ears. Strauss's Clytaemnestra says, "was die wahrheit ist, das dringt kein mensch heraus" ["what is true, what is untrue, no one can know"], but during her encounter with Elektra it is *music* that Clytaemnestra cannot hear that (ironically) tells us the truth that she claims must elude us. We know, long before she does, that she is doomed, as Strauss exploits operatic music's capacity to speak the ineffable and otherwise unknowable.

Indeed, we generally assume that the message conveyed by that music—whatever form it takes—possesses absolute moral authority, that whatever falsehoods are spoken by a character, the music will speak across and thus expose the lies. This thought (which has been adumbrated in Chapters 1–4) reverberates through most writing on opera; Peter Conrad's *Romatic Opera and Literary Form* (to cite one example) is, in some senses, an extended exploration of how music smoothes and fulfills what language cannot define. Conrad, writing of Isolde's narration in *Tristan* Act I, proposed that "Wagner's people are characterized by music, not drama: the truth about the vengeful Isolde of the first act is intimated by the orchestra, with its unappeased yearnings which betray her own fictitious, dramatic version of events."[1] Music, in his view, is bound to flatten out what words make ambiguous. It has an "appetite for disclosure," for "it is only in words that we can tell lies"; music is "unable to cope with the prevarications of allegory."[2] When we encounter an inspired and truthful character, his rectitude is confirmed, his voice enhanced by music: this, for instance, is Caryl Emerson's interpretation of the narrator Pimen in Musorgsky's *Boris Godunov*, whose "*truthful* stories" need only be told to shape history, and to kill kings. When the Writing Theme that first accompanies his storytelling in the monastery scene becomes the sound of Boris's guilt-ridden thought, we *know* (for the music has told us) that Pimen has truly exposed Boris's secret crimes. As Emerson puts it, Pimen does not "rely on the powers of *this* world"—he is endorsed by musical signs that multiply and secure his moral force.[3]

Later Wagnerian opera—the *Ring* in particular—nonetheless confutes the moral authority of music by giving us music that may ring false. In the *Ring*, music exists as only one strain in a polyphonic web of narration in different voices, which includes the words of the character, his or her singing voice, the voices within the musical fabric of a given passage as a whole. But far from validating or conferring security on narrative words, music can speak itself equally doubtful. This is what happens in one particular case—the *Ring*'s longest narration, sung by Wotan in Act II of *Die Walküre*—where the music is called into question because it exists as the monologic utterance of a dubious narrator, Wotan himself.

The *Ring* is able to attain its narrative multiplications, and to present music that rings false, in part because it is saturated with scenes of narration: no other operatic work rivals it in this respect. This saturation was a perverse and unanticipated consequence of the *Ring* poem's genesis in the years 1848–1853. Wagner wrote three of the four *Ring* libretti to *eliminate* narration from the fourth, *Siegfrieds Tod* (*Götterdämmerung*), the original single-opera version of the drama. In transposing what was originally narrated into onstage action, he believed that he could better compel belief in his mythic world. Yet as the text evolved, scenes of narration crept back in. Thus the *Ring*'s evolution circles around artistic questions of enactment and narration that are also played out in moral terms within the operas themselves. What follows—an account of both the *Ring*'s evolution and interpretations of that evolution—forms a prelude, in asking again how music is *assumed to narrate*, to understanding Wotan's Monologue as monophonic, Wotan's music as his own fabrication.

I

The history of the *Ring* text's evolution from a single opera has itself become a Wagnerian legend. In the last months of 1848, Wagner wrote a libretto for a "tragic, heroic" opera called *Siegfrieds Tod*. The libretto depicts Siegfried's arrival at the Gibichung court, his betrayal of Brünnhilde, Brünnhilde's conspiracy with Hagen and Gunther, how Hagen murdered Siegfried, how Brünnhilde dies with Siegfried on his funeral pyre, returning his magic ring to the waters of the

Rhine. *Siegfrieds Tod* is *Götterdämmerung*—with some surprising differences.

Brünnhilde is visited not by Waltraute but by all the Valkyries; they scold her for yielding to mortal love, but bring no gloomy reports of Valhalla. The Norns are far less loquacious; they report only briefly on Alberich, the giants and Wotan's bartering for Valhalla, Siegfried and the dragon. The apocalyptic visions of the *Götterdämmerung* Norns are missing. In *Siegfrieds Tod*, finally, there is no apocalypse. Brünnhilde springs into the flames, which flare higher. The Rheinmaidens get the ring; Hagen runs into the Rhine in pursuit and drowns. Alberich appears and makes "mournful" gestures. "Suddenly," the stage directions report, "out of the smoke there emerges a brilliant light, in which we see Brünnhilde, in her helmet and shining armor, on a glowing horse, as a Valkyrie, leading Siegfried by the hand up through the clouds."[4] No world-destroying flood, no flames to annihilate Valhalla. Indeed, it seems clear that Brünnhilde, restored to her status as Valkyrie, ushers Siegfried up to heaven, to sit in splendor at Wotan's side as a valkyrized Senta who is transfigured through death and united with her beloved in the end.

Between 1848 and 1850, Wagner made revised versions of the *Siegfrieds Tod* text, and in the summer of 1850 he began writing the music. He sketched a passage for the scolding Valkyrie chorus in Act I, inventing music for them that was used later in the orchestral prelude to *Die Walküre* Act III. He also started a draft for the Prologue, the Norns' narrative scene and the Brünnhilde-Siegfried love scene.[5] But he broke off the draft about a hundred measures through the love scene. Why? This is one of the great riddles of Wagner's creative biography. He was ready with answers in 1851, in "Eine Mitteilung an meine Freunde," and much later, in retrospect, in *Mein Leben*. He writes of practical difficulties, of depression, of a growing certainty that no theater could produce the opera. It seems clear, however, that these are less explanations than rationalizations. *Siegfrieds Tod* was flawed, and the failed attempt to compose music for it drove Wagner to an obsession with the abstract side of his art, with philosophical and theoretical speculations on opera texts and operatic music. *Oper und Drama*—one of the most important operatic treatises ever written—was one product of this intense speculation.

Wagner's inability to complete music for *Siegfrieds Tod* was nonetheless directly tied to the narrative nodes in its text. Many famous incidents surrounding Siegfried's death, from Siegfried's arrival at the Gibichung court to the murder and the apotheosis, are played out before us. *Siegfrieds Tod* also included long passages of narrative exposition, devised to convey critical prehistories. Without knowing that Brünnhilde was set on the fiery rock as punishment, without knowing how Siegfried got the ring from Fafner, that Brünnhilde is Wotan's daughter, that Hagen is the son of Alberich, that Alberich forged and cursed the ring—we cannot comprehend the action in *Siegfrieds Tod*. In *Siegfrieds Tod*, not only exposition but also development and catastrophe were articulated at every turn by narrative, and narrative infuses the text to an extraordinary degree—so much so that storytelling becomes by far the most common activity on stage. In these narrations, events unseen and past are continually conjured up by allusion, and the allusions create untenanted spaces that we fill by envisaging the events they sing. For Wagner, these frequent narrative points and the tension wound into them became intolerable. He wrote *Der junge Siegfried* (1851) to release the tension by bringing unseen events described in *Siegfrieds Tod* before his audience's eyes. In describing the decision to write *Der junge Siegfried*, Wagner referred significantly to "making plastic"—palpable, visible—what was originally told only in narrative:

> *Der junge Siegfried* would have the tremendous advantage of conveying the important myths to the audience in the form of a *play*, in the way one conveys a fairy tale to a child. Everything makes a plastic impact, through sharply focused sensual impressions; everything will be understood. Then comes the serious opera *Siegfrieds Tod*, and the audience knows everything that originally had to be narrated as prehistory [vorausgesetzt], or even merely touched upon by allusion.[6]

Wagner nonetheless darts between myth, stage play, and fairy tale in a way that seems to blur the distinctions between the genres. *Der junge Siegfried* casts myth—previously only *narrated* (as myth usually is)—into temporal form in the stage play. But this "making plastic" is analogous to the way that one conveys a fairy tale to a child, which is not literally to convert the fairy tale into a stage play (suppressing the narrator, adding dialogue), but rather to read the story out loud. *Performing* narrative is thus associated with *transposing* narrative into staged enactment, since the aural excitements of reading narrative or hearing narrative out loud, and the enacting of action in live theater, both make a far deeper plastic impression (though in different ways) than stories that are merely written down. Wagner's tacit acknowledgment of both forms' sensual provocations suggests that the performed narratives in *Siegfrieds Tod* had some hold on him, even as he denied their right to exist at all.

The entire *Ring* grew in some sense out of this readerly impulse to constitute events *out of* narrative representation. Converting the narrations in *Siegfrieds Tod* did not stop with *Der junge Siegfried*; the first sketches for the action of *Die Walküre* and *Das Rheingold* were made in the fall of 1851, the *Walküre* poem was finished in June 1852, and that for *Rheingold* in November. In a famous letter to Liszt (20 November 1851) Wagner predicted that the two new libretti would enable him to eliminate "everything of a narrative nature" from *Der junge Siegfried* and *Siegfrieds Tod*.[7] Once more, he protests that the force of enactment will overcome the "weakening" contingent upon narrative representation, and a clarity of presentation that heightens the audience's emotional engagement.

The favor granted to concrete portrayal over narrative representation stems ultimately from Wagner's practical experience as opera librettist and composer. Both static and detached, narration was difficult to manage in traditional opera precisely because it involves neither confrontational action nor moments of intense emotion—the dramaturgical raw matter of conventional ensembles and arias. The tone of Wagner's letter to Liszt is triumphant, suggesting boisterous joy in vanquishing some stubborn enemy. By rejecting narrative, Wagner was in fact adopting familiar, proven operatic means, and the *Ring* would be impelled by its own scenic wonders (the Rainbow Bridge, Brünnhilde's fire, Fafner as a dragon) as well as by its physical action and dramatic confrontations (Wotan's seizure of the ring, the death of Siegmund, Brünnhilde's dialogue with Wotan in *Walküre* Act III, Wotan and Siegfried). All of these bring to life what *Siegfrieds Tod* only represents in language as a recited text. Wagner's action nonetheless speaks beyond mere application of conventional theatrical-operatic sense. The very genesis of the *Ring* attests to a longing for presentation, for the physical force of embodiment in performance, over representation and the suspicions attached to the written and silently read word. (Performed narratives—like those in *Siegfrieds Tod*—lie somewhere between these dualistic extremes; on one hand, they are narrative representations, while on the other, the act of narrating is live, the voice of the narrator speaks and sings.) We could thus see the evolution of the *Ring* as Wagner's labor against suspicious texts. By stripping away narrators whose reliability will always be uncertain, by eliminating narrations whose significance is not wholly assured, by replacing them with visible incidents, Wagner was attempting to ensure *belief* in his myth. While immediacy, force, and traditional operatic spectacle and action may have been gained, along with them came (he hoped) epistemological certainty, for in the stage's world enactments are always more trustworthy than reports (characters in theater confirm this when, like Othello, they themselves desire ocular proof, and suspect narrative). Within a world of textual genres that includes performed/heard as well as written/read texts, the former, no matter how fantastic their conceits, have the subversive force of compelling belief.

How, then, can we explain the great paradox in the *Ring*'s history, and what many consider to be the great flaw in its text: that the narratives, despite Wagner's glee over their elimination, were kept, and that in the *Ring*'s final form, these narratives give contradictory accounts of the events we have witnessed? In December 1852, after finishing the *Walküre* and *Rheingold* poems, Wagner returned to *Der junge Siegfried* and *Siegfrieds Tod*, and began revising them for publication. Not only did he retain the narratives in the two operas, but he expanded many of them. Beyond this, he included in the new epic passages narratives of events older than *Das Rheingold*, occurring in a primeval time that we do not see enacted in the *Ring*—such as the Norns' description of how Wotan destroyed the World Ash Tree. He also included narratives of events that occur offstage, between the times defined within the four libretti (Siegmund's and Sieglinde's stories of their childhoods; Wotan's seduction of Erda). He had already planned, in the winter of 1851–1852, extensive scenes of narration for *Walküre* and *Rheingold*. Between the letter to Liszt on 20 November 1851 and the first extensive prose draft for *Walküre* in the spring of 1852, Wagner came to believe that narrative—far from being made expendable by the expansion of *Walküre* and *Rheingold*—was, after all, crucial to the kind of work that he had conceived.

Knowing the *Ring* text's history, we may indeed be inclined toward an explanation of the *Ring*'s narratives in terms of Wagner's creative evolution. The narratives in the finished tetralogy are his way of insinuating his authorial self into the *Ring* text. The final *Ring* text contains both narrative accounts—we might think of them as scenario, sketch, or source—and dramatic enactment, writing out or realizing source stories. By retaining both modes, Wagner reminds us that our experience of the sequence—enactment, followed by narrative retelling—is the inversion of his own creative process—making enactment from a précis. By inventing narratives that deal in unseen actions, he urges us as listeners to complete gaps and form our own supplementary stretches of libretto. At these nodes, we replay the same Wagnerian process of "making plastic" that drew forth dialogue and stage action from epic summaries, to make the *Ring* from *Siegfrieds Tod*.

II

The retrograde evolution of the *Ring* text has thus cast up this series of biographical enigmas, and attempts to explain them: what came to seem unsatisfactory in the *Siegfrieds Tod* text? Why did Wagner abandon the musical draft for the opera in the summer of 1850? Having claimed that the expansion of *Siegfrieds Tod* into three prefacing operas would eliminate the need for narrative exposition, why did Wagner keep the *Siegfrieds Tod* narratives, extend them, and add narratives in the three other operas? Changing forms in the answers proposed to these questions also reflect changes in historical conceptions of narrative's *role* in dramatic texts. The answers also reflect the speaker's assumptions about how, precisely, music can be said to narrate; indeed, it is these assumptions that have most forcefully shaped the solutions proposed to the biographical enigmas.

For Thomas Mann, the answers were unequivocal, and Mann's account has been the model for most music-analytical interpretations since.[8] Mann appealed to Wagner's authority and cited the letters quoted previously (to Theodor Uhlig on 10 May 1851, and to Franz Liszt on 20 November 1851) with their predictions that narrative would disappear from the *Ring*. "Abneigung gegen Vorgeschichten, die hinter der Szene spuken" ["a distaste for prehistories that are lurking about offstage"]: Mann's famous phrase imputes to Wagner a disinclination to let history lurk somewhere out of the public's view, as well as a practical theatrical penchant for stage action.[9] From Wagner, Mann absorbed certain structures of value, favor granted to the "real," "plastic," and to what is temporal and played out over fictions and static narrating. In Mann's view, those original *Siegfrieds Tod* narratives, by mutating into physical enactments, took on overwhelming force. But Mann went farther than this: he proposed, by sleight of hand, an analogy between the *Ring*'s creation and the trajectory of Wagner's own creative life. Just as the various narrative précis in *Siegfrieds Tod* become something lived-out, as *Rheingold*, *Walküre*, and *Siegfried*, so Wagner's early plans for future work—for the *Ring*, for *Meistersinger*, for *Parsifal*, all conceived as scenarios by 1848—were later *written out* when he created finished works of them over the next thirty-five years. Here enactment or execution of a summary précis is literally a creative life lived. Mann's equation of the *Siegfrieds Tod* narratives with Wagner's meager working scenarios is a sly gesture. Those scenarios are mere telegraphic hints of the full text and music that was based on them. And what would we have made of Wagner's artistic life had he died in 1848, leaving only his plans? So fierce now is the privileging of enactment and execution, of the "stern, creative force" that could make *Parsifal* out of a brief scenario, that, by analogy, the *Siegfrieds Tod* narratives must also be reduced to mere potential, to source texts plundered to build up the full *Ring*.

While Mann found the first biographical enigma straightforward, the second and third claimed a greater share of his attention—and with good reason: if the status of the *Siegfrieds Tod* narratives is denigrated, then the third question—why Wagner, after all, kept narrative in the *Ring*—seems a portal into paradox.

Narrative came back into the *Ring* on the heels of what Mann called the "great letter to Liszt,"[10] the very letter that announced the death of narrative in the *Ring*. Indeed, the first brief prose scenarios for *Walküre* and *Rheingold* (probably made in October 1851) already hint at narrative moments.[11] In the first sketches for the Wotan-Fricka scene in Act II, for instance, there are indications that both characters will refer to "prehistories that lurk about offstage"—Wotan to Alberich's purchase of Grimhilde's body, and Fricka, in turn, to Wotan's own seduction of Erda:

Wodan und Fricka: streit über Siegmund's und Sieglind's that. Fricka's vorwürfe: ihre eifersucht und eherechtslaune. Alberich hat Grimhilde durch goldenen schmuck bezaubert und geschändet: Wodan schmäht auf Grimh. und die frauen, die Fricka, schiene es, am eifrigsten dreuten.—Wodan erblickt die Walküre Brünnhilde durch die lüfte reitend sich nähern. «Sie wittert todesstreit.» Fricka wirft ihm eine älterere Untreue vor: er habe die Wala bewältigt und mit ihr eben diese Brünnhilde gezeugt.[12]

[Wotan and Fricka: an argument about Siegmund's and Sieglinde's crime. Fricka's reproaches: her jealousy and complaints about marital rights. Alberich has seduced Grimhilde by means of golden jewels, and violated her: Wotan reviles Grimhilde and women, whom, it seems, Fricka is most enthusiastic about defending.—Wotan sees Brünnhilde the Valkyrie approaching, riding through the air. "She senses a mortal battle." Fricka reproaches him with an old infidelity: that he overpowered the Wala and, with her, fathered Brünnhilde.]

Both these stories—parallel tales of rape and a payment for it (the golden jewels, the child)—were later transposed to the Wotan-Brünnhilde scene, which at this early stage involved no narrating. This first prose sketch presents it as a series of emotional outbursts for Wotan:

Wodan und Brünnh allein. Wodan's tiefer schmerz, sich ewig im widerspruch mit sich selbst befinden zu müssen: «freiere muß es geben, als wir unselige götter es sind.»—Er sehnt nach dem lande «Vergessenheit». Brünnhilde sucht ihn schmeichelnd aufzurichten: Wodan verräth, ohne es zu wollen, seine geheime Absicht mit den Wälsungen, seine sprossen. Brünnhilde erräth ihn vollends: sie erbietet sich, Siegmund zu retten. *Wodan* ergrimmt: und befiehlt zornig, mit höchster selbstüberwindender kraft, Siegmunds tod.[13]

[Wotan alone with Brünnhilde. Wotan's deep pain, in finding himself constantly in contradiction against himself: "there must be freer beings than we, the unlucky gods."—He longs for the land of "forgetfulness." Brünnhilde tries to comfort him and cheer him: without wanting to, Wotan betrays his secret plans for the Wälsungs, his descendents. Brünnhilde guesses fully his desire: she offers herself as Siegmund's rescuer. *Wotan* becomes furious: and orders—angrily and with ultimate self-denial—the death of Siegmund.]

Wotan's "deep grief," his wish for a "free hero," his "longing for the land of forgetfulness," and his final fury fill the scene and leave little room for storytelling. Yet narration gradually twisted away from other parts of the nascent *Walküre* text, and migrated to the scene as if to some magnet for narrative revelations. The accretions began some weeks later, in December 1851 or January 1852, with a new idea for the scene:

Walküre II act. Nach dem streit mit Fricka berichtet Wodan—als er mit Brünnhilde allein ist—vor sich hinbrütend, sein verhältniß zur Wala (Erda): nachdem sie ihn vor dem ringe gewarnt und ihm zum erstenmale den götteruntergang angedeutet hatte, war ihm die sorglosigkeit benommen; er strebte der Wala nach, weiteres von ihr zu wissen; er übermannte sie endlich um sich ein pfand von ihr zu gewinnen; sie gebar ihm Brünnhilde.—[14]

[Walküre Act II. After the argument with Fricka, when he is alone with Brünnhilde, Wotan, as if lost in a dream, tells of his relationship with the Wala (Erda): after she had warned him about the ring and predicted to him, for the first time, the downfall of the gods, he was seized with care; he pursued the Wala to learn more from her; he overpowered her in order, at last, to obtain a pledge from her; she bore him Brünnhilde.—]

Storytelling is suddenly the heart of the matter, and is given in its most intense and concentrated form: the speaker (singer), the listener, and a single tale. But once storytelling entered, and the original substance of the scene was breached by a single retrospective tale, *narrating* could come in at length and the brief narrative moment become an epic. In the full prose draft (May 1852) and the final poem (June 1852), the single tale had become many; the story of Alberich and Grimhilde shifted from its original locus in the Wotan-Fricka argument, and others flowed in as well. Migrations, accretions, tales engendering other tales—these are marked in Wagner's manuscripts, as marginal additions, insertions, index signs, arrows pointed at stories written within circles, all crowding upon the places where Wotan's narrative is written down. The original emotional outbursts of the first sketch are reduced in the final poem to digressions, points of articulation within an immense epic narration.

III

Mann knew nothing of this genetic drama, but he knew that the final *Ring* text was saturated with narrating despite Wagner's predictions to Liszt. His explanation of the paradox was musical. In the summer of 1850, Wagner abandoned the musical draft for *Siegfrieds Tod*, Mann explained, *because* of the narrative texts that open the poem— the Norns' scene and the Siegfried-Brünnhilde scene. Wagner had no means to symbolize these narratives in music, Mann claimed, since (for him) musical symbolization of text meant leitmotivic symbolization:

> His relationship to music [was not] purely musical; it was literary or po-
> etic to the extent that it was decisively influenced by the spiritual and
> symbolic content of his music, [that music's] richness of meaning, evoc-
> ative power and allusive magic [Beziehungszauber]. It was, after all, his
> specifically musical poetic gift that had led him gradually to abandon
> traditional operatic forms, and had suggested to him his new technique
> of weaving a fabric of themes and motifs . . . and now here, in the case
> of the Nibelung myth, this brilliant and ingenious technique promised
> delights and effects of unparalleled splendor and solemnity—but subject
> to certain conditions that forced Wagner to reflect and pause: for as he
> was proposing to plunge straight into the composition of *Siegfrieds Tod*
> [in the summer of 1850], these conditions (it seemed to him) had not
> been satisfied. The drama he could step into at will; parts of the long
> epic prehistory (he could assume) were already familiar to his audience,
> the rest could be filled in by exposition. But he could not step into the
> music *in medias res*, for *the music required its own prehistory, just as deep-rooted*
> *as that of the drama: and this could not be communicated by indirect means . . .*
> *Wagner's new technique of weaving an interconnected fabric of themes could not*
> *celebrate its highest and most moving triumphs unless this primal music had ac-*
> *tually been played and heard in present conjunction with the dramatic moment to*
> *which it alluded* [emphasis mine].[15]

Music, for Mann, cannot narrate "by indirect means"; when it cannot recapitulate or repeat a leitmotif actually heard earlier, in the past time of hearing, it can have no narrative force. The *Siegfrieds Tod* text begins, like *Götterdämmerung*, with a scene for the three Norns, the Fates who see past, present, and future, who weave their visions into a continuous rope of time. The two versions are different in their details, but similar in structure and import. In the *Siegfrieds Tod* text, as in *Götterdämmerung*, the Norns recount events that precede the tragedy about to be played. They tell how Alberich stole the gold, how the giants bartered for Valhalla, how Siegfried killed Fafner the dragon. In *Götterdämmerung* the stories selected are different, but they are equally concerned with the past. There is, nonetheless, one difference that Mann would see as critical: when the Norns in *Götterdämmerung* narrate the past, they call upon a past musical world as well, a musical world that exists in *Rheingold, Walküre, Siegfried*. Loge's trickery, the giants and Valhalla, Alberich, the ring, Brünnhilde's fire—all these have been enacted *to music*, they are events with a musical presence, associated with particular musical motives. When the *Götterdämmerung* Norns recall these events, these motives are recalled as well, musically transformed. But in the summer of 1850, there was only one opera; *Siegfrieds Tod* was to stand alone. The Norns in *Siegfrieds Tod* have no "musical past" that they can invoke, no leitmotivic hoard stored up in three previous operas. They are the beginning. Wagner's discarded music of 1850 gives us Norns who sing of giants, Alberich, and the ring not in motives that have accumulated meaning over three previous nights, but to chords and arpeggios that are neutral, without established symbolic significance. As Mann might have put it, they cannot invoke the past *in medias res musicalis*. Thus Wagner, with a vision of the leitmotivic system already fully formed in 1850, was *compelled* to give up on *Siegfrieds Tod*.

Despite his obvious pleasure in leitmotivic narration, Mann nonetheless covertly favors the "dramatic moment" of the enactment and its "primal music" above the retrospective moment of narrating and its recapitulative music. Because it is alleged to be unrepresentable *except* by leitmotifs, narration became the goad for creating that prefacing and primal leitmotivic hoard. But by putting it in these terms, Mann again makes the moment of narration parasitic on the moment of enactment; it can only be a repetition and transformation of something a priori. Mann's structure of value, with its bias toward enactment, undermines his lyrical effusions in praise of "narrative" music such as Siegfried's Funeral March:

> The lament for the death of Siegfried—the *Trauermarsch*, as it is known—would [now] be something more than a conventional operatic *pompe funèbre*, no matter how impressive. It would be an overwhelming celebration of thought and remembrance. The young boy's longing enquiry after his mother; the "hero" motif of his race, created by a captive god to act in godless freedom; the "love" motif of his brother-sister parents, rising up so marvelously from the depths; the mighty sword being unsheathed from its scabbard; the great fanfare phrase that signifies his

own essential being, first heard long ago on the prophetic lips of the Valkyrie; the sound of his horn, drawn out in rhythmic cadences; the sweet music of his love for the once-awakened one; the ancient lament of the Rheinmaidens for the stolen gold, and the dark motif that symbolizes Alberich's curse: all these sublime reminders, pregnant with feeling and destiny, would pass before us with the body on the bier, while the earth shook and the sky was rent with thunder and lightning.[16]

Mann's rhetorical bloom seems intended to distract, to draw us away from our realization that he himself has deemed the *Ring*'s narratives secondary and derivative gestures. The passage is not merely proof that "the 'deadly' power of music is a myth that cannot withstand the ridicule of literal description."[17] It is weak because it is a feinting motion, because its praise for narrative is undermined within the essay in which it appears, and by the very terms in which it describes the narrative music. To describe musical narration, Mann can do no more than enumerate a series of "primal" motives that already exist elsewhere (the "hero" motif, the "love" motif, the "great fanfare phrase that symbolizes his own essential being"). The narrative music itself has no essence; without quotation, it does not exist.

IV

Mann's explanation for Wagner's abandonment of *Siegfrieds Tod* falters twice. The first precarious moment is simply historical: if Wagner, in the summer of 1850, envisaged a leitmotivic concept that demanded "primal music," eventually to be grandly recapitulated in a veritable "feast of [musical] associations" during retrospective narratives, if this was his reason for abandoning the *Siegfrieds Tod* music, then why was he still crowing over the elimination of narrative in the fall of 1851? Eliminating narrative would have meant eliminating many verbal opportunities or signals for the "feast of associations," the repetitions and recollections that Mann claims are so powerful. The history of the *Ring*'s evolution, in which narrative gradually flows into *Walküre* and *Rheingold* in the fall of 1851–1852, suggests rather that Wagner came to realize only at a later time that narrative was, after all, critical to the kind of musical and literary work that he had conceived. Carl Dahlhaus, who reduplicated Mann's arguments in *Richard Wagner's Music Dramas*, explains the historical contradiction by suggesting that the "great letter" to Liszt was specious, that Wagner could not really have intended to eliminate "everything of a narrative nature" from the *Ring*, for the " 'abundance of associations' that Wagner also wanted to create was inseparable from epic presentation."[18]

Mann's second precarious moment emerges when his praise for the narratives is systematically undermined by his presentation of them: he assumes that music narrates leitmotivically. For Mann, narrative music is comprised of signs quoted and decoded in sequence; the listener should be able to remember their associations and assemble a series of remembered past events. But such music is inevitably dependent upon the initial moment when the sign is established; as Mann put it, the "primal music" of the "dramatic moment."

Mann's reading raises a number of theoretical issues that can inflect interpretation of Wotan's Monologue. The first has to do with "leitmotivic" analysis itself. We tend to read the *Ring* leitmotivically because motives *tend* to have specific associations at their first occurrences. But these associations also escape; they cannot be held by the music, and become imprecise. Wagner's motifs may, in short, absorb specific meaning at exceptional and solemn moments, but unless they are maintained in this semiotic state, they shed their meaning and become musical thoughts. (The *Ring* is unique in that so much energy is used to keep the motives suspended against gravity, against reversion to pure music.) If poetic meaning is far from immanent in the motives, then Mann's vision of narrative music can hardly stand unquestioned. Motives can shed their associations; they also shed their ability to symbolize cardinal moments in the story of Siegfried's life, and the "hero" motif, the "love" motif, and the "great fanfare phrase that symbolizes his own essential being" are potentially no more than a splendid assemblage of musical ideas.

The second issue raised by Mann's account concerns favoring action and "primal" music in interpreting the *Ring*'s narrative music. Mann's covertly negative judgment of the narratives (even as their fascination has forced them to become an object of contemplation for him) recurs again and again in accounts of Wotan's Monologue. For Dahlhaus, who returned frequently to the scene in his writings on Wagner, the monologue suffered from "gaps in the musical fabric, filled in by . . . recitative-like declamation, which creates the impression of monotony from which the scene suffers."[19] His perception of "gaps" is generated precisely by his traditional ear; he hears the scene as a narrative assembly of leitmotifs. So "the motives associated with the gods and the myth that predominate elsewhere [in the scene]— the motives of Erda, Valhalla and the ring—appear as sporadic quotations, summoned up by specific verbal references, but without musical motivation or consequence."[20] Dahlhaus is bolder than Mann, openly declaring this particular narrative music to be thin and unstructured. Yet in this, he is overt where Mann was covert; in both cases, narrative music *fails* because it quotes primal motives and depends on them. Anthony Newcomb, in referring to the monologue's "relative looseness," to "musically unformed recitative," also explained these "unstructured" passages by indicating how narrative text calls up appropriate citations of leitmotifs.[21]

Mann's account projects a general view of operatic music that we have encountered before, one that deems such music's proper sphere as *representational*, mimicking actions on stage and existing as a redundant shadow of action. Yet by fastening upon narration as leitmotivic, Mann hints at one refutation of this view, since leitmotivically narrative music may exist, as it were, in a time different from that of the stage action. At the end of *Walküre*, for instance, there is a notorious symbolic gesture: the Siegfried motif sounds as Wotan sings, "wer meines Speeres Spitze fürchtet / durchschreitet das Feuer nie" ["he who fears my spear's sharp point / will never pass through the fire"]. The moment is sometimes seen as banal, silly, the point painfully obvious; it is Siegfried who will come to awaken Brünnhilde. The orchestra (to paraphrase Joseph Kerman on *Tosca*) has screamed the first thing that comes into its head, a piece of information about the future.[22] But as silly as the gesture may seem, it can open up radical interpretive possibilities. One is struck by Kerman's phrase, the image of the screaming orchestra with a single head, an image sufficiently grotesque to inspire strange fantasies: if it has a head, it also has a mouth, a consciousness, and a voice. The music that it speaks is a commentary. The voice of the orchestra is sometimes assumed to be the "voice of the composer."[23] But the orchestra's voice is, rather, the voice of a narrator, who, in an proleptic move, conveys information about a future event: that Siegfried will rescue Brünnhilde. This voice knows the outcome of the plot, and can design prolepses because it *looks back* upon the *Ring* as if all action in it were already past at the moment that it speaks in music. What we *see* at this moment in the *Ring* is action in the present, Wotan making a speech over sleeping Brünnhilde. But what we see, the orchestral prolepsis implies, is also somehow *past*, for it has been cast into the realm of the long-ago-enacted by the orchestral narrator, who knows what happened long after Wotan departed from the mountain. The banal conjunction of poetic line and symbolic motif is a complex stroke, in which time is layered within a temporal art. When the musical voice thus seems precognizant of actions still in the future, the music of the *Ring* becomes a filter, pushing the words of the characters, and the actions that they perform before us, into the past, distancing them even as we experience them played out in the present before our eyes. These places of layered time—when a voice is heard from outside the present action—give the *Ring* its occasional sense of veiledness, of the surreal and the mythic. And in this reading, the scenes of narration become extremely complex nodes indeed, as the characters' sung narrating of past myths become performances themselves pushed into the past by a second narrating voice.

V

The narratives are layered, complex, and primary, rather than thin, monotonous, and parasitic: this is the place from which we can begin if we try to escape the terms of Mann's interpretation. For one thing: if the narrators in the *Ring* are unreliable and their narrations are inadequate representations of real events, then *narrating*—the act—is indeed autonomous, freed from the dualistic model that regards narrating as dependent upon an a priori set of events or actions. And if we free ourselves from the dualistic model, even momentarily as a heuristic move, then the questions we will ask of narrative become fundamentally different: for instance, is Wotan's musical act of narrating shaped more by an older imperative for the form of musical narration than by the specific events that he recounts? I shall argue that his music is not dependent on leitmotifs for its meaning; it draws upon formal gestures peculiar to operatic narrative music. Wotan may be the maker of his own music; how, then, must we rehear that music? But the point is more than a theoretical recuperation of Wotan's Monologue, or of the narratives in general, or even to reject the "dualistic model" of narrative and hence to discard or deny the "leitmotivic" gestures in the score. Wagner may call upon many different musics, and these musical voices of narration may contradict the text—or seem to affirm its meaning. But whether thus "polyphonic" or "monologic," do these voices ring true?

VI

"As if lost in a dream," Wotan tells Brünnhilde how he visited and overpowered Erda, how she yielded to him, and bore a daughter. This second sketch for the Wotan-Brünnhilde scene (cited previously) gives us a single narrative moment, and represents a turning point in Wagner's transmutation of the scene from a grieving lyric soliloquy to an epic tale of the world's history. The sketch is the epic in microcosm: the narrator, the listener, and the single tale. The other stories that were drawn into the narration were, however, variations upon the Erda narrative. What Wotan narrates is, in effect, a single myth, repeated in many guises, each variation located at another point in past, present, and future time. His narrative is cyclic and an invariable sequence recurs in variant forms.

The first part of his narrative is concerned with the most distant past, before *Rheingold*:

> Als junger Liebe
> Lust mir verblich,
> verlangte nach Macht mein Mut:
> von jäher Wünsche
> Wüten gejagt,
> gewann ich mir die Welt.
> Unwissend trugvoll,
> Untreue übt' ich,
> band durch Verträge,
> was Unheil barg:
> listig verlockte mich Loge,
> der schweifend nun verschwand.
> Von der Liebe doch
> mocht' ich nicht lassen,
> in der Macht verlangt' ich nach Minne.

[When the pleasures of youthful love had grown pale for me, my spirit longed for power: driven by the force of impetuous desires, I won the world for myself. Unwittingly treacherous, I committed wrongs, and established contracts bound up with things that were evil. Craftily Loge encouraged me, then silently disappeared. But I regretted abandoning love; even in my power I longed for passion.]

The "evil" contract with the giants, offering Freia in exchange for Valhalla, is established before the beginning of *Rheingold*; when we encounter the gods in scene 2, we are *in medias res*, and the giants are ready to claim their wages. The primeval time of Wotan's first statement is immediately juxtaposed with the time of *Rheingold* itself:

> Den Nacht gebar,
> der bange Nibelung,
> Alberich, brach ihren Bund:
> er fluchte der Lieb'
> und gewann durch den Fluch
> des Rheines glänzendes Gold
> und mit ihm maßlose Macht.
> Den Ring, den er schuf,
> entriß ich ihm listig;
> doch nicht dem Rhein

gab ich ihn zurück:
mit ihm bezahlt' ich
Walhalls Zinnen,
der Burg, die Riesen mir bauten,
aus der ich der Welt nun gebot.
Die alles weiß,
was einsten war,
Erda, die weihlich
weiseste Wala,
riet mir ab von dem Ring,
warnte vor ewigem Ende.
Von dem Ende wollt' ich
mehr noch wissen;
doch schweigend entschwand mir das Weib.—

[Born of night, the craven Nibelung Alberich broke from love's bonds: he cursed love and won through the curse the glittering Rheingold, and with it boundless power. The ring that he forged I cunningly seized from him, but to the Rhine I did not return it: with it, I paid the price of Valhalla, the castle the giants built me, whence I ruled over the world. She who knows all that once was, Erda, the solemn wisest Wala, advised me to avoid the ring, warned of the end of the gods. I wished to hear more of that end, but in silence she vanished from my sight.]

By "cursing love," Alberich—fulfilling the secret condition set for forging the ring—breaks a bond that still constrains Wotan. But Wotan has revealed that he, in a more covert way, has also "cursed" love, by "abandoning" it in favor of power, and allegorically by offering Freia (the goddess of love) in exchange for the castle that becomes the physical locus and visual sign of his power.[24]

The narrative passes next to recent events, to the time after *Rheingold* but before *Walküre*. Wotan descended into the earth, found Erda, and seduced her in order to learn what she knows of the future; in exchange for her knowledge, Wotan gave her Brünnhilde the Valkyrie, who was raised with eight sisters as defenders of Valhalla. But Erda had prophesied dangers. At this point, the verb tenses shift from past to present forms, as Wotan describes a continuing situation: Alberich could turn the heroes in Valhalla against Wotan, should he ever regain the ring. Fafner guards the ring; Wotan cannot take it from him, for it was given as the price of Valhalla, in an agreement that Wotan (as the lawgiver) must respect. The narrative is then interrupted by a lyric digression, as Wotan expresses dismay over his inability to father a free individual who could take the ring from Fafner.

Brünnhilde asks about Siegmund; is he not this free hero? In response, Wotan recounts his altercation with Fricka in the previous scene, and Siegmund's history. Brünnhilde's incredulous question, "so nimmst du von Siegmund den Sieg?" ["you will take the victory away from Siegmund?"] marks the opening of the most terrible of the stories. Rather than delay closure by lingering on details, this tale compresses narrative within a series of cardinal events:

> Ich berührte Alberichs Ring,
> gierig hielt ich das Gold!
>   Der Fluch, den ich floh,
>   nicht flieht er nun mich:
> Was ich liebe, muß ich verlassen,
> morden, wen je ich minne,
>   trügend verraten,
>   wer mir traut!
> (Wotans Gebärde geht aus dem Ausdruck des furchtbarsten
> Schmerzes zu dem der Verzweiflung über.)
>   Fahre denn hin,
>   herrische Pracht,
>   göttlichen Prunkes
>   prahlende Schmach!
>   Zusammenbreche,
>   was ich gebaut!
> Auf geb' ich mein Werk;
> nur eines will ich noch:
>   das Ende,
>   das Ende.—

[I touched Alberich's ring, in greed I clutched the gold! The curse that I fled, now it will not leave me: all that I love, I must abandon, murder whomever I cherish, betray treacherously whomever I hold dear! (Wotan's demeanor transforms itself from the expression of a most terrible pain to that of despair.) Away then, lordly splendor, the boasting shame of godlike glory! Let it fall in ruins, what I have built! I abandon all my works, I desire only one thing: the end, the end.]

Because he once touched the ring, Wotan will be forced to rehearse or replay his original gesture—giving away love for power—in its deadly form as the murder of his son. At this nadir of the narration the cumulative force of all the semantic repetitions—the recurring sequence of abandonment, force, and payment—has pressed Wotan into foreseeing the one fatal future repetition. His moment of revelation, which brings him to "abandon all his works," is brought about by the formal structure that his *narrating* has engendered, and the cyclic repetition in his narrative has compelled him to a future action. An epilogue follows this moment of revelation, the twofold cry "das Ende, das Ende":

> (Er hält sinnend ein.)
>   Und für das Ende
>   sorgt Alberich!
>   Jetzt versteh' ich
>   den stummen Sinn
> des wilden Wortes der Wala:
> «Wenn der Liebe finstrer Feind
> zürnend zeugt einen Sohn,
>   der Sel'gen Ende
>   säumt dann nicht!»
>   Vom Niblung jüngst
>   vernahm ich die Mär,
> daß ein Weib der Zwerg bewältigt,
> des Gunst Gold ihm erzwang:

[(He stops, struck by a thought.) And the end will be brought by Alberich. Now I understand the hidden meaning of the Wala's strange words: "When the dark enemy of love in contempt fathers a son, the end of the gods will not long be delayed!" About the Nibelung I recently heard a story, that the dwarf has forced a woman, who gave herself for gold:]

This is, of course, the story of Grimhilde, Hagen's mother, and the prediction of Hagen's future birth. The stage direction—"er hält sinnend ein"—suggests that the narrative structure's power over Wotan continues in the final moments. Wotan is stopped by a thought; he projects again from past repetitions and is suddenly able to understand Erda's prediction, whose significance had remained obscure, to be unlocked only by the narrative spiral. Though Wotan stops, the compounded energy of the narrative impels him forward. The gesture of "giving away love" for power has in Grimhilde become prostitution, and the gesture will end in Hagen's birth.

Recurring in Wotan's narrative are variations, dilated and compressed forms of a myth, a familiar (for Adorno, simpleminded)[25] parable that is the center of the *Ring*: a sin of violence, the renunciation of love, is committed to acquire power; agreements, contracts, and laws confirm the original exchange, but the consequence of the first sin is death, "the end." This narrative sequence is anchored in four words that recur in a series through the text of the Monologue:

Liebe, Macht, Vertrag, Ende [love, power, the contract, the end]. Lucid and unfragmented variations, the stories of Wotan before *Rheingold* and Alberich in *Rheingold*, are heard first. In these, the parallelism of the two tales is clear, for the same cardinal *words* are used in both. Later, in *Götterdämmerung* Act I, the first Norn finally reveals that Wotan's primeval sin was against nature, and that it was Wotan who killed the World Ash Tree by breaking a branch from it. The branch becomes the spear, carved with the symbols of Wotan's law. Wotan's sin lies deeper, we finally learn, and occurs much earlier in history than Alberich's: it is Wotan who first brought violence into the world.

As the monologue progresses, Wotan's narrating progressively extends and breaks the purer form of the sequence. In the Erda tale, the terms are different; the parable survives. Love is misused, to overpower; the agreement is the exchange of knowledge for a child; the prophecy of death is, however, delayed by a long excursus on the Valkyries and Valhalla. Yet for all the expansions and digressions, one can hardly speak here of narrative *suspense*. Sounds are recycled; a narrative sequence becomes, through recurrence, a master trope for the monologue. We anticipate no closure, no resolution, but rather a continuation of the process. The text's force, then, derives from its rhetorical strategy, from *repetitio*. A disaster set long ago in motion, now touching the whole world, marks sonority and formal shape in the text. Thus, the text is *strophic*. It is not strophic in the conventional sense, not divided into verses with repeating rhyme schemes. But it is strophic semantically, strophic in that the master trope is repeated many times, strophic in its asymmetrical sonorous recurrences, in the frequent repetition of a single bleak line concerning Erda's prophecy of the end. In this, the text is also *musical*, for the repetitions suggest one musical strategy in fact used in the scene, successive transformations of a musical master sequence that trace the unfolding historical cycles. To hear the monologue, we hear beyond mere leitmotivic bursts, which match references to *Rheingold* events with *Rheingold* motifs. We hear how a mastering gesture of recurrence emerges from Wotan's narrating, and how his perception of this gesture shapes his vision of the future. The form of Wotan's narration, the fatal cycles that cannot be broken by a cry for "the end," *create* rather than describe the *Ring*'s doomed real world.

VII

The monologue is marked by nested repetitions, yet these are not simply the negatively charged repetitions that critics like Peter

Brooks, writing from a Freudian bias, have identified in the nineteenth-century novel. Verbal repetition on a small scale is often read as a degradation of language, as the sign of a flattened self, as something to be feared, struggled against: as uncanny.[26] To be sure, Wotan's Monologue exploits repetition—phonetic, figural, and rhetorical—in order to oppress us, to convey a sense of widening arcs of disaster. Repetition of a narrative sequence, however, also brings Wotan to his discovery that Siegmund's murder is a replaying, in different terms, of his own original sin. If repetition teaches him despair, it also forces his willing of the world's end, and the Hegelian cry for a break to the spiral (if ultimately impotent) is all the more forceful for coming near the end of so many recurrences of the cycle.

Repetition in *music* is as manifold as repetition in language, yet it tends to be accorded a higher value. In music, small- and large-scale recurrence is generally read as a fundamental means of coherence. Repetition in a temporal art reminds us of a past moment in our experience of hearing; recurrences will bind together more digressive, improvisatory, unrepetitive passages. One of Wagner's most familiar formal gambits is the binding together of rhapsodic, harmonically and thematically amorphous discourse by means of recurring refrains: Tristan's delirium scene, the Norns' scene and the conspiracy scene in *Götterdämmerung*, and the Wanderer-Mime riddle contest in *Siegfried* are only a few examples. Many Wagnerian critics have argued that entire operas are articulated by recapitulations of tonal patterns that bind up the hours of hearing.[27] Small wonder, of course, that critics fasten upon forms of repetition in music. Music will bear far more repetition than any literary art—a thousand times more, say, than the language of the novel; even "musical" writers like Thomas Mann were sparing in their attempts to bring repeated sonorities or small verbal formulas into the novel. Music analysts interpret music almost without exception as straying from recurring nodal points of familiarity. So entrenched is this move in formalist analytical writing on music that it transcends great differences in style, technique, and genre in the object scrutinized. Thus tonal analyses trace the motions away from and back to (recurring) tonal centers, thematic analyses seek out the (recurring) forms of melodic matter, and analyses of atonal music enumerate the (re)appearances of "important" atonal sets, row forms, or motivic gestures.

In Wotan's Monologue (as we shall see) a recurring musical sequence coincides with the recurring narrative gesture. But given the contradictory meanings that certain literary theories and certain music-analytical strategies have attached to repetition, there seems to be some inversion of values when we move from text to music, or vice versa. The monologue presents history as marked by replaying, time that has had development leached away from it by recurrence. But in the music, tendencies toward digression, toward "degeneration" into "unstructured monotony" (to paraphrase Dahlhaus) are combatted by the *repetition* of certain identifiable swatches. The musical representation of the historical tragedy thus involves a kind of dissonance; and the moral import of the text may seem to be contradicted in the music, in which chaos is brought around by recurrence.[28] Perhaps the only way to define the monologue's polyphony is to hear it with ears as morally acute as Brünnhilde's. She is (as we shall see in Chapter 6) the listener who refuses to be satisfied with a single meaning, and who constantly shifts the frame of her assumptions to see what another turn of the theoretical kaleidoscope can do to the image she hears.

VIII

Mann claimed that music could not communicate pastness by indirect means. In other words: Wagner's music could narrate only by citing leitmotifs heard in the past, with associations established in the past. Mann could have put it in other terms—that only music parasitic on established and previous musical matter can narrate, and that its narrative consists of references that force memory back to a past hearing. This is a view already explored, though in other terms, in Chapters 1 and 2, in which I stressed how recapitulation alone cannot engender the sense of detachment, even the uncanniness, that marks the narrating voice. In the monologue, this sense of musical detachment is, significantly, absent.

The monologue begins as Wotan intones "in a completely muffled voice" his first tale, of the time before *Rheingold*. The only accompaniment to his vocal line, which is free, declamatory recitative, are pedal-point drones sustained in the lowest registers of the contrabasses. He sings, for the most part, against a single note (Example 5.1). Only two motivic gestures intrude upon this recitation, the opening descending theme (Wolzogen labeled it "Wotans Verzweiflung," ["Wotan's Despair"]), which is repeated and spun out as a transition at the end of the passage. And the only harmonic motion comes in measure 10 (the shift to the dominant), and then finally in measures 16–17 (the modulation out of A♭ minor). Music has been stripped of almost all that we might consider "content," reduced almost to inaudible rumble, without rhythmic character (the vocal line takes its free rhythm from the text; the low bass pitches are unrhythmicized), without thematic presence. The passage is also empty of

Example 5.1. Die Walküre Act II: the first cycle in Wotan's Monologue.

leitmotifs, a lack that could be smoothly explained in Mann's terms. This is a tale of the world before *Rheingold*, a world that has no "primal" music, hence no music that could be recalled here. Absence of leitmotifs in the first tale is set in relief by the music for the second tale, the story of *Rheingold*, and by a sudden invasion of quoted motives from that opera (Example 5.2). The quotations include the Rheinmaidens' cry at "des Rheines glänzenden Gold" ["the glittering Rheingold"], the Ring motif at "maßlose Macht" ["boundless power"], and the Valhalla motif at "die Burg, die Riesen mir bauten" ["the castle that the giants built for me"]. The reference to Erda (in m. 31) casts up the music that had accompanied her entrance—characteristic theme and key (C♯ minor) both.

Example 5.2. The second cycle in Wotan's Monologue.

Rhein gab ich ihm zu-rück: mit ihm be-zahlt' ich Wal-hall's Zin-nen, der Burg, die Rie-sen mir bau-ten, aus der ich der Welt nun ge-bot. Die Al-les weiss, was eins-ten war, Er-da, die weih-lich wei-ses-te Wa-la, rieth mir ab von dem Ring, war-nte vor

Ex. 5.2 (cont.)

Leitmotivically, the two tales must be heard as unlike, for the first is bare of motives, while in the second, "primal" musical material has come flooding in. The first is empty—the sort of monotonous recitative that Dahlhaus saw as the scene's chief weakness—and the second is an assembly of fragments, dependent on *Rheingold*. Two musical tales that are different in the leitmotivic reading can be heard nonetheless as variations on the same sequence, but only when their points of identity are unmasked, made audible in discarding the leitmotivic bias. In this reading, the second passage is simply the first, dilated and extended by accretions of leitmotivic quotation. Both musical sequences, for instance, are set off by a similar opening flourish, the descending motif with its brief internal turn (Example 5.3). Both close with a similar cadential recitation for Wotan (Example 5.4). This is not to say that the two passages are *the same*, only that a certain series—opening motif, recitation against a drone, recited close—is unfolded in both, and that the second delays the moment of closure with leitmotifs. The invariables in the series are like cardinal moments or fixed action-sequences, while the end is delayed by excurses, cultural references, symbols lingered upon, description.[29] When the musical cycle begins a third time, for the Erda story, the sequence has become even richer (Example 5.5). Teased out of the opening motif is a long and chromatic sequence; the leitmotivic dilation of the inte-

Example 5.3. Beginnings of the first and second cycles.

Example 5.4. Ends of the first and second cycles.

rior is extended, and Brünnhilde takes over the closing recitation (mm. 87–89), which now coincides with the *motivic* end of the second tale, the citation of Erda's C♯ minor arpeggio.

Two readings, then, set their claims against one another. In the leitmotivic reading, the three passages are significant only as they contain quotations determined by critical images in the text (the Rheingold, the ring, Valhalla, Erda, the Valkyries, and so forth). The formalist reading presses away the leitmotifs as ornament, as filling out time within a recurring musical sequence. The first, like Mann's

Example 5.5. The third cycle (beginning and end).

(Beginning, Third Cycle)

40 Wotan

Da ver -lor ich den leich - ten Muth,   zu wis-sen be-gehrt' es den Gott: in den

Schoss der Welt   schwang ich mich hi - nab,   mit Lie - bes-zau-ber zwang ich die Wa- la,

45

stört' ih - res Wis- sens Stolz,   dass sie Re - de nun mir stand.

Kun - de emp-fing ich von ihr;   von   mir doch emp - fing sie ein

Pfand: der Welt wei-ses-tes Weib ge-bar mir, Brünn - hil - de, dich.

Ein wenig bewegter.

Mit acht Schwes-tern zog ich dich auf; durch euch

Wal - kü - ren wollt' ich wen - den, was mir die Wa la zu fürch-ten

schuf, ein schmäh - li - ches En - de der Ew' - gen. Dass

Ex. 5.5 (cont.)

essay on the *Ring*, must regard a narrative scene as musically dependent, as secondary creation. The second is apparently able to present the narrative scene as autonomous, a recurring sequence that is defined uniquely in this context. The second reading, however, by no means denies the conspiracy between musical process and the narrative unfolded in the text. The recurrences of the sequence correspond to the repetition of the text's "master trope"—the tale of power, love abandoned, the exchanges and agreements, and the disaster. Just as the tale may be compressed, or extended by discursive moments, so may the musical sequence become more leisurely in its unfolding, and absorb more time.

IX

Two readings, one leitmotivic and one formalist, seem to expose the ways in which music reacts with text. When the words "Erda," "Valhalla," and "ring" are reinforced by leitmotivic references, the reinforcement is tautological. The monologue presents the motives as redundant, seeming never to speak beyond the images they accompany. In the formalist reading, the same redundancy seems to be at work. To be sure, cyclic *repetition* in the music belies the text to the extent that it belies the overt temporal and historical *progression* described in the narrative. Yet they confirm covert similarities between events in the distant past and the present, and disasters still to come. A grimmer conception of historical time as discontinuous, marked by reversion to flawed origins, is pressed into and spoken by the musical cycles.

Recurrence in the monologue's music creates a clock with many hands defining circuits within circuits, a cyclic effect that is felt on many levels. The repetitions of the musical master-sequence exist within larger cycles marked by recurring refrains. Twice in the monologue, Wotan sings a particular vocal fragment, set over an inverted E minor chord. His second tale, the retelling of *Rheingold*, begins in this way (mm. 18–19), and the musical moment returns well into the monologue, during the present-tense account of Fafner and the *Ring* (Example 5.6). There is a return of both the intoned, recitativelike texture of the monologue's opening, and of a specific musical idea. The two recurrences are widely spaced in time. More importantly, however, the recurring musical element is not a leitmotif, and its repetition is not engendered by some textual signal. The images of which Wotan sings are unlike (Alberich, Fafner); the precise words that he sings are different. In another large-scale repetition, the music that opens the Wotan-Brünnhilde scene, for Wotan's "O heilige

Example 5.6. Repetition without verbal pretext.

Schamch," is recapitulated at the beginning of his grim realization
that he himself must allow Siegmund to be murdered (Example 5.7).
Repetition in larger cycles such as this also ends Wotan's excursus on
the "free hero" (mm. 128–81), and the same tale of Siegmund's fate
(mm. 203–61). Again, there is no specific textual motivation for the
repetition. The second time, the cadence accompanies a critical moment in the text, Wotan's cry for "the end" and his attempt to halt
the spiral of repetition. The cadence is expanded; its conventional
initial resolution to A minor is deflected to C minor, in a famous moment of harmonic irrationality and incongruence, in a fall from the
E major dominant to the minor key a third below (Example 5.8). The
C minor chord is "fallen into" in many senses: from the full orchestra
to the low brass, from the E major chord, from fortissimo to pianissimo, with the changes mediated by the prolonged silence. It is fallen
into as a *change* as well, as a radical rewriting of the cadence in measures 179–82. So Wotan's demand for an end may seem to be written
into the music locally—the cadence is deflected, cut off by silence; not
resolved, but severed by the final chord. But it is also an end to repetition in that it *changes* radically the harmonic direction of that cadence, which has begun to unwind once more as Wotan sings.

What may be most significant about all these instances of recurrence is that they are not equivalent musical responses to similar
texts, not coy and parallel musical commentaries on the particular
words spoken. The musical repetitions are independent of the text's
details. In the case of the inverted E minor chord, the vocal filip for
"den Nacht gebar, der bange Niblung" and "der Riesen einer," one
would be led into specious contrivances indeed in attempting to explain the repetition in terms of these specific words (what do Alberich
and Fafner have in common?). Repetition is nonetheless not without
moral or symbolic meaning. Rather, the image of history embedded
in Wotan's account—history not as progress but as a recurrent
wrenching-back, as error replayed—has been replicated in the music
in a sphere that transcends any ordinary or direct correspondences
between music and word.

X

The transformed cadences seem to point to one progressive element
of the monologue's music: its harmonic trajectory. Juxtaposing the
two cadences brings together two points of tonal articulation in the
monologue, two different keys—A minor and C minor. A "modulation" seems to occur in the time between the two cadences, one which
might define a developing harmonic course. Yet this "modulation"

Example 5.7. The scene's opening material repeated within the monologue.

Example 5.8. A cadence reinterpreted.

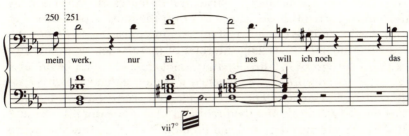

(and all progress that the word implies) is itself illusory. Within the monologue, there are few passages that can be said to be "in" a key, in the sense that they are consistently oriented toward and governed by that key; the A minor excursus on the "free hero" is one instance. The monologue is instead punctuated by cadences that refer to other keys. These cadences mime self-importantly the "establishment" of a key; their point is to create the effect of various controlling tonalities. The C minor chord that severs Wotan's cadence at "das Ende" is recalled as a C minor cadence at the monologue's close (Example 5.9). Such cadences, mimicking the structural cadences of conventionally tonal music, actually have little power over the musical discourse that they divide, and we cannot read intervening music as shaped by the cadential tonalities.[30] Telling the roles of these cadences would give us a neat "progression" through the monologue. A♭ minor begins and ends the first, pre-*Rheingold* sequence, a sequence that is, in effect, no more than an extended and incomplete cadence pattern in that key. The tales of *Rheingold* and the prehistory of *Walküre* (mm. 18–39 and 40–82) are articulated by and end (in mm. 79–82) in ironically secure A major, unfolded within the Valhalla chords; yet this resolution is always undone by a turn to C♯ minor, arpeggiated as Erda's Warning motif (cf. Example 5.2). The tale of the present, the lyric digression concerning the "free hero," is shut off by the A minor cadence of Example 5.8; the Siegmund tales and the monologue as a whole end in C minor. Continuity and metamorphosis could be read into these turns from A♭ minor, through A major and A minor, to C minor. Mutation through tonalities a third apart, or a gradual inflection of chordal pitches through a collection of accidentals (A♭–C♭–E♭, to A–C♯–E, to A–C–E, to C–E♭–G) accounts for the pattern. Wagnerian tonal analysis—which tends to take note of cadence points and extrapolate their relationships—might find "progression" or "modulation" an adequate description, for both words are charged with comfortable values; both imply that there is a coherent arc traced by the monologue's harmonic course. Yet the cadence points are detached from the musical matter that they punctuate; they are not integral to it. It is as if these cadences are laid over unstructured harmonic improvisation; the cadences create localized wrinkles, but draw only a few instants into their tonal sphere. Their real isolation calls into question the very notion of modulation or harmonic progression. To insist that any given cadence is a sign for previous, coherent harmonic progress to this end is to mistake irony for the naiveté of conventional tonal music, a figure for literal description.

Hearing the cadences' detachment from the surrounding harmonic flux is critical to understanding one symbolic function of those

Example 5.9. The cadence at the end of the monologue.

cadences. As illusory ends that regenerate beginnings, they also work to replicate the monologue's view of history. The progression that they define (from A♭ minor, to A major, to A minor, to C minor) is a false progression—not a progression but itself a *motif*, a musical figure for modulation, modulation that no longer moves because it is reified as an object.[31] The tale of the cadences presents us with a kind of pseudo-progression that mocks modulation: the monologue itself proposes this reading of its own "important" cadences. At two brief moments, the chords of the initial and final cadences—A♭ minor, C minor—are juxtaposed in deliberately exposed, almost ceremonial fashion. The juxtaposition is a momentary allusion, in the form of the two chords, to the two cadences that span the entire monologue. Brought together, the two chords are nonetheless no summary or mystic paraphrase of harmonic *progress*. For one thing, the chords are juxtaposed in inverted order, C minor first, A♭ minor second. Moreover, they are presented as autonomous individual sounds, as chords that, so to speak, cannot be heard as a logical harmonic progression. Their temporal successiveness actually emphasizes the disjunctive gap between them. Just as the two chords, on a small scale, cannot be formed into a progression, so they warn against reading "progression" into the series of cadences that punctuate the monologue. Within Wotan's outburst of despair, the sound is woven into a longer series of sonorities (Example 5.10). This sound—C major or minor "falling into" A♭ minor—is, from this moment, a repeated motif. Heard rarely in the *Ring*, it recurs at moments inhabited by Hagen and by intimations of the apocalypse. In the trio in *Götterdämmerung* Act II, the motif takes on the rhythmic guise of the Valhalla chords, as Brünnhilde's and Gunther's overt invocation of Wotan as avenger is mingled with Hagen's secret appeal to Alberich and his own hidden cause (Example 5.11). In Wotan's monologue, the sound spans the silence between Wotan's wish for "the end" and his bleak realization that "the end will be brought by Alberich." Silence marks the moment when Wotan "pauses in thought," or is "struck by a thought" ("er hält sinnend ein") (Example 5.12). Wotan is propelled into the future by the repetitions described within his own discourse, and suddenly understands Erda's prophecies, once obscure. The moment is extraordinary not only as sonority, but for its concentration of the tensions and impulses explored throughout the monologue. Wotan calls for an end, and his own voice is immediately and literally stopped by the thought that strikes him into silence—a thought that nonetheless rushes on to another repetition of the now-fatal narrative sequence. Love is traded for gold; Hagen's birth is the disastrous outcome. The C minor chord that so violently severs the progress of the

Example 5.10. Wotan's Peroration.

Ex. 5.10 (cont.)

Ei - nes will ich noch:

255

das En - de, das En - de!

Langsam

260
(He pauses in thought)

Und für das En - de sorgt Al - be-rich;

Example 5.11. The C–A♭ minor motif in *Götterdämmerung* Act II.

preceding cadence is similarly no end—or only a momentary illusion of an end, for it becomes, in the next instant, the initial gesture of a motif already minted. Yet this motif (which itself recurs) by juxtaposing C minor with A♭ minor has only served to suggest again that there is no progress, no development toward an end, but rather a repeated succession of discontinuous chords. Finally, by "falling" from C minor to A♭ minor, the motif acts out another sweep through a vast

Example 5.12. The C–A♭ minor motif in the monologue.

circuit: the monologue's final chord, C minor, will fall again and again into its A♭ minor beginning, as the fatal cycle recurs.

XI

A tautology emerges from these readings of the monologue's music. At every moment, the music can be heard as transposing the controlling and despairing historical vision of the words. The music no more escapes the words of Wotan's narrative than Wotan can elude the repetitions that degrade the tale of his world's story. What does the tautology mean?

The question is pointed precisely because such sustained and multivalent musicotextual correspondence is actually rare in the *Ring*, where music can more often be understood as an independent voice, one that may speak across the words, seem to ignore them, or (as Peter Conrad pointed out in the essay cited at the opening of this chapter) reveal what their speakers cannot know. Wagner's music can make its own contradictions or predictions (in leitmotivic fashion), and speaks interpretations that cannot be heard by the characters who speak the words. The notorious leitmotivic asides (such as the quotation of the Siegfried motif at Wotan's final words in *Walküre*)—while overcalculated—also force us, brutally, to consider the autonomy of the musical voice. In speaking with the text, the musical voice has means beyond leitmotif—but the conversation, whatever music's means, is not always one of bland agreements or redundant echoings. Interpretations of opera occasionally seem unaware of this polyphony, in positing absolute correspondence between words and music as an aesthetic value.[32]

The monologue is thus anomalous. However we hear and interpret its music, the music seems to rebound upon Wotan's understanding of the story that he tells. He hears the form that his story has taken, hears its sonorous and significant recurrences, and is driven by narrative to despair, because he hears recurrence become fatal even as he sings. When leitmotifs mechanically shadow the images that he makes, without bringing any unrealized meanings, when a musical sequence unwinds coevally with his repeating narrative trope, when cadence serves only to mock harmonic modulation, when tonal sequence becomes progress blocked and frozen, as motif—then music is replicating Wotan's perceptions in many tongues. Wherever we touch the monologue's music, it seems to cast back its singer's view of history and its singer's discursive habits. Such absolute redundancy (rare in the *Ring*, as in any opera) informs us that the monologue's sonic world is set apart from the normal sound of the *Ring*. Thus the tautologies in the monologue are significant, for they tell us that the music comes from the singer of the tale, who cannot step outside the circle of his narrative—the music comes from Wotan. There is no untainted or external musical narrator, and all that we hear assumes shape as a projection of the world that Wotan has constituted. This is the reason that the monologue sounds so unlike most of the *Ring*. This is also the reason that it has seemed so inaccessible to analysis. Any interpretation that assumes that the monologue's music originates in the external orchestral voices that sing most of the *Ring* will fail. The monologue, too, will fail: it will be parasitic on preexisting leitmotifs, and will be formally incomprehensible.

The monologue is in fact a *song*, and so is signaled by the break from its context that *song* will always engender within opera. Linked to historical prototypes, the narrative ballads of an earlier time (those discussed in Chapter 3), it assumes something of a balladic existence as a performed song lying apart from the normal musical discourse of opera. It shows signs of phenomenal narrative song's characteristic musical conceits. In the cyclic repetitions, we hear the remnants of the strict and invariable repeated verse and refrain; both performed narrative song and the monologue share a contradiction between a text that describes unfolded time, and music's obstinate repetition. The monologue—*pace* Mann—can thus seem to evoke the past *in medias res musicales*, because it makes those musical gestures that belong to a historically established epic genre. Identifying ballad as a historical prototype for the monologue, or designating the monologue a much distorted, improvisatory play upon the ballad lodges the monologue within operatic history and the tale of its genres. Formalist analysis of the monologue, by identifying its recurring musical sequences and other instances of cyclic repetition, may reply to those critics who puzzle over the monologue's musical "amorphousness." Indeed, the two can serve together as a riposte to claims that Wagner, as an antioperatic composer, invariably invokes instrumental or symphonic forms.[33] The image of the monologue as a song that Wotan invents and sings, however, goes beyond the older institutional wrangles of Wagnerian interpretation, to rebound upon certain urgent questions that will recur in Chapter 6. How do we understand narrative—musical or textual—in a work that oscillates between proposing overmastering force for narrative, and undermining narrative's claim to describe or constitute reality? How reliable is Wotan's narrative of the world's history? This question cannot be answered by the monologue alone—because the monologue, language and music alike, originates with Wotan and is one of his performances. No witty or ironic musical narrator frames Wotan's speech and no autonomous musical voice reports his words.

Wotan's monologue is not, of course, the only narrative song in the *Ring*, and in its other presentations of narrative song, the *Ring* may attempt to drag us back from this moment of doubt. It is in its presentation of narrative song that the *Ring* questions what might be called the morality of musical narration. Other narrative songs in the *Ring* are, like the monologue, identified as phenomenal song in various ways. In the Norns' scene, the sisters refer to "singing" their narrative of past, present, and future. Loge's narrative (*Rheingold* scene 2) and Sieglinde's "der Männer Sippe" in *Walküre* Act I are both prepared by the kind of signals—introductory recitative, exhortations to the listeners—that traditionally announce phenomenal song in opera. Siegfried's narrative in *Götterdämmerung* Act III is the clearest case, since Siegfried tells Gunther, "I will *sing* to you stories of my youthful days" ["singe ich dir Mären aus meiner Jugendzeit"]. This conception of Siegfried's narration as a sung performance goes back to the "Der Nibelungen-Mythus: Als Entwurf zu einem Drama," the 1848 essay that was to serve as scenario for the *Siegfrieds Tod* libretto and, eventually, for much of the *Ring*. In his description of the murder scene, Wagner writes:

Hagen nimmt beim Trinken die scherzhafte Weise auf: ob er dann wirklich der Vögel Gesang und Sprache verstehe?—Gunther ist trüb und schweigsam. Siegfried will ihn aufheitern und *erzählt in Liedern* von seiner Jugend: sein Abenteuer mit Mime, die Erlegung des Wurmes, und wie er dazugekommen, die Vögel zu verstehen. In der folgerecht geleiteten Erinnerung kommt ihm auch der Zuruf der Vögel bei, Brünnhilde aufzusuchen, die ihm beschieden sei; wie er dann zu dem flammenden Felsen gezogen und Brünnhild erweckt habe. Die Erinnerung dämmert immer heller in ihm auf. Zwei Raben fliegen jäh über sein Haupt dahin. Hagen unterbricht Siegfried: "was sagen dir diese Raben?" Siegfried fährt heftig auf. Hagen: "ich verstand sie, sie eilen, dich Wotan anzumelden." Er stößt seinen Speer in Siegfrieds Rücken [emphasis mine].[34]

[Hagen, in drinking, takes up the joking mood. Does Siegfried really understand the song and speech of birds? Gunther is sad and silent. Siegfried wishes to cheer him up, and *narrates in songs* about his youth: his adventure with Mime, the defeat of the dragon, and how it came about that he understands the speech of birds. Next, in order of memory, he thinks of the birdcall that told him to search for Brünnhilde, who was destined to be his, how he then came to the fiery cliffs and awakened her. Memory dawns ever clearer in him. Two ravens fly close over his head. Hagen interrupts Siegfried: "And what do these ravens say to you?" Siegfried springs up. Hagen: "I understand them: they hurry to announce you before Wotan." He thrusts his spear into Siegfried's back.]

In the final version as well, Siegfried performs his narrative songs to "lighten" Gunther's mood, in a gesture calculated to remind us that music is good, and has therapeutic capabilities. And Siegfried is thus struck down in the midst of phenomenal song, singing music that he, Gunther, the vassals, and Hagen—as well as the theater audience— can hear. Within the stage-world, Hagen's violent blow, by stopping Siegfried's voice, brings the cessation of music itself. It is followed by silence. In the stage-world, that silence continues, and only we (not the characters on stage) hear the sublime music of Siegfried's rhapsody to Brünnhilde.

Hagen's spear stops the song. His blow is, however, only one of many such fatal moments that arrest narrative song throughout the tetralogy. In the Norns' long narrative, Alberich's curse "gnaws on the threads" of time's rope and dooms the world's future course. Brutally, the Norns' song is ended as the curse severs the thread of the future, in a symbolic coupling devised once more to equate cessation of narrative singing with the silence of a disastrous end. Yet, in a curious inversion, Hagen's blow—along with other arresting moments in the *Ring*—actually works *for* narrative by making narrative song the affirmative and positive term that collides with death. Music is more than medicine for melancholy; it battles with mortality, and even those narratives delivered in the voices of liars or mythmakers (and Wotan is both) exist as music and singing set against that deadly silence. The *Ring* thus appears to propose all narrative as overmastering, because sung narration borrows music's great virtue as a sign of living presence amid murder and decay. (Wotan, as we recall, resumes singing almost heroically *against* the dead silence that follows "das Ende, das Ende.") This glorification of singing—so that song, as sheer sonority, will eliminate doubts about the singer—is nonetheless a fundamentally suspicious gesture, though perhaps one that rightly points to one source of opera's terrible fascinations. It leaves us with a system in which buffoons, liars, and the most dubious narrative voices can seem to overmaster us—for their lies are preferable to *that* silence. Thus the *Ring*'s narrative songs appear to assign this force to all narrative in constructing a complicated trap, involving the familiar allegory of music's transcendence; it is this construction that is played out repeatedly in these scenes of music against murder. Once the listener accepts music as an absolute voice lying *outside* the human world, he or she may never again question narration—so long as it is *sung*.

In the end, listeners like Conrad and Emerson, who so elegantly postulate and celebrate operatic music's capacity to "disclose" ineffable reality, may forget to resist operatic music's other face—its capacity to speak "falsely." Interpreting Wotan's monologue works to expose the trap, as I have argued, by uncovering Wotan's music as a solipsistic enunciation that originates in an immoral god. The monologue asks us to distrust music's voice: that voice may *ring false*. Yet there is one figure within the *Ring* itself who is able to perceive Wotan's monologue in precisely this way, and that is Brünnhilde, the all-but-silent person who sits, only faintly illuminated, at the edge of the spotlight that tracks Wotan's performance. As the second individual in the scene, the listener that every narration (in being a performance) must postulate, she may seem to represent a merely passive function, or a reflexive projection of opera's own real audience. So, too, she might be taken as a character who seems merely to follow the dictates of others' desires. She is often defined as a conduit for Wotan's thought, as "Wotan's will," and her final action—returning the ring to the Rhine—corresponds to his wish for "the end." Her initial act of subversive misbehavior (the decision to side with Siegmund against Wotan's command) is inspired by Siegmund's own persuasive voice. Her presence and identity as a listener, however, is in fact extremely complex, extending back from the *Ring* to its mythic sources; this identity reconstrues Brünnhilde as a focus of moral acuity and tragic skepticism, one whose interpretation of narration is predicated on a unique gift of hearing. This ambiguous gift—rather than some blind execution of Wotanic commands—is what brings her to the Hegelian stroke that ends the *Ring*'s world. My final move, therefore, is from a narrating performer to a listener whose aural acuity is one factor in her wholly unique voice.

Chapter Six

BRÜNNHILDE WALKS BY NIGHT

Das Motiv welches Sieglinde der Brünnhilde zusingt,
[ist] die Verherrlichung Brünnhilden's, welche am
Schluß des Werkes gleichsam von der Gesamtheit
aufgenommen wird. [The motif sung by Sieglinde to
Brünnhilde is the glorification of Brünnhilde, which
at the end of the work will be taken up by the whole.][1]

Two THINGS will concern us: an instant of laughter, and a narrative prophecy.

Laughter first: legend tells us that Brünnhilde laughed in exultation upon witnessing (or, in some versions, upon hearing of) the death of Siegfried. Brünnhilde's laughter recurs in most of the sources for her story; in the three versions of the Eddic Sigurd poems, one source (*Sigurdarkviða in forna*, the *Old Lay of Sigurd*) tells how Brünnhilde "triumphs" at the news of Sigurd's [Siegfried's] death; another (*Sigurdarkviða in skamma*, the *Short Lay of Sigurd*) tells how she "laughed when she hears Gutrune's shrill laments"; the German *Thidreks saga* reports that she displayed good cheer; in the Norse *Volsunga saga*, she "laughed aloud when she hears Gutrune gasp"; and finally in the German *Nibelungenlied* (in which her enthusiasm is muffled), she is "indifferent to Kriemhilt's [Gutrune's] mourning."[2] In Wagner's text for *Siegfrieds Tod* Act III, this laughter is never heard, but only described; it is the sound that woke Gutrune from her sleep:

(Die Halle der Gibichungen mit dem Uferraum, wie im ersten Akte.—
Nacht. Mondschein spiegelt sich im Rheine. *Gutrune* tritt aus
ihrem Gemache in die Halle heraus.)
    War das sein Horn?—
(Sie lauscht.)
Nein! Noch kehrt er nicht Heim.—
Schlimme Träume hab' ich geträumt!—
Wild hört' ich wiehern sein Roß,—
Lachen Brünnhilde's weckte mich auf.
    —Wer war das Weib,

daß ich zum Rheine schreiten sah?—
(Sie Lauscht an einer Thüre rechts, und ruft dann leise.)
Brünnhild!—Brünnhilde!—bist du wach?
   (Sie öffnet schüchtern und blickt hinein.)
Leer das Gemach!—So war es sie,
die zum Rhein ich wandeln sah?—
   (Sie erschrickt und lauscht nach der Ferne.)
Hört' ich ein Horn?—Nein, öde Alles:— —
Kehrte Siegfried nun bald heim![3]

[(The Gibichung Hall with view to the Rhine, as in Act I.—Night. Moonlight is mirrored in the Rhine. *Gutrune* comes out of her chamber into the hall.) Was that his horn? (She listens.) No! He is not on the way home.—I have dreamed evil dreams!—I heard his horse neighing,— Brünnhilde's laughter woke me.—Who was the woman whom I saw walking to the Rhine?—(She listens at a door to the right, then calls out softly.) Brünnhild!—Brünnhilde!—are you awake? (She opens the door timidly and looks in.) Her room is empty!—So it was she whom I saw walking to the Rhine?—(She starts and listens into the distance.) Did I hear a horn?—No, all is desolate:— — If only Siegfried would come home soon!]

This is one of the *Ring*'s oddest scenes; its music is marked (as Christopher Wintle points out) by prolonged silences that mirror its repeated images of emptiness and desolation. Siegfried's Funeral March (the densest of the *Ring*'s orchestral interludes) precedes it, and the juxtaposition of the Funeral March with Gutrune's solo sets two wholly different musical conceits against one another. The "feast of associations" in the interlude (which develops motivic material from the whole of the *Ring* into a fortissimo symphonic passage) reverts in Gutrune's scene to a reduced and minimal music, in which alternating silences and motivic fragments (played pianissimo) follow inconsequentially upon one another.[4]

Seen on the page, the text itself is broken by the long black lines that trace the silences in between, ending with the longest—the duplex stroke after "Nein, öde Alles." Wagner's music punctuates those silences with sounds, yet they are not merely instrumental simulacra of what Gutrune does or does not hear, drawn from the *Ring*'s motivic hoard. The orchestra instead produces sounds that Gutrune *imagines* she hears: when she asks, "was that his horn?" she sings to a distorted version of the Horncall motif, whose musical distortion we hear as if we were eavesdropping on Gutrune's own aural hallucination. Yet when she pauses to listen, she is never rewarded by any trace of that horn's sound. During Gutrune's first listening silence, the orchestra winds through a languid, dissonant version of the Rheinmaidens' lament (it had underpinned the horncall, and now continues on its own) (Example 6.1). The distorted horncall recurs as she describes her "evil dreams," and now this once-familiar sound is heard as if through the sick confusions of sleep. The "wild neighing of the horse," however, is not some wind-choir onomatopoeia; instead, we hear the uneasy ruffle of Loge's fire. In a final turn (m. 13) the triadic arpeggiation of the horncall is rhythmically altered to become the B minor of Brünnhilde's own Valkyrie music, and Gutrune reaches the highest note in her monologue (F♯), falling to B at "lachen" ["laughter"]. Brünnhilde's laughter, something we never hear, is thus conveyed to us in mediated form, through the agency of Gutrune's memory and her imitation of its sound (her falling F♯–B). Gutrune (preceded and aided by the orchestra's valkyrizing) is resinging one of the most famous of Brünnhilde's vocal moments, the final rising F♯–B of that eldritch laughter (yes, "hoijotoho") that ushers her in as both character and voice-object in the first moments of *Walküre* Act II. Gutrune's "lachen" thus reminds us of Brünnhilde's first and fabulous appearance before us, reminds us that Brünnhilde (in one of opera's most astonishing vocal entrances) originated aurally as sheer musical voice and as prolonged and unfettered laughter: only after she has been brought back to earth by Fricka's approach does she begin to speak in words. By introducing her as laughter itself, Wagner alludes obliquely and proleptically to the terrible laughter that lies in her future, and leaves the secret imprint of that moment (which, in his version of the legend, we will never directly hear) on this triumphant debut.

Brünnhilde's laughter at Siegfried's death—one of the famous moments in her legend—has been a thorn in interpretations of her character because it seems to define her moral relationship to that death. The many poetic narrators assume differing stances toward her laughing, all depending upon their individual presentations of Brünnhilde's persona.[5] Why does Brünnhilde laugh? Or why, in some versions, does she continue to laugh, and why, in others, does she suddenly revert to grief? Both laughter and grief set out the terms of a relationship to Siegfried. In *Sigurdarkviða in forna* (the simplest and probably the oldest of the Eddic versions), Sigurd [Siegfried] is a vassal of Gunther, and is married to Gunther's sister, Gutrune. Disguised as Gunther, Sigurd acts as his overlord's proxy in winning Brünnhilde, and though he puts a sword between himself and Brünnhilde on their "wedding night," he also takes a ring from her. Brünnhilde is brought to Gunther's court, but discovers the deception from Gutrune, who shows her the ring in the course of an

Example 6.1. Götterdämmerung Act III: Gutrune's solo scene (beginning).

Ex. 6.1 (cont.)

argument about precedence. Brünnhilde is outraged, and demands
Sigurd's death—and Gunther and Hogni [Hagen, Gunther's brother]
execute it. Yet after his death, her laughter becomes grief; she awak-
ens before dawn the next day, reports that she has experienced a sad
dream, and gives in to a sorrow that the court finds puzzling.[6] This
juxtaposition of laughter with enigmatic sorrow is a hermeneutic
crux, for while her sadness may be simply a reaction to her dream, it
may also suggest some secret (long-standing) emotional obsession
with Sigurd, a relationship that predates Sigurd's marriage to Gutrune. A prior betrothal between Brünnhilde and Sigurd is, of
course, made explicit in certain versions, including the *Volsunga saga*
(Wagner's main source), in which Brünnhilde and Sigurd are lovers
and Gutrune steals Sigurd away through the magic potion. Brünnhilde, in sorrow, commits suicide after his murder.[7] Thus in *Sigurdarkviða in skamma* and the *Volsunga saga*, Brünnhilde's laughter is described by the narrator as perceptibly *false laughter*, for she is secretly
devastated by Sigurd's death.[8]

If Brünnhilde laughs truly and without regret (a queen has
avenged a slight to her integrity and her will) she is heroic; if her
laughter is false and turns to lament (a jealous woman has struck out
at a false lover, and discovered grief at his death) she is romantic:
"tragic heroine" and "romantic victim" are the paradigms that Anderssen proposes to explain the differing Brünnhildes, whose separate identities are defined by that instant of laughter (is it true or
false?). The oldest Brünnhilde (the *Ur*-Brünnhilde, one might say)
was the "heroic" figure who had no prior connection to Siegfried,
who loved no man and existed within no family romance, and who
followed her own will. This *Ur*-Brünnhilde did not kill herself at the
end, but lives (as she does in several surviving sources) to celebrate

her just revenge upon a man whose deceit has bespoken his dishonor.[9] She laughs eternally.

The Germanic and German-influenced sources (with their "romantic" leanings and their eroticizations) denigrate Brünnhilde, judge her personality "barren," kill her off, and, under various cultural and social pressures, erase the "other Brynhild, who was cheated, took revenge, and survived to exult."[10] Anderssen writes that the full German tradition (represented chiefly by *Thidreks saga* and the *Nibelungenlied*)

> converts her forceful and somewhat mysterious personality into truculence and muscle. [Siegfried's] magic wooing in the northern variant appears as a prosaic arrangement in *Thidreks saga* and as the taming of a bully in the *Nibelungenlied*. Still more disenchanting is the second phase of Brynhild's subjection, her unceremonious deflowering in *Thidreks saga* and Siegfried's wrestling contest in the *Niebelungenlied*. It is tempting to think that this denigration of Brynhild in the German variant is connected with her status as victim . . . the southern milieu, or a particular poet, reacted negatively to such an overwhelming apparition and proceeded to neutralize her by making her a slave of passion and devising crasser forms of humiliation—jilting, physical subjection, defloration.[11]

Brünnhilde as comic relief, as athletic female wrestled to the ground: in these mutations, we are well on the way to the Brünnhilde who inhabits popular imagination in our century, the thick-set screeching figure of fun, with her armor and braids. Wagner, who borrowed his Brünnhilde-plot, on the whole, from the *Volsunga saga* (Norse poem, but German-influenced), gives us Brünnhilde faintly colored by some of this poetic ridicule; he generally followed the "romantic victim" paradigm for her plot-character. Certainly Wagner dislocates her famous instant of laughter and revoices it musically through Gutrune's recollection, thus seeming in his own way (and like the poetic narrator in *Sigurdarkviða in skamma* or the *Volsunga saga*) to make it *false*.

Locating and recuperating the ancient Brünnhilde (as Anderssen does) is more than a philological and ideological quest, more than a feminist rescue action, though both are salutary correctives. As Anderssen asks, why has Siegfried ever been seen as the "hero" of ancient legends that so obviously center on Brünnhilde?[12] One might echo his plaint by asking why Wagner, having written a tetralogy whose central figure is Brünnhilde, continued to pen Hegelian rhapsodies to his pallid World-historical hero, Siegfried. Such displacement of critical attention from the female figure parallels and reenacts synchronically the diachronic progress of Brünnhilde's mutations as she moves through time and space (toward the south) in the medieval sources. This same displacement occurs in arch demythicizations of Brünnhilde that have become one topos of modern *Ring* commentaries. The *Götterdämmerung* Brünnhilde is, for Clément, a "frumpy homebody Brünnhilde now, patiently waiting for her man to come home," and a "nasty" wife who "tells" on her husband Siegfried, and betrays him. She "becomes a woman, at least a woman as Wagner describes them, totally without virtue unless they are sisters . . . as wives [women] are [merely] annoyed."[13] For Conrad, "Brünnhilde's warrior-maid heroism declines into shrewishness, allowing Siegfried to treat her shrieks of rage on the spear as ill-bred scolding . . . Brünnhilde herself strides into the final scene shrewishly, mocking Gutrune's grief as childish puling over spilt milk; but she goes on to revise her own motives in apologetic retrospect and to effect her own transformation while music submerges drama and the pyre is ignited in the orchestra."[14] Nietzscheans both, they allow music to redeem ignobilities in plot-characters, in a dispensation not specific to Brünnhilde and applying to everybody. Clément writes that the whole sordid plot is saved by the final repetitions of a melody originally sung by Sieglinde in *Die Walküre* ("O hehrstes Wunder! Herrliche Maid!" "Oh most magnificent wonder! Oh beautiful maiden!") at the end of *Götterdämmerung*. This tells of something "beyond the death of the gods."[15] For Conrad, "though defeated and humbled in the drama, the characters [in general] are raised aloft by the music."[16] Such music is not *ringing false*, or, put another way, the *Ring* establishes a true music-character that is at odds with the silly plot-characters; both sets of characters coexist, imperfectly overlaid on one another.

The apotheosis of Sieglinde's melody from *Walküre* Act III at the end of the *Ring* could, however, be read quite explicitly as a musical celebration of Brünnhilde herself, for Sieglinde sings the motif (otherwise heard nowhere else) to exalt Brünnhilde for her deeds. (Wagner, asked about the motif's significance, straightforwardly said: glorification of Brünnhilde.)[17] In what follows (which in certain ways grew as a meditation upon that idea), I will recuperate the opposition explored by Conrad and Clément, but will not make my distinction in terms of "plot-Brünnhilde" and her "musical rescue." I will hold on to "plot-Brünnhilde" but broaden that idea: "plot-Brünnhilde" is the woman in Wagner's *Ring* libretto as she exemplifies the "romantic victim." The opposing (or complementary) figure is "voice-Brünnhilde," who is harder to define, and whose identity will emerge here only gradually. But "voice-Brünnhilde" is not simply some generalized redeeming music; rather, she is a "tragic-heroic" persona who continued to inhabit the medieval sources even as they debased "plot-

Brünnhilde," and who exists, as it were, "in between," constituted in the *Ring* through both her verbal and her musical discourse.

II

The Wagnerian Brünnhilde's initial *identity* as unfettered laughter (that appearance in *Walküre* names her sonically and confers this voice) is a portal, a place that brings another Brünnhilde, the *Ur*-Brünnhilde with her undying laughter, into a plot that has seemingly debased her. A similar force accrues to my second (related) theme: the narrative prophecy.

Anderssen points out that the older Brünnhilde, in her sheer heroic status, acts as a magnet for ancillary tales, *enfances* or stories about her childhood. Many motifs concerning her past—her strength, her warlike nature, her supernatural gifts, and her identity as the daughter of a god—are clustered around her adult identity.[18] Of her supernatural gifts, clairvoyance is described with obsessive focus. In *Sigurdarkviða in forna*, she experiences an ominous dream after Sigurd's death, in which she sees Gunther in defeat, and foretells disaster that will ensue from the broken oaths of blood-brotherhood.[19] In *Sigurdarkviða in skamma* (in which a more romantic Brünnhilde stabs herself in grief), she makes a long prophecy before dying; the scene is repeated in a number of other versions, including the *Volsunga saga*, in which she is granted numerous visions of the future. Before she ever comes to the court, she foresees Sigurd's beguilement through the magic potion, a prophecy that is fulfilled. At her death, she again tells of a disastrous future.[20] (The full German sources, *Thidreks saga* and the *Nibelungenlied*, strip her of this power in an action consistent with their other debasements of her character.) The antemortem moment of narrative clairvoyance mutated in Wagner's text as he altered the endings for *Götterdämmerung*. In the "Schopenhauer" ending of 1855–1856, for instance, the moment of prophecy is given in one simple line: "Trauender Liebe / tiefstes Leiden / schloß die Augen mir auf: / enden sah ich die Welt" ["The deepest suffering of tragic love opened my eyes: I saw the world end"].[21] Even the bleak economy of this single vision—"I saw the world end"—was reduced further in the definitive text set to music, in which Brünnhilde states, "alles, alles weiß ich" ["I know all, all"], but does not actually describe what she foresees.

Sibyls (and clairvoyant Brünnhilde is one) have a unique relationship to what they say in their moments of prophecy, and we hear their speech in a special way. Their speech is oracular; that is, sibyls are heard as a sounding board for speech that originates elsewhere.

Such speech is the sound of an aeolian harp played by an unseen presence, or the speech of a ventriloquist's doll; that speech seems to have complete authority since we sense an ultimate speaker (the speaker whom we assume to speak through the sibyl) who is mysterious and omniscient. The sibyl, on one level, articulates *truth* in a way that no other narrator can. We might speak of sibylline speech as always ringing true (this is why Cassandra's lot is so piteous since her sibylline speech is doomed—unlike all other oracular utterance—to be taken as false). Our assumption of truth is thus directly tied to our assumption that the sibyl is a conduit, and that she does not *intervene* in the vision that she receives. Yet in all this, the sibyl is also a "hybrid, double, ambiguous figure," who "introduce[s] the fantastic and the supernatural into the 'real' world and retain[s] only a highly tenuous relationship with the transcendental idea."[22] For Kristeva, the sibyl— by making *terrible* prophecies, by introducing alterity or negativity into the signifier—also suggests that *any* signifier might break away from one stable (transcendental, positive) meaning, and float unfixed, "belonging to this and not the other world, the Sibyl speaks all languages, possesses the future, reunites improbable elements both in and through the word. The unlimited possibilities of discourse . . . are symbolized in this transitory figure."[23] Thus she is at once a speaker of transcendent truths, yet—because she is peculiarly doubled—hybrid, androgynous, simultaneously mortal (she "belongs to this and not the other world") and clairvoyant—she functions to undermine the security of any speech's claim to transcendence.

The sibyl, however, can also be defined in another way, not only as a speaker but as a *listener*. Her clairvoyance is actually *clair-entendement* (in the double sense of hearing and understanding), and it is granted because she can hear what others cannot, because she possesses a hyperacusis for an otherwise inaudible voice. That inaudible voice speaks, as Barthes has written,

> The *secret*: that which, concealed in reality, can reach human consciousness only through a code, which serves simultaneously to encipher and decipher that reality . . . listening is religious and *deciphering*: it intentionalizes at once the sacred and secret (to listen in order to decipher history, society, the body, is *still*, under various lay alibis, a religious attitude). What is it that listening, then, seeks to decipher? Essentially, it would appear, two things: the future (insofar as it belongs to the gods) or transgression (insofar as transgression is engendered by God's gaze). By her noises, Nature shudders with meaning: at least, this is how, according to Hegel, the ancient Greeks listened to her. The oaks of Dordona, by the murmur of their boughs, uttered prophecies.[24]

While we all listen to seek meaning, only the sibyl can *hear* (understand) what the oaks of Dordona say.

Brünnhilde is, then, at once a commanding prophetic voice and a unique listening ear. In her operatic form, both elements are greatly multiplied. Her commanding *voice* is (in general) multiplied as her immense and sharply focused soprano. Her hearing, however, is set in relief as Wagner stages, again and again, a scene of Brünnhilde's listening. As Valkyrie, she hears (and executes) Wotan's choices, of course, but she also hears his monologue. She hears (understands) Siegmund's voice in the *Todesverkündigung*, which begins as her ritual statement and ends when she hears (and is changed by) what lies beneath his words. In *Götterdämmerung* Act I, Wagner stages her *refusal* to hear Waltraute as a new aberration in her character, one followed (as if causally) by the disaster of Gunther's/Siegfried's arrival.

The commanding prophecy and the sibylline ear are finally brought together at the end of *Götterdämmerung*. Brünnhilde appears far upstage, silences everyone, and begins the monologue that ends the *Ring*; her review of the past is punctuated by incomplete allusions to a future that only she can see, and ends in farewell. Structurally, of course, this monologue occupies the position of Brünnhilde's antemortem narrative prophecy as it recurs through many versions of her tale in the Norse sources. It has become less a voiced prediction than a summing-up in which "knowing all" means not only foreseeing the future, but understanding a past whose sense had eluded her; in the first moments of Act II scene 5, Brünnhilde refers to that past as "dies Wirrsal . . . dies Rätsel" ["this disorder . . . this riddle"]. Yet Brünnhilde obliquely reveals that this overarching retrospective vision of her own narrative's true form has come to her because she is a sibyl, because she *listened* to a mysterious and omniscient voice:

> Mein Erbe nun
> nehm' ich zu eigen.
> Verfluchter Reif!
> Furchtbarer Ring!
> Dein Gold fass' ich
> und geb' es nun fort.
> Der Wassertiefe
> weise Schwestern,
> des Rheines schwimmende Töchter,
> euch dank' ich redlichen Rat.
> War ihr begehrt,
> ich geb' es euch:
> aus meiner Asche

         nehmt es zu eigen!
         Das Feuer, das mich verbrennt,
         rein'ge vom Fluche den Ring!

[My inheritance I now claim. Accursed treasure! Terrible ring! I grasp
the gold and give it away. Wise sisters of the water's depths, swimming
daughters of the Rhine, I am grateful for your truthful counsel. I give
you what you want: take it out of my ashes! Let the fire that consumes
me cleanse the ring of its curse.]

Brünnhilde (as Gutrune told us) had laughed cruelly: she was rejoicing at Siegfried's fate. Gutrune also tells us that Brünnhilde had gone
to the Rhine, by referring twice to a woman who walks in the night:
"who was the woman whom I saw walking to the river bank?" (the
answer is given by the orchestra); "So it was she whom I saw walking
to the Rhine" (Example 6.2). Her references to Brünnhilde's absence,
the empty room, and silence are thus the debris left by a secret, an
enigma solved by two other clues. While Brünnhilde is elsewhere, she
has changed because she listened—to the Rheinmaidens. Her meeting with the Rheinmaidens is predicted by them in Act III scene 1,
after their futile effort to warn Siegfried against the ring:

         Leb' wohl, Siegfried!
         Ein stolzes Weib
         wird noch heut dich beerben:
         sie gibt uns bess'res Gehör.

[Farewell, Siegfried! A proud woman even today shall become your heir:
She will hear us better than you.]

This "bess'res Gehör"—a "better hearing" that implies the listener's
special acuity—might stand as motto for Brünnhilde's capacity for
perceiving meanings that others cannot. The series of clues is finally
closed in the Immolation Monologue, which reveals fully how the
sibylline voice revoices its immortal source in the Rheinmaidens' unheard narrative. Thus *Götterdämmerung* buries within itself an unheard narrative, whose telling we do not witness. Yet this is the critical
narrative in the *Ring*, the last in the long series that Brünnhilde
hears, an unsung narrative that enables Brünnhilde to "know everything," to know how the story must end in her own self-willed destruction and the destruction of the world. Her transformation has
been engendered by listening to a narrative *elsewhere*, a narrative that
is therefore as fugitive as all else that deserts the strange untenanted
rooms described by Gutrune.

Example 6.2. Gutrune's solo scene (continuation and end).

Ex. 6.2 (cont.)

So war es sie, die ich zum Rhei- ne schrei-ten sah?

War das sein Horn?   Nein!   Öd' — al-les!

Horn *(on the stage, in the distance.)*

Bewegt, und immer bewegter.
(She starts and listens to a sound in the distance.)

Säh' ich Sieg- fried nur bald!

zart

III

Brünnhilde is a heroic character because she is endowed with acute hearing; she is able to hear falsehoods narrated by other characters, and hear as well when music rings false. Wotan's Monologue trains her to hyperacusis. She loses her immortality and with it some of her aural acuity, only to regain it in the end.

Gutrune, "Gunther's gentle sister," is her inverted double within the *Ring*. They are very different; in many Norse and German sources they are overtly enemies—yet interpretations of Brünnhilde have been shaped by her gentler foil. Gutrune is seldom noticed among the stronger personalities in Wagner's *Ring*—and with reason. As a lyric soprano who can hardly compete in the vocal arena with Brünnhilde, she seems rather colorless: negligible female, minor character. She is shaped by what she lacks. Lacking a will, she becomes Hagen's puppet; without knowledge, she accepts unresisting others' explanations of action and motivation. She can modulate to absorb any narrative, be it Hagen's lies about Siegfried in Act I, or Siegfried's lies about himself and Brünnhilde in Act II, or Brünnhilde's truthful account in Act III. Yet in one significant instance, in the final act, Gutrune forms her own interpretation of what she sees, and insists upon it against a lie (Gunther's and Hagen's tale of the "wild boar" that has killed Siegfried):

> *Hagen*: Eines wilden Ebers Beute:
>   Siegfried, deinen toten Mann.
> (Gutrune schreit auf und stürzt über die Leiche.
> Allgemeine Erschütterung und Trauer.)
> *Gunther* (bemüht um die Ohnmächtige):
>   Gutrun, holde Schwester,
>   hebe dein Auge,
>   schweige mir micht!
> *Gutrune* (wieder zu sich kommend):
>   Siegfried—Siegfried erschlagen!
> (Sie stößt Gunther heftig zurück.)
>   Fort, treuloser Bruder,
>   du Mörder meines Mannes!
>   O Hilfe! Hilfe!
>   Wehe! Wehe!
>   Sie haben Siegfried erschlagen!

[*Hagen*: We bring a wild boar's victim: Siegfried, your dead husband! (Gutrune cries out and casts herself upon the body, which has been laid down in the middle of the hall. General consternation and grief.) *Gunther*

[(attending his unconscious sister): Gutrune, dear sister! Open your eyes!
Speak to me! *Gutrune* (regaining her senses): Siegfried!—Siegfried
killed! (With some force she pushes Gunther away.) Away, faithless
brother! My husband's murderer! Help! Help! Alas! Alas! They have
killed Siegfried!]

Her cry is a sonorous motif also present in the medieval sources as a
countersound to Brünnhilde's laughter, with which it is often paired
(as in *Sigurdarkviða in forna*, where Brünnhilde triumphs while Gutrune laments). Gutrune's sorrow is generally accorded narrative es-
teem in direct proportion to narrative dismissal of Brünnhilde. In the
Volsunga saga, Gutrune "gasps" and Brünnhilde laughs. By the time
of the German *Nibelungenlied* (in which Kriemhild [Gutrune] has replaced Brünnhilde as the central tragic figure), she breaks into
"boundless lamentation . . . she sank speechless to the ground and lay
there for a while, wretched beyond all measure till, reviving from her
swoon, she uttered a shriek that set the whole room echoing."[25] The
Gutrune-figure's cry has been dilated into this ear-splitting noise,
while Brünnhilde's laughter (and Brünnhilde herself) are erased
from the scene. In the *Ring* (as in the *Nibelungenlied*) Gutrune faints,
and regains her senses. During this instant of unconsciousness, she is
visited by prescience: she *knows* that Siegfried was murdered by the
men who tell of his death. An ability to see clearly, to know which
story is true and which is false—an ability that Gutrune had lacked—
is bestowed while she resides in a place that we cannot see or know.
A few moments later, she accuses Brünnhilde of conspiring in Siegfried's death. Brünnhilde does not address the accusation (which is
true), but rather the question of her own motivation, by stating simply that she was Siegfried's true bride.

Brünnhilde's arrival presages Gutrune's death. Her "confident and
solemn" interruption of the squabbling Gibichungs—"Schweigt eures
Jammers / jauchzenden Schwall" ["Silence the noisy sound of your
squabbling"]—is hardly "shrewish," for, as her final entrance, it bal-
ances her first, and is *the* great entrance in the *Ring*: an unforgettable
moment.[26] She appears far upstage; she appears as if summoned by
the magic of dead Siegfried's raised hand; she appears transformed.
The Götterdämmerung motif enters with her as her escort, a musical
gesture that links her with other sibylline singers (her mother Erda,
who first made the motif, and her half-sisters the Norns, who em-
broidered upon it). When we saw her last, at the end of Act II, she
was betrayed and furious, conspiring with Siegfried's murderers.
Now she appears as the singer of threnodies to a doomed world, no
longer blind and ignorant but omniscient. When she declares once

again that she is Siegfried's true bride, the truth of the matter is clear.
As Wintle puts it,

> the allusion [to the Götterdämmerung motif] reveals a number of things:
> that Brünnhilde's nocturnal communion described in Gutrune's mono-
> logue is now complete; that through her new wisdom and maturity she
> has gained a hieratic authority aligning her with the eternally feminine
> forces of Erda, the Norns, and the Rheinmaidens; that she herself has
> entered into the mechanism of eschatology set in train at the outset of
> this work; and that by virtue of all this she is now fit to act as the re-
> deemer of her dead husband's image.[27]

Only the last of these phrases is a letdown, suggesting as it does that
Brünnhilde sets a keystone in the eschatological arch to a relatively
trivial end, to clear pallid Siegfried's damaged reputation. (It seems
especially curious, given that Brünnhilde's analysis of Siegfried's ambiguous character in the Immolation Monologue ends with the line
"doch . . . trog keiner wie er" ["yet . . . no one betrayed so thoroughly
as he"].) I shall propose a different reading of her singing presently.

That Brünnhilde's voice has assumed its complete prophetic authority is clear, certainly, to Gutrune. In Act II she had worried about
Brünnhilde's version of the story; now (after a brief struggle) she believes, and Brünnhilde's voice literally kills her—she "turns, full of
shame, from Siegfried and bends down, dying, over the body of Gunther: so she remains motionless until the end." Brünnhilde's ability
to kill Gutrune with her voice may subtly realign her with another
supernatural axis—that represented by her father, who kills Hunding
in the same way at the end of *Walküre* Act II. But Gutrune's death is
not merely mysterious in its cause; it is unmarked in time. Gutrune
dies sometime during Brünnhilde's Immolation Monologue, the
lighting of the pyre, the burning of Valhalla, the Rhine's flood, the
return of the ring to its waters, and the world's destruction. Given the
distractions of this apocalypse, few might worry why we cannot know
when one insignificant character passes on. Yet the very fact that Gutrune dies by Brünnhilde's voice, that she dies at a moment that is
completely unmarked—can this be said of any other operatic de-
mise?—attaches some magnetism to her empty character. Her unlo-
catable death, her being elsewhere (in unconsciousness) at her moment of clairvoyance, her curious moral emptiness, occupied by
others' plots and interpretations—all these are so *marked* as to become
a source of irritation, demanding the creation of a soothing hermeneutic pearl.

If Gutrune functions as a figure who points to or warns of something, she warns especially of misconstruing Brünnhilde's offstage

transformation from vengeful conspirator to transfigured heroine, of misreading that transformation in terms of her own behavior. Readings of the *Ring* text have found the transformation to be a precarious spot in its dramatic edifice. Brünnhilde's only overt causal explanation for the change—"mich mußte / der Reinste verraten, / daß wissend würde ein Weib!" ["the purest one had to betray me, so that a woman might become wise!"]—has served as a focus for interpretations that insist upon Siegfried's death as a tragic catalyst that clears Brünnhilde's head of Hagen's lies. Such a reading follows the "romantic victim" paradigm of Brünnhilde in which her emotional bond to Siegfried is identified as the central clue to interpretation. Embraced by certain narrators of the medieval tradition, the "romantic victim" paradigm enables them (as we have seen) to soothe that key interpretive irritant—the question of Brünnhilde's laughter. Sagely, they declare that her laughter at his death *rings false*. Modern Siegfried-centered interpretations replay the medieval narrators' strategies, and their account of the Wagnerian Brünnhilde's transformation thus imposes Gutrune's pattern—sudden grief inspired by knowledge of Siegfried's death, and inspiration gained while she is elsewhere (unconscious)—on Brünnhilde. Labile Gutrune, molded by everyone else's plots and explanations, is (ironically) deployed as an interpretive template that molds Brünnhilde once more into the "romantic victim."

That Brünnhilde's transformation is enigmatic is beyond doubt; but some have seen it merely as typical of the many miscalculations and unexplained turns that are characteristic of the *Götterdämmerung* text. After the *Ring* evolved from *Siegfrieds Tod*, Wagner adjusted that original in order to bring it in line with the three poems that came to precede it in the tetralogy. Inconsistencies in *Götterdämmerung* might well be considered the residue of its layered genesis; the availability of a practical explanation for *Götterdämmerung*'s flaws has meant that they have been excused—and, in being excused, ignored. Yet it is the inconsistencies and the moments of confusion that are precisely the point, that indicate a critical characteristic of the *Ring*'s narrative passages. Since the many narrators in the *Ring* seem to recapitulate accurately events that we ourselves have witnessed on the stage, we assume that they are honest and their narratives are true. But many are nonetheless telling tales, and if we listen more closely we hear the contradictions. Wotan tells Fricka in *Das Rheingold* that he sacrificed his eye to win her; the Norns say that he gave it in exchange for the branch that becomes his spear. In *Götterdämmerung* Act I, Hagen lies to Gutrune and Gunther about the existing relationship between Siegfried and Brünnhilde. In Act II, Brünnhilde and Siegfried tell conflicting stories about the nights they spent together, and Siegfried's contains one obvious lie (he denies having taken the ring from Brünnhilde when, disguised as Gunther, he overpowered her).[28] In Act III, Siegfried narrates for the hunting party "stories from my youth," including (under the influence of Hagen's memory-restoring potion) his quest for Brünnhilde: yet he omits entirely the critical symbolic encounter in that quest, his defeat of Wotan. The *Ring* is full of magic tricks—disguising helmets, mysterious liquids, the ring itself—that, as props, are tiny reinscriptions of its larger narrative sleights of hand. Indeed, one central plot-motif in *Götterdämmerung*—Hagen's potion of forgetfulness—overtly projects the *Ring*'s underlying doubt of narration into a stage-object, making a traditional device of sorcery into a sign for epistemological irresolution. The potion beclouds Siegfried's internal narrative grasp of his own past existence, and through its agency Siegfried mutates into a happy and uncontrollable fountain of narrative untruths. When the *Ring* stages these scenes of narrative misrepresentation, when it puts before us narrators whose "point of view" ensures that they will omit and fabricate, the reliability of *all* narrating (even that we assume to speak the truth) is impugned. This uncertainty is reflected in the opposition of Gutrune and Brünnhilde: the former believes the narratives offered for her consumption; the latter has learned skepticism.

IV

Brünnhilde was transformed not by erotic panic at the news of Siegfried's death, but through her act of *clair-entendement*; she possesses sibylline listening that can decipher acoustically couched narratives. Unlike her inverted double Gutrune (who listens anxiously but hears nothing, or hears wrongly and believes almost all that she hears), Brünnhilde strains the contrapuntal voices out of the stories that she is told. She listens below the words.

Having first been introduced as pure laughter (in *Walküre* Act II scene 1), she appears next as a listener who hears Wotan's Monologue in *Walküre* Act II scene 3. Comparing the Brünnhilde who exists at the beginning of the narrative to the one at the end reveals her as a skeptic. Brünnhilde invites the narrative by effacing herself, assuring Wotan that he speaks only to himself in speaking to her:

> *Wotan*: Lass ich's verlauten,
>   lös' ich dann nicht
>   meines Willens haltenden Haft?
> *Brünnhilde* (sehr leise): Zu Wotans Willen sprichst du,

> sagst du mir, was du willst;
> wer bin ich,
> wär ich dein Wille nicht?

[*Wotan*: If I speak out loud, do I not loosen the binding power of my will? *Brünnhilde* (very quietly): But you are speaking to Wotan's will, tell me what you wish; who am I, if I were not your will?]

This identification of Brünnhilde as Wotan's will is straightforward enough; as Valkyrie, her task is to execute Wotan's decisions about who will live or die in battle. Wotan thus believes his narrative to be "unausgesprochen"—literally, not spoken out loud and not narrated—because Brünnhilde is the listener. This nonnarrated narrative should be subject to no outside interpretation and should produce no external consequences not willed by Wotan himself. The narrative that Brünnhilde elicits is (as we have seen in Chapter 5) Wotan's historical justification for deciding that Siegmund must die in the upcoming battle with Hunding; his hand is forced to the murder of his own son, as the outcome of his entanglements in agreements and laws. But having listened to the entire narrative, Brünnhilde refuses to accept its demand for proper closure in Siegmund's death. In interpreting Wotan's narrative, she becomes autonomous and can no longer be understood as a blind agent for Wotan's choices. Her refusal outrages Wotan; her refusal brings her to the *Todesverkündigung* without conviction, so that she is moved by Siegmund's despair and decides to save him. Her refusal of the narrative closure that Wotan proposes thus brings her punishment upon her at the opera's end. She declares this refusal (significantly) as grounded in listening and interpreting:

> Den du zu lieben
> stets mich gelehrt,
> der in hehrer Tugend
> dem Herzen dir teuer—
> gegen ihn zwingt mich nimmer
> dein zwiespältig Wort!

[Against him whom you always taught me to love, who in his noble virtue is dear to your heart, to fight against him—that your divided words will never force me to do!]

"Gegen ihn zwingt mich nimmer / dein zwiespältig Wort": in Wotan's Monologue, the "word" (both verbal and musical) is, for Brünnhilde, both schismatic and *contrapuntal*; she rejects the monophonic line and an ending that Wotan would set before her (and us). In a gesture that aligns her with yet another mythic axis (now, that of Prometheus) she liberates the "word" from its authorial source and frees it to live in her rehearing and reinterpretation. This action is also self-liberating; by splitting Wotan's narration into layers and identifying conflicting imports, she can split herself from Wotan and become more than his will. When she disobeys his will at the end of the monologue, she takes the first step into that alternative eschatology (one controlled by female figures) that will eventually break the unending cycles that she perceives in his singing. *In his singing*: that is deliberate. Wotan's Monologue is a long and clouded phenomenal song; as such, its music can be heard by his onstage listener. Brünnhilde hears his discursive habit of cyclical recurrence in both verbal and musical forms, hears musical circles that are not always bound to specific textual events and, in being unbound to the poem, are all the more powerful. There is thus an ironic reversal of traditional male/female polarities. Wotan—the man who wishes for the end—sings only in (feminine) circles, while Brünnhilde will eventually fulfill the (masculine) role when she brings down the sword that cuts the knot, and *creates* that end at the cost of her life.

The fundamental opposition that Brünnhilde hears in Wotan's Monologue is, in simplest form, Wotan's and the story's demand for Siegmund's death, set against Wotan's unspoken desire to let his son live. Splitting the narrative nonetheless implies more than recognition of Wotan's divided heart, for oppositions of other sorts emerge. Wotan's musical rhetoric sometimes belies, yet eventually revoices, the history that he recounts. The musical setting in certain respects denies the words, yet in the end endorses the vision they convey. Brünnhilde's "zwiespältiges Wort" thus expresses her recognition that narrative itself must divide into strata, none of which bear complete meaning or moral truth. Her sibylline ears are attuned to such polyphonic layers of music and words in several restagings of this scene of listening. She is represented as one who is aware that she inhabits opera, aware of its music, able to parse it out. She will repeatedly characterize her ability to fracture others' stories and understand their oppositions as *hearing*.

Such, for instance, is her retrospective analysis of the *Todesverkündigung*, her dialogue with Siegmund in *Walküre* Act II scene 4. Brünnhilde appears to Siegmund and commands that he look upon her. Their dialogue begins with a ritual series of questions and answers (a first round), during which Brünnhilde tells Siegmund of Valhalla. Upon discovering that Sieglinde cannot accompany him, Siegmund refuses the proposed honor (in death) of a place at Wotan's side. The second and belligerent round of exchanges involves declarations on both sides, in which Brünnhilde warns Siegmund that he must die; Siegmund breaks off to observe the sleeping Sieglinde, and the third round (in which Brünnhilde is gradually convinced to spare him) is ushered in by a reversal of their positions: now *Brünnhilde* is ignorant and asks, "so wenig achtest du / ewige Wonne?" ["does it mean so little to you, eternal glory?"][29] Musically, the scene obsessively repeats and recomposes a harmonic question-and-response in a series of thematic waves dominated by two elements—the slow, spondaic chord-pair of the Fate motif and the long line of a melody heard for the first time in this scene.[30] That melody, harmonically open-ended in most of its mutations, is first heard instrumentally in the ritual music for Brünnhilde's appearance and subsequently *sung* repeatedly by Siegmund (and later by Brünnhilde as well) (Example 6.3). Siegmund's questions tend, at first, to take their harmonic opening from a point determined by Brünnhilde's singing; initially, her answers to each question *turn* Siegmund's endpoint (by means of the modulatory Fate motif) in another tonal direction. This relationship (imputing musical control to Brünnhilde's singing) is gradually inverted. The musical unscrolling of the scene involves a progressive dissolution of that hieratic ritual-musical period, which is both Brünnhilde's appearance (mm. 1–29) and, when repeated (mm. 29–55), her first utterance.

Later (in *Walküre* Act III scene 3), she describes her meeting with Siegmund to Wotan in order to explain why she disobeyed his command, and tells what she witnessed when he "turned his back on" Siegmund: "die im Kampfe Wotan / den Rücken bewacht, / die sah nun das nur, / was du nicht sahst: / Siegmund mußt' ich sehn" ["she who guards Wotan's back in battle, she saw what you did not see: I had to see Siegmund"]. While her experience is initially recounted in ocular terms (the same word—*sehen*—is repeated three times to echo her grim command to Siegmund: "seht auf mich" ["look upon me"]), she immediately turns to verbs of hearing:

> Tod kündend
> trat ich vor ihn,
> gewahrte sein Auge,
> hörte sein Wort;
> ich vernahm des Helden
> heilige Not;
> tönend erklang' mir
> des Tapfersten Klage;
> freiester Liebe
> fürchtbares Leid,

Example 6.3. Die Walküre Act II: Brünnhilde's first statement in the *Todesverkündigung.*

Ex. 6.3 (cont.)

> traurigsten Mutes
> mächtigster Trotz!
> Meinem Ohr erscholl,
> mein Aug' erschaute.

[I became aware of his eyes, heard his words; I understood the hero's sacred need; ringing out it resounded to me: this most brave man's plaint; the terrible pain of a most free love, the powerful defiance of tragic courage! My ear thundered with it, my eye saw.]

Seeing is neutral (sehen, gewahren, erschauen). But hearing is charged, as "heard" words "ring, resound" with sound that thunders into her ear (hören, tönen, erklingen, erschallen). Phonic energy explodes in the line *tönend erklang mir*, which might even be understood as Brünnhilde's reference to her own musical ear and the proof that she has no deaf spot: "[His words] resounded to me (*erklang mir*) 'musically' (*tönend*)."[31] The music that is heard as she sings paraphrases musically her dialogue with Siegmund (Example 6.4). Remaking the *Todesverkündigung*'s ritual opening music (the Fate motif on bass D–C♯ in mm. 5–7, and the characteristic F♯ minor melody in mm. 8–12), this passage both *quotes* that formal opening and simultaneously lays over it a distinct rhythmic and harmonic loosening that had previously affected it only gradually over the course of a long encounter. The music, in other words, embraces as polyphony what was originally separate (the formal ritual music, and the temporal process that dissolves it). This return-transformation multiplies the phonic energy invoked in Brünnhilde's description by compelling us to rehear not Siegmund's precise words, but rather the musical process that accompanied them. Having heard this music, Brünnhilde sings it as a special polyphony, layering music by isolating and then assimilating once-separate strains. Arriving at the full texture of truth, as she has explained, entails not seeing (reading a face, or a text) but, rather, hearing (voices).

V

Brünnhilde has one seeming deaf spot: she refuses to hear her sister Waltraute in *Götterdämmerung* Act I, whose plea "hör' mich, hör' meine Angst" ["hear me, hear my fear"] is ignored, and whose words are calmly dismissed as "banger Träume Mären" ["stories born of anxious dreams"]. This refusal to listen is made ironic by subtle and fragmentary musical references to the *Todesverkündigung* within Waltraute's narrative, and music that Brünnhilde once heard so acutely (and acted upon so completely) now apparently goes unnoticed.

Example 6.4. Die Walküre Act III: Brünnhilde remakes the *Todesverkündigung* music.

trat ich vor ihn, ge-wahr - te sein

Au - ge, hör - te sein Wort; ich ver-

nahm des Hel - den hei - li - ge

poco cresc.

Ex. 6.4 (cont.)

trau - rig - sten Mu - thes mäch - tig - ster

Trotz! MeinemOhr er - scholl,

mein Aug' er - schau - te, was tief im

Ex. 6.4 (cont.)

Bu - sen   das Herz   zu   heil' - gem

Be - ben mir traf.

When Waltraute, describing Wotan, sings, "so sitzt er, / sagt kein Wort" ["so he sits, saying nothing"], she does so to music that resonates (though partially transposed, from bass E to bass F♯) from Brünnhilde's pivotal question in the *Todesverkündigung*, "does it mean so little to you, eternal glory?" Waltraute tells how Wotan felled the World Ash Tree and heaped its wood around Valhalla (an act recounted by the Second Norn). She resings music belonging to the Third Norn at "die Weltesche zu fällen" ["to fell the World Ash Tree"] and "des Stammes Scheite / hieß er schichten" ["he ordered that pieces of its trunk be piled up"], thus slipping, as musical presence, into the female eschatology. But her chief purpose is to urge Brünnhilde to return the ring to the Rhine—a demand that is summarily dismissed as sheer madness. The entire argument about the ring should serve to remind us that the curse (for the moment) touches Brünnhilde: it is the cause of her deafness. The curse, which acts to kill narrators and narration, acts here to defeat Waltraute's narrative by veiling it from Brünnhilde's ears, and when the curse filters that narration, Brünnhilde hears it as *meaningless* sound, "wirr und wild" ["confused and wild"].

Brünnhilde as "romantic victim" is in no psychological condition to interest herself in Waltraute's account of disaster in Valhalla, having herself been stripped of divinity, and discovered earthly love with Siegfried. In *Götterdämmerung* Act II, however, Brünnhilde's deafness to Waltraute's narrative cedes to despair in narrative meaning, born of her own previous acuity. Hagen brings this about, for like all great tacticians, he knows his antagonist and exploits Brünnhilde's tendency to listen and interpret, along with the wariness toward narrative consequent upon both. Hagen arranges that Brünnhilde see Siegfried in wedding dress, see him with Gutrune, see him with the ring. Hagen, however, also elicits *narration* from Siegfried, a false retelling of certain critical events. Siegfried's narration (which is false), and not his behavior, dooms him; his narration justifies his murder and brings Brünnhilde into the conspiracy.

To us, Siegfried is not accountable for omitting from his narrative something that he cannot recall. But to the listener—Brünnhilde—there is only the false narrative, lacking all reference to the first night. By *forgetting*—whether intentional or not—Siegfried betrays Brünnhilde. A narrative gap becomes fatal to the teller:

> Hört, ob ich Treue brach!
>   Blutbrüderschaft
> hab' ich Gunther geschworen.
> Nothung, das werte Schwert,
> wahrte der Treue Eid:
> mich trennte seine Schärfe
> von diesem traur'gen Weib.

[Hear now whether I broke faith! Blood-brotherhood I swore with Gunther. Nothung, my valiant sword, preserved my faith's oath: its sharpness separated me from this sad woman.]

Brünnhilde's opposing story is fuller, and takes account of both nights:

> Du listiger Held,
> sieh, wie du lugst!
> Wie auf dein Schwert
> du schlecht dich berufst!
> Wohl kenn' ich seine Schärfe,
> doch kenn' ich auch die Scheide,
>   darin so wonnig
>   ruht' an der Wand
> Nothung, der treue Freund
> als die Traute sein Herr sich gewann.

[Crafty hero, see how you lie, falsely alluding to your sword! I know its sharpness, but I also know the sheath, in which so gently that true friend Nothung rested on the wall, while its lord won a beloved for himself.]

This exchange of stories (which adapts and plays out in public an intense private Brünnhilde-Sigurd dialogue in the *Volsunga saga*) culminates in a famous *coup de théâtre*, the conflicting oaths ("Helle Wehr, / heilige Waffe") sworn on Hagen's spear as the means of punishing the perjurer. The passage is a tenor-soprano duel in which Brünnhilde usurps Siegfried's music, repeating it, reharmonized, with rhythmic distensions, and hitting a higher note at the end. The exchange is also a nodal point at which the contradictory narratives heard previously are pressed into an essence, an oath sworn, an accusation of perjury in which Brünnhilde's claim is set higher. In the German text for the Spear Oaths, an imperfect verbal parallelism on the smallest scale—*Eid* (Siegfried's oath) and *Meineid* (Brünnhilde's accusation of perjury)—is the last essence distilled from the conflicting narratives. The coup de théâtre causes an uproar, and sends Siegfried and Gutrune, with male and female choruses, running for the wings. (The three who remain—Hagen, Gunther, and Brünnhilde—will enter into the murder conspiracy.) Only Brünnhilde realizes that there has been a more frightening chaos, an epistemological uproar. Siegfried's narrative, the latest in a long series that she has heard, has brought a vertiginous reflexive moment: it has suggested to her that no narrative *represents* or stands for past events, that all narratives refer only to themselves as artifice. Caught in this moment, Brünnhilde slips into despair, expressed in a single critical remark made to Hagen, in which she can equate *Eid* and *Meineid* by calling the difference between them "müßige Acht"—a "distinction not worth making" (Example 6.5). The musical oscillation—augmented triad turning to augmented triad—creates a harmonic wobble in which neither chord prevails (this particular oscillation is derived from the refrain "Singe, Schwester" in the Norn's scene). Just as one word contains the other, or is a fragment of the other, so are the opposing narrations for which they stand—truth and perjury, Brünnhilde's story and Siegfried's—equally fragile. Either could be false.

VI

The *Ring* text asks us to be suspicious of narrative. Gutrune's blankness and passivity, the way she recedes beside the other characters, and finally her characteristic solo scene function to underscore this demand. Gutrune (as we have seen) is a character whose solo scene

Example 6.5. Götterdämmerung *Act II scene 5:* Eid und Meineid.

points to a secret. For Gutrune not only *is* passive, always filled up by others' explanations; she also *speaks* of emptiness. Her soliloquy concerns what is not present, for Siegfried is gone, and Brünnhilde's chamber is bare: "öd alles" ["everything desolate"], she laments at the end. Sounds are left to hint at what has fled; Brünnhilde's wild laughter is heard at the edge of consciousness, but when Gutrune wakes, it has become the horse's panicked neighing. Siegfried, murdered, cannot even be represented by sound—his horn is silent. "Öd alles" summarizes all these empty spaces that have been abandoned, and the sounds that cannot be trusted to signify as they should.

Brünnhilde has gone away to enact her last sibylline function, and to listen to the oaks of Dordona by hearing the Rheinmaidens' narrative. This narrative seems at first to be cast as a master narrative for the tetralogy. Sung by primordial creatures belonging to a prelapsarian order, it overcomes Brünnhilde and dictates the end of the *Ring*'s world. Brünnhilde's "Eid und Meineid—müß'ge Acht"—envisaging all narrative as potentially tainted and meaningless—seems reversed entirely when she submits to the Rheinmaiden's narrative, with its transcendent meaning.

Her transformation is thus in no sense merely from woman

scorned to forgiving spouse, but rather from relativistic despair to absolute faith in meaning. The proper closure made for the master narrative has a certain musical presence. At the opening of the Immolation Monologue ("Starke Scheite / schichtet mir dort" ["Let massive logs be heaped there for me"], there is a famous effect of large-scale musical recapitulation, created by the final return of the hieratic, half-dissonant march music that had first been heard in the *Götterdämmerung* prologue, for the Third Norn's vision of Valhalla in flames. This march also accompanies Waltraute's description of how Wotan ordered the World Ash Tree's branches to be heaped around Valhalla, and how Wotan sits silent at their center, waiting for the end. For several hours, the march disappears, and recurs only with Brünnhilde's antemortem speech. Widely spaced recapitulation of this sort is a typical Wagnerian gambit, which both articulates long expanses of time, and creates a sense of closure in its effect of musical anticipation finally realized, completed. Other gestures of closure are themselves amassed around the Immolation Monologue's opening, as Brünnhilde obeys the demands of a narrative without questioning, and acts out its end in several ways. In demanding the construction of her own funeral pyre, she repeats Wotan's orders to pile wood around Valhalla, rephrasing Wotan's very words as Waltraute had reported them.[32] Beyond this, she *enacts* the ending required by the Rheinmaidens' master narrative, an end she now senses as "demanded by [her] own body" ("denn des Helden heiligste / Ehre zu teilen, / verlangt mein eigener Leib"). Her transformation is transfiguration, in which a Brünnhilde purged of her doubts toward narrative is willing to execute the story's closure with her own death.

On the face of it, the Rheinmaidens' unheard narrative, which so masters Brünnhilde, seems to be a moral and epistemological happy end for the *Ring*. Narrative succeeds in representing truth (Brünnhilde deems the Rheinmaidens' words "redlich" ["honest" or "candid"]) and changing the course of the world. This happy end would be in line with the *Ring*'s myth of cyclic renewal in which evil is purged in destruction, and the ring returned to the Rhine in a new beginning. The tetralogy would thus seem to undermine narrative throughout, only to assuage this doubt by implying that the Rheinmaidens' narrative has absolute power over a listener whose hyperacuity is everywhere celebrated, and who has repeatedly exposed the ambiguities of narrative performance. Like all happy endings, this one is dubious, for the Rheinmaidens' narrative takes place offstage, and its banishment has moral implications. As a perfect narrative, an overwhelming narrative, a narrative that omits nothing, a narrative that proposes itself as *representing* truth, this narrative cannot actually be sung or heard.

There were (of course) practical reasons for having Brünnhilde's transformation and the narrative that engenders it occur offstage. Wagner knew well enough that denouements should never be arrested by epic exposition; in opera, especially, swift pacing for endings is critical. Narrative that halts action and changes our perception of passing time has dilating properties that should always serve some purpose. The last long narrative in *Götterdämmerung*—Siegfried's "stories from my young days" in Act III scene 2—provides the pretext for Siegfried's murder in revealing, before witnesses, his first night with Brünnhilde. It also extends time between the hunting party's arrival and the murder, and makes us unnaturally sensitive to Hagen's waiting. We wait, with him, for the moment to strike. Some hypothetical Rheinmaiden-Brünnhilde narrative scene would suspend time where suspense is miscalculated; dramaturgically, the idea is ludicrous. Yet whatever practical considerations existed to suggest that this narrative *might* happen offstage, the *Ring* itself *demands* that it be unheard. Should the Rheinmaidens' narrative have entered the drama, it would have fallen under the *Ring*'s own subversion of narrative. Thus embodied and performed, it would be insecure, its moral authority and its mastery of Brünnhilde destroyed. "Offstage" is the only place where the transcendent idea can possibly reside. Wotan hints at this when he says of his own monologue, "unausgesprochen / bleib' es denn ewig: / mit mir nur rat ich, / red' ich zu dir" ["unspoken let it remain forever: I speak only to myself, if I tell it to you"]. Narrative not performed aloud cannot be challenged. Wotan's narrative is, of course, as flawed as others; it is spoken loudly and at length. Only because Wotan has mistaken Brünnhilde for himself, for his will, can he believe that he has narrated silently, unwitnessed, and in this sense offstage. "Offstage" is thus the place that ultimately thwarts the *Ring*'s attempt to propose a last transcendent narrative. Within the stage-world, offstage is not noumenal but phenomenal; it is as full of events as "onstage"; it is the rest of the world. To the characters, offstage can be reached by walking. Within the performance, however, nothing (to us as the audience) exists offstage; the entire world is contained within what we see and hear, in the performance. Offstage is merely constituted by what is said or enacted onstage. So the Rheinmaidens' narrative is an event *alluded to* by fragmentary clues cast out in onstage speech; in being constituted by onstage narrative, its existence, like that of all events that the *Ring* narrates, becomes dubious. Since the *Ring*, in its constant juxtaposition of live enactments of events and narratives that may lie, has repeatedly warned us against assuming that events are truly constituted in representations, even the marks that seem to have been left by a last narrative may be false. They may be empty signs (there is nothing offstage). Narrative's capacity to mean has been made precarious in the *Ring* text, which thus comes to modulate between proposing this absent and overwhelming narrative and acting upon its force, and denying both its perfection and its very existence elsewhere.

VII

"Öd alles": Gutrune's pentultimate line in her solo scene could mean that everything is empty, or desolate, laid waste, deserted. This would describe, for many, the musical effect of her scene. By comparison, the actual end of *Götterdämmerung*, which depicts an apocalypse, functions musically as an extensive, symphonically developed close. In some sense, it constitutes a coherent musical end to the *Ring*, for it winds up the *Ring*'s harmonic tensions in that its tonality—Db—refers back to the end of *Rheingold*, and thus creates a cyclic return at the end. That Wagner lingers for many minutes on this single key seems a necessary expansiveness within the proportions of *Götterdämmerung* itself, for five hours of wandering tonality demands a long final drone. Gutrune's scene is, as a musical conceit, far more exaggerated, more subversive than the opera's final gesture of resolution. Its disjunctions—the juxtapositions of unrelated motivic fragments, the abandonment of the motives to silence—radically challenge musical values. In this broad sense, it would seem to modern aesthetic sensibilities (preferring simpler musical analogies for textual images) to be a better representation of the collapse of order.

Gutrune's remarks about mysteriously missing Brünnhilde and her idiosyncratic music are not merely a touch of uncanniness calculated to lend color to *Götterdämmerung*'s last hour, nor are they merely some musical depiction of her own sketchy character. Her remarks generate narrative tension by creating a riddle: what is Brünnhilde up to at the Rhine? The *Ring* nudges us toward an answer (that she hears the Rheinmaiden's overmastering narrative), but we in effect construct the answer urged by lines of text, by an account of how Brünnhilde has left her room and walked by night. Are the traces left by the Rheinmaidens' narrative left by an event gone missing onstage, or are they self-referential empty signs that require no interpretive pursuit? The *Ring* will not allow us to pause; it will force us to modulate (as it does) between trust in the Rheinmaidens' narrative and skepticism about its existence. This modulation must not be seen as merely paradoxical, or, worse, as the mark of a morally noncommittal

or confused libretto. If we are left without critical certainty about the
meaning of the Rheinmaidens' narrative, then we are also left with a
lively and life-giving kinesis—for the *Ring* text's uneasiness is, in some
sense, *musical*. It plays, as well, on the human impulse to imagine
events on the basis of allusions or narrative descriptions—the very
impulse that created the *Ring* libretti as we know them. Critical reflections on Gutrune and Brünnhilde and the *Ring*'s narratives turn
back, finally, to the history of the *Ring*, for our own tendencies to
decode the riddle of Brünnhilde's transformation by postulating offstage events replicate Wagner's creative work in making the *Ring*
text.

The *Ring*'s narratives (as we saw in Chapter 5) survived their precarious moment under the ax, but they themselves continue to form
precarious points in its text. As contradictory accounts of events we
do not see, as imperfect representations of actions that we have witnessed, the narratives serve to maintain the *Ring*'s epistemological
tensions. The *Ring*'s denouement and Brünnhilde's transfiguration
propose the Rheinmaidens' narrative as overmastering. Yet that narrative is forced offstage, and we are forced to modulate between belief in that narrative and the concomitant mistrust of narrative proposed by the *Ring*. The *Ring* cannot resolve this dissonance, yet the
dissonance, in the end, animates an extraordinarily complex text.
Dissonance also marks the *music* in the *Ring*'s narratives. No matter
how warmly we might wish that operatic music be an outside and
truthful voice, imposing a sovereign reading on the text that it sets
this cozy vision of yet another overmastering voice is itself suspect.
Music in the *Ring*'s world is potentially as marked by contradiction
(or dissonance) as words are. In the *Ring*'s world, not even the sonorous narrator is above reproach.

IX

Brünnhilde and Gutrune traveled together through all versions of
their stories. Their great disagreement over precedence, the "Quar-
rel of the Queens" (during which Gutrune sets in motion the events
that will culminate in Siegfried's death by revealing his deception to
Brünnhilde), is a central episode in many versions, though it has disappeared in the *Ring*. These two figures seem to exist through historical time in a reciprocal economy of feminine energy: as one (Brünnhilde) dwindles, the other (Gutrune) puffs out with narrative
interest.[33] Gutrune is a "romantic victim" in even the most ancient
sources (she loves Siegfried; she is properly married to him; he dies;
she mourns him). As a paradigm for Woman, she is imposed on the

Ur-Brünnhilde who once remained outside, creating the middle-Brünnhilde who appears (for example) in the *Volsunga saga* (deemed to love Siegfried; secretly married to him; eventually he dies; she mourns him and kills herself). This appears to be Brünnhilde as she exists in the *Ring* plot. In the history of her subsequent medieval mutations, it seems that the more Brünnhilde resembled Gutrune, the less she was needed by poetic narrators; late-Brünnhilde is drained out of *Thidreks saga* and the *Nibelungenlied*; her supernatural attributes are denied. The sibylline voice is forgotten. The magic strength becomes risible.

Yet Wagner's Brünnhilde is *not* just the middle-Brünnhilde proposed by the *Ring*'s plot. Wagner's Brünnhilde enfolds within herself the *Ur*-Brünnhilde; she is secretly *laughing*, and is burning up all along from the phonic energy of the voices that she hears. Twice she is surrounded by an onstage fire: it alludes visually to that internal combustion. Her double identity as laughter and the sibylline ear creates a Brünnhilde who is neither a plot-Brünnhilde (the personality, the woman in the plot) nor a purely musical Brünnhilde (equivalent to Conrad's idea of some generalized sublime music that redeems the plot-character). She is, rather, what I called "voice-Brünnhilde" (a concept that is only indirectly related to Poizat's operatic voice-object).[34] This figure is constituted through the texture of her language (for instance, through her repeated allusions to her own hearing), through the moments at which she seems to hear (and at times, to recompose) the music. She first peers out during plot-Brünnhilde's entrance in *Walküre* Act II, as laughter in B. She hovers throughout the *Ring*, but reemerges fully only in the Immolation Monologue, the locus that draws together what we can now understand as numerous voice-Brünnhilde strains.

As a version of the traditional antemortem prophecy, the Immolation Monologue is, in part, Brünnhilde's final revoicing of the mysterious "transcendent" narrative heard during the night. The monologue is divided into six large poetic and musical waves. First, Brünnhilde requests that the pyre be built. She then apostrophizes Siegfried, and describes the contradictions in his character:

> Echter als er
> schwur keiner Eide;
> treuer als er
> hielt keiner Verträge;
> lauter als er
> liebte kein andrer!
> Und doch alle Eide,

> alle Verträge,
> die treueste Liebe
> trog keiner wie er!

[No one swore oaths more truly than he, no one kept contracts more faithfully than he, no one loved more honestly than he; and yet all oaths, all contracts, the most faithful love—no one betrayed them so thoroughly as he!]

No one demythicizes Siegfried so thoroughly as she, and the fourfold musical hammering at "trog keiner wie er!" (a repetition of the cadential close that ends *Götterdämmerung* Act I) underscores her own emphatic break with the Siegfried myth. Like everything else described in the Immolation Monologue, Siegfried is seen with cleared sight.

In the third part of the monologue, Brünnhilde addresses Wotan; the passage famously defuses accumulated musical distortions of the *Ring*'s main motifs at the line "ruhe, du Gott" ["rest, oh god"]. In the fourth (initiated by a return of the march music from the first), she describes how she listened to the Rheinmaidens. The fifth section begins when she seizes the torch and sends Wotan's ravens to Valhalla; the final part follows the lighting of the pyre.

Most listeners (I suspect) regret the words in this final section, thinking it one of Wagner's tasteless miscalculations: the invitation to Grane, Brünnhilde's magic horse, to join her on the pyre of "dein Herr, Siegfried, mein seliger Held" ["your master, Siegfried, my blessed hero"]. One can, like Clément, simply listen to the music, including the repetitions of Sieglinde's great melodic peroration, now taken up by Brünnhilde. But Brünnhilde's words, which may seem merely embarrassing, are far more than a self-effacing and final glorification of Siegfried. To hear their import, one must hear them not as the cloying speech of plot-Brünnhilde, but as part of a final textual-musical utterance by voice-Brünnhilde, coming in the context of *her* continued presence and identity throughout the *Ring*. The utterance is "double-voiced" in Bakhtin's sense of being "directed both toward the referential object of speech, as in ordinary discourse, and toward *another's discourse*, toward *someone else's speech* . . . incorporating a relationship to someone else's utterance as an indispensible element."[35] Voice-Brünnhilde enunciates the rhapsodic references to Siegfried. Yet in Bakhtin's terms, she does not so much evoke Siegfried (the referential object) as the characteristic discourse of a plot-Brünnhilde whose voice she thus stands above and transcends. (She also mixes this evocation of plot-Brünnhilde's discourse with words of her own.) The sixth phase of the monologue is thus linguistically polyphonic, and voice-Brünnhilde *quotes and revoices* the "romantic victim," using the occasion of references to Siegfried as the pretext for underscoring and celebrating her own presence.

As a presence, she constitutes herself (as she has all along) through both language and musical sound. To understand the extent of her self-celebration, rehearing the sixth part of her monologue is critical. It is—most significantly—woven almost wholly of music that she has unequivocally *heard* or herself *invented* (Example 6.6). The melody of Sieglinde's "O hehrstes Wunder! Herrliche Maid!" recurs (at mm. 4–7, and then repeatedly until the end of the opera) for the first time in the *Ring* at this moment. The melody's exclusion from the *Ring*—to reappear only in its final minutes—is an enigmatic and highly charged musical gesture (so much so that nearly everyone who hears the *Ring* notices it). Voice-Brünnhilde speaks at this moment from within the score, for the motivic recurrence hypostatizes, Brünnhilde's ear: only Brünnhilde *heard* this music. It never otherwise returns, and Brünnhilde alone can bring it back by resinging it at the end. Her vocal entry in measure 4 is precisely timed to twist a sustained instrumental high D into the melody that she wants; with that eighth-note D, she whips the orchestra around and forms it into *her* voice. The polyphonic web of her singing and its orchestral echos is further spun of musical ideas that she *authored*, as the first voice in the *Ring* to sing them—the Siegfried motif in measures 7–9, and the laughter music from her debut in *Walküre* Act II (mm. 11–14). So the Siegfried motif is not some semiotic reference to Siegfried; rather, it revoices the sound of her own singing voice in *Walküre* Act III, in which she had first created this particular music. (Put another way, the musical discourse alludes not to the referential object, but to her own earlier utterance.)

Example 6.6. Götterdämmerung Act III: the Immolation Monologue (final part).

Ex. 6.6 (cont.)

Ex. 6.6 (cont.)

die la - chen-de Lo - he?

Fühl' — mei - ne Brust auch, wie sie ent - brennt, — hel - les

Feu - er das Herz mir er - fasst, ——

(etc.)

Revoicing her own music, Brünnhilde finally rejoins her initial
identity as laughter, a fusion that she acknowledges verbally:

> Lockt dich zu ihm
> die lachende Lohe?
> Fühl meine Brust auch,
> wie sie entbrennt,
> helles Feuer
> das Herz mir erfaßt,
> ihn zu umschlingen,
> umschlossen von ihm,
> in mächtigster Minne,
> vermählt ihm zu sein!
> Heiajaho, Grane!
> Grüß deinen Herren!
> Siegfried! Siegfried! Sieh!
> Selig grüßt dich dein Weib!

[Do they draw you to him, the laughing flames? Feel my body, how it
burns, how pure fire seizes my heart. To embrace him, surrounded by
him, in a most powerful passion, to be united with him! Heiajaho, Grane,
greet your master! Siegfried! Look! Joyfully your beloved greets you!]

What seems to be plot-Brünnhilde's erotic desire (for union with
Siegfried) is revoiced as intoxication or madness that bypasses that
object as voice-Brünnhilde reasserts her identity. The fire that now
"laughs" is also a Brünnhilde who senses herself as "burning"—with
fire and laughter both. With the highest note in the Immolation
Monologue, the B at "[lachende] Lohe" (along with the music surrounding it),[36] Brünnhilde's end refers to her beginning, and to that
unfettered laughter in B that is her first voice. And after the music
for the apocalypse, the *Ring* itself ends with the sound of *her* voice,
re-sounding in the high violins.

Brünnhilde (to return to my own beginning) in her "heroic" form
can be summarized by a moment of laughter, and by a sibylline voice
that utters a narrative prophecy: this form inhabits Wagner's *Ring* in
ways that I have tried to describe. But the sibyl, we should recall, is
marked by alterity; she is not an unambiguous figure, and does not
simply transmit divine or transcendent truth. Being of this world,
yet hearing another, she symbolizes (as Kristeva saw it) the possibility
that a signifier (words *or* music) might lose any attachment to a transcendent signified. In her identity as sibyl, then, Brünnhilde proposes
that we doubt narration—even (or especially) the master-narration

that comes to her through her sibylline ear. As a sibyl, she is paradoxically able to suggest this doubt even as she seems to obey the dictates of the master-narrative by returning the ring to the Rhine, and as the listener who can hear and shatter narration, she suggests the same skepticism in a different way. "Voice-Brünnhilde" thus resembles the *Ring* itself, which calls into question the probity of narrators and the truth of their tales. The Brünnhilde enfolded by the *Ring*, as I have suggested, reflects in these ways the traces of the "heroic queen" who is erased from most other forms of her story. She walks by night, brings no solace, no romantic ending, and no feminine or maternal comforts; she offers in the end only laughter itself. She laughs—eternally.

NOTES

Preface

1. Catherine Clément, *Opera, or the Undoing of Women*, trans. Betsy Wing (Minneapolis: University of Minnesota Press, 1988).

2. *New York Times Book Review*, (1 January 1989), 3. See also his essay "A Deconstructive Postscript: Reading Libretti and Misreading Opera," in *Reading Opera*, ed. Arthur Groos and Roger Parker (Princeton: Princeton University Press, 1988), 328–46.

3. I am thinking here of such apparently disparate forms as nineteenth-century literary programs, more abstract late twentieth-century narratological analyses of musical plots such as those of Leo Treitler, Anthony Newcomb, Hermann Danuser, and Hans-Heinrich Eggebrecht (see Chapters 1 and 4), play-by-play descriptive analyses such as Tovey's, and the work of musical hermeneuticists such as Albert Schering, whose *Beethoven und die Dichtung* (Berlin: Junker und Dünnhaupt, 1936) is a classic of narratological interpretation.

4. Edward T. Cone, *The Composer's Voice* (Berkeley and Los Angeles: University of California Press, 1974).

5. There are two ways in which my definition of "voice" diverges from that proposed by Cone. First, I do not postulate a monophonic, single "voice" associated with the utterance of a virtual author ("the Composer's voice"). Second, I do not hear entire pieces, at every moment, as the utterances of a virtual-author voice. The moments of enunciation are set apart, and in many cases disrupt the flux of the piece around them, and decenter our sense of a single originating speaker.

6. This point was made by René Leibowitz, in *Le compositeur et son double* (Paris: Gallimard, 1971), 26.

7. Narrative is a text that urges completion and imputation of causality, according to one classic description in E. M. Forster, *Aspects of the Novel* (1927; reprint, New York: Harcourt, Brace, 1955), 86.

8. Seymour Chatman, "What Novels Can Do That Films Can't (and Vice Versa)," in *On Narrative*, ed. W.J.T. Mitchell (Chicago: University of Chicago Press, 1981), will only admit music for ballet and opera, or music with a specific dramatic program as possessing narrative discourse (i.e., music retells or comments on a series of actions constituted by the dancers, the stage action, or the program); Paul Ricoeur, *Time and Narrative* vol. 2, trans. Kathleen McLaughlin and David Pellauer (Chicago: University of Chicago Press, 1985), 29–30, omits music from his litany of narrative genres.

9. Emile Benveniste, *Problems in General Linguistics*, trans. Mary Elizabeth Meek (Coral Gables: University of Miami Press, 1971), 208.

10. One typical interpretation along these lines is Max Brod's reading of

Mahler's symphonies as "Opern ohne Worte," in *Prager Sternenhimmel: Musik-und Theatererlebnisse der zwanziger Jahre* (Vienna: Paul Zsolnay Verlag, 1966), 248–54.

11. George Steiner's *Real Presences* (Chicago: University of Chicago Press, 1989), with its recurring rhapsodies to music, is a recent work in this traditional line.

12. The term (and its provenance and definition) is given in Jean-Jacques Nattiez, *Musicologie générale et sémiologie* (Paris: Christian Bourgois, 1987), 15–17.

13. Whether music possesses immanent cultural or sociological content—the central issue in Adorno's music criticism—is a question honored more in the asking than in the resolution; for a summary of the issues involved, see Janet Wolff, "The Ideology of Autonomous Art," in *Music and Society*, ed. Richard Leppert and Susan McClary (Cambridge: Cambridge University Press, 1987), 1–12; and Christopher Norris, "Introduction," in *Music and the Politics of Culture* (New York: St. Martin's Press, 1989), 7–19.

14. This commonplace has yet to unsettle the assumptions of most music analysis, but is eloquently set out in such works as Marie-Elisabeth Duchez's "La représentation de la musique," *Actes du XVIIIe Congrès de Philosophie de langue française* (Strassburg: Strassburg University Press, 1980), 178–82; Susan McClary's afterword to Jacques Attili's *Noise*, trans. Brian Massumi (Minneapolis: University of Minnesota Press, 1985), 154–56; and Nattiez's *Musicologie générale et sémiologie*.

CHAPTER ONE

1. Cone refers to a similar phenomenon as "virtual song"; see *The Composer's Voice*, 35. The distinction between which music is heard and which is not heard by the characters in opera is taken up in Chapters 3 and 4.

2. I borrow this Lacanian term from Michel Poizat's *L'Opéra ou le cri de l'ange* (Paris: A. M. Métailié, 1986).

3. The second verse, of course, shifts for the description of the stranger as Vishnu, and so reacts in one passage to the changing events of the tale. On the issues raised by contradiction between textual narrative and musical verse structure, see Chapter 3.

4. For an exploration of Austinian speech-act categories within performed theater, see Anne Ubersfeld, *L'Ecole du spectateur: Lire le théâtre II* (Paris: Editions Sociales, 1981); Marie Maclean, *Narrative as Performance* (London: Routledge, 1988), 28–33; and Shoshana Felman, *The Literary Speech Act*, trans. Catherine Porter (Ithaca: Cornell University Press, 1983), 25–58. Kaja Silverman discusses a feminine "capacity to effect through discourse" lodged specifically in a voice that is "disembodied" in a way similar to Lakmé's. See *The Acoustic Mirror* (Bloomington: Indiana University Press, 1988), 81–84.

5. Poizat, *Le cri de l'ange*, 81–82.

6. Ibid., 98–100.

7. In this, *voice* is understood in a Bakhtinian sense, not literally as the reported dialogue of this or that character within the novel, but as registers

of speaking that are the mark of narrator-speakers inhabiting the text. That Bakhtin chooses musical terminology (such as "polyphony") to describe phenomena that he perceives in literature does, of course, suggests that there is something tautological in the ease with which his theory may be manipulated to illuminate music. See *The Dialogic Imagination*, ed. Michael Holquist, trans. Caryl Emerson and Michael Holquist (Austin: University of Texas Press, 1981), xix–xx and 41–61.

8. Cone, *The Composer's Voice*, 35.

9. See Gérard Genette, *Narrative Discourse*, trans. Jane E. Lewin (Ithaca: Cornell University Press, 1980), 213–14.

10. These distinct musics are technically distinguishable from one another—a notion of "voice" explored in greater length in Carolyn Abbate, "Elektra's Voice," in *Richard Strauss: Elektra*, ed. Derrick Puffett (Cambridge: Cambridge University Press, 1989), 107–27.

11. This claim is deliberately one-sided; for arguments about the nature of the musical text, see Nelson Goodman, *The Languages of Art* (Indianapolis: Bobbs-Merrill, 1968), 176–80; on the nature of music as sound, see Nicholas Ruwet, "Typography, Rhyme, and Linguistic Structure in Poetry," in *The Sign in Music and Literature*, ed. Wendy Steiner (Austin: University of Texas Press, 1981) 131–37; and especially Roman Ingarden's *The Work of Music and the Problem of Its Identity*, trans. Adam Czerniawski, ed. Jean G. Harrell (Berkeley and Los Angeles: University of California Press, 1986).

12. Drama, in the sense of acted-out events, is the literary concept that seems most convenient in musical description; examples of "dramatic language" in music-analytical writing, and "dramatic" analyses are given in Fred Maus, "Music as Drama," *Music Theory Spectrum* 10 (1988): 65–72. The familiar notion of music as drama, of drama as "ersichtlich gewordene Taten der Musik" (the phrase coined by Wagner, "Über die Benennung *Musikdrama*," *Sämtliche Schriften* vol. 9, 306), coalesced with particular force in Wagner's musical writings, which gave the music-drama model its great impetus in the nineteenth century.

13. See Hermann Danuser, "Zu den Programmen von Mahlers frühen Symphonien," *Melos/Neue Zeitschrift* (1975): 15.

14. Hayden White cites Benveniste's distinction between "discourse" as subjective, and "narrative" as objective, lacking references to a narrator: "Here no one speaks. The events seem to tell themselves." See "The Value of Narrativity in the Representation of Reality," in Mitchell, *On Narrative*, 3.

15. Roland Barthes, *The Responsibility of Forms*, trans. Richard Howard (New York: Hill and Wang, 1985), 307.

16. Ibid., 276. For a critique of Barthes' "carnal stereophony," see Silverman, *The Acoustic Mirror*, 187–93. For a provocative discussion of the relationship between the body, voice, song, and presence, see also Sheila Murnaghan, "Voice and Body in Greek Tragedy," *Yale Journal of Criticism* 1/2 (1987): 23–45.

17. Paul de Man's "Autobiography as De-Facement," in *The Rhetoric of Romanticism* (New York: Columbia University Press, 1984), 67–82, is in part a

meditation upon prosopopoeia that dwells on its visual implications; Michael Fried's *Realism, Writing, Disfiguration* (Chicago: University of Chicage Press, 1987), which draws on de Man's essay, considers at some length the figure's visualizing appetites. I am indebted to Stanley Corngold for his suggestions about how prosopopoeia might be reconstrued in a musical context.

18. *In Search of Wagner*, trans. Rodney Livingstone (London: Verso, 1981), 82.

19. Ibid., 83–84.

20. Poizat, *Le cri de l'ange*, 53–64.

21. Rousseau, *On the Origin of Language*, trans. John H. Moran (Chicago: University of Chicago Press, 1966), 50–58, and especially 65.

22. See, for example, *The Birth of Tragedy*, trans. Walter Kaufmann, in *Basic Writings of Nietzsche* (New York: Random House, 1968), 55:

> Our whole discussion insists that lyric poetry is dependent upon the spirit of music just as music itself in its absolute sovereignty does not *need* the image and the concept, but merely *endures* them as accompaniments. The poems of the lyricist can express nothing that did not already lie hidden in that vast universality and absoluteness in the music that compelled him to figurative speech. Language can never adequately render the cosmic symbolism of music, because music stands in symbolic relation to the primordial contradiction and primordial pain in the heart of the primal unity, and therefore symbolizes a sphere which is beyond and prior to all phenomena.

See also 114–16 (on the origins of opera).

23. Ibid., 126–27. The passage is discussed by Paul de Man in "Genesis and Geneology," in *Allegories of Reading* (New Haven: Yale University Press, 1979), 96–99.

24. See *Prose Works* vol. 4, 322.

25. See, for instance *Oper und Drama* part 3; it has been my claim that Wagner privileged his own "nonabsolute" music as a constant feature of his prose writings—one that survived his encounter with Schopenhauer's musical metaphysics, though in altered form. This claim, of course, runs contrary to other readings of Wagner's prose works, including those of Carl Dahlhaus; for a summary of the issues, see Carolyn Abbate, "Symphonic Opera, a Wagnerian Myth," in *Analyzing Opera*, ed. Carolyn Abbate and Roger Parker (Berkeley and Los Angeles: University of California Press, 1989), 92–123.

26. *Of Grammatology*, trans. Gayatri Chakravorty Spivak (Baltimore: Johns Hopkins University Press, 1976), 203.

27. The string of texts that ends in de Man's reading includes (besides Rousseau's *Essay on the Origins of Language*) *The Birth of Tragedy*; Lévi-Strauss's *Tristes tropiques*; Derrida's "Genesis and Structure of the *Essay on the Origins of Language*"; *Of Grammatology*, 165–94; and de Man's "The Rhetoric of Blindness: Jacques Derrida's Reading of Rousseau," in *Blindness and Insight* (Minneapolis: University of Minnesota Press, 1983), 102–41.

28. De Man, "The Rhetoric of Blindness," 117–19. For commentaries on de Man's writing about music, see John Neubauer, *The Emancipation of Music from Language* (New Haven: Yale University Press, 1986), 85–89 and 101–2;

and Christopher Norris, "Utopian Deconstruction: Ernst Bloch, Paul de Man, and the Politics of Music," in *Music and the Politics of Culture*, ed. Norris, 305–43, especially 335–43.

29. See Carolyn Abbate, "Ventriloquism" (forthcoming).

30. "Rhetoric of Blindness," 128–29.

31. Ibid., 128.

32. *Essai sur l'origine des langues* (Paris: A. Belin, 1817), 537; *Essay*, 63.

33. See Jean-Jacques Nattiez, "Introduction à l'esthétique de Hanslick," in Eduard Hanslick, *Du beau dans la musique*, trans. Charles Bannelier and Georges Pucher (Paris: Christian Bourgois, 1986), 16–28.

34. *Essai*, 538; *Essay*, 65.

35. See Jean-Jacques Nattiez, *Musicologie générale et sémiologie*, 20–27.

36. "Rhetoric of Blindness," 129: "music is the diachronic version of the pattern of non-coincidence within the moment."

37. See Abbate, "Ventriloquism," (forthcoming). Exploring the implications of music's paradoxical muteness in a linguistic universe would, perhaps, illuminate music's consistent assignment to the female gender, especially in eighteenth- and nineteenth-century texts. In Wagner's early writings, for instance, music was the "woman" whose marriage to male poetry engendered the *Gesamtkunstwerk*. See *Oper und Drama* part 2.

38. This is a commonplace that still meets with violent resistance from music analysts who see themselves as mere describers of structures that are immanent in the musical work. For most Schenkerians, the *Urlinie* has the same epistemological status as the roundness of the earth.

39. The point, as a sobering rather than despairing one, was made by Carl Dahlhaus in his "Das 'Verstehen' von Musik und die Sprache der musikalischen Analyse," *Musik und Verstehen*, ed. Peter Faltin and Hans-Peter Reinecke (Cologne: Arno Volk Verlag, 1973), 41: "Die Sprache, 'als' die Musik erscheint, ist nicht unabhängig von der Sprache, 'in' der über Musik geredet wird"; and 46: "Das Denken 'über' Musik ist also ein Teil der 'Sache selbst,' nicht ein bloßer Appendix . . . Das Verstehen von Musik erscheint demnach als Aneignung einer sowohl musikalischen als auch musikalisch-sprachlichen (oder musikalisch-literarischen) Tradition: eine Überlieferung, in der die 'Interpretation' als 'Musik machen' und die 'Interpretation' als 'Musik auslegen' ineinanderfliessen." The distinction between the two "interpretations" goes back to Adorno's "Fragment über Musik und Sprache," in *Quasi una fantasia* (Frankfurt am Main: Fischer, 1963), 1.

40. *The Beethoven Quartets* (New York: Alfred A. Knopf, 1967), 191–222. See also Jeffrey Kallberg's discussion of the "singing voice" and genre in Chopin's nocturnes, in "The Rhetoric of Genre: Chopin's Nocturne in G Minor," *19th-Century Music* 11, no. 3 (Spring 1988): 238–61.

41. I shall not enter into debates on the relative merits, or claims, of narratology in its "structuralist," "discourse-oriented," and "pragmatics" phases; one familiar polemical essay, which argues for transcending concerns with structure in order to arrive at an engagement with discursive strategies and the contexts of telling, is Barbara Herrnstein Smith's "Narrative Versions, Narrative Theories," in Mitchell, ed., *On Narrative*, 209–32.

42. The assumption is pervasive and unquestioned in most writing on opera; Joseph Kerman's superb operatic meditation, *Opera as Drama* (Berkeley and Los Angeles: University of California Press, 1988), perhaps illustrates my point by means of title alone. See also Chapter 3.

43. For one survey of the issues raised by so-called program music, see Peter Kivy, *Sound and Semblance: Reflections on Musical Representation* (Princeton: Princeton University Press, 1984).

44. See Carl Dahlhaus, *Die Idee der absoluten Musik* (Kassel: Bärenreiter, 1978), 128–39.

45. On the debate over the immanent versus the ancillary status of the program, see Edward T. Cone, *Hector Berlioz: Fantastic Symphony* (New York: Norton, 1971), and Kivy, *Music as Representation*, 169–96.

46. Dahlhaus, *Die Idee der absoluten Musik*, 130–32.

47. Ibid., 134.

48. See Abbate, "Symphonic Opera, A Wagnerian Myth," in *Analyzing Opera*, ed. Carolyn Abbate and Roger Parker, 97–102.

49. Dahlhaus claims that Nietzsche viewed anything other than the absolute musical essence as "accidental" or "irrelevant"; this is perhaps an overstatement: in *The Birth of Tragedy*, the words defuse, but in so doing, save the listener.

50. Hector Berlioz, *A Travers chants* (Paris: Michel Lévy frères, 1862), 21.

51. Adolf Bernard Marx, *Ludwig von Beethoven* vol. 1 (Berlin: Verlag von Otto Janke, 1859; facsimile reprint, Hildesheim: Georg Olms Verlag, 1979), 258: "es wurde nicht einmal ein ikonisches Bild des Helden, sondern mehr, ein volles Drama des Lebens, das er in und um sich entzündet. Der *erste Akt* stellt das Geistesbild des Heldengangs auf, vom stillen, kaum bemerkten Anfang, durch die Welt hindurch."

52. *A Travers chants*, 22: "Le fin surtout émeut profondément, Le thème de la marche reparait, mais par des fragments coupés de silences et sans autre accompagnement que trois coups *pizzicato* de contre-basse; et quand ces lambeaux de la lugubre mélodie, seuls, nus, brisés, effacés, sont tombés un à un jusque sur tonique, les instruments à vent poussent un cri, dernier adieu des guerriers à leur compagnon d'armes, et tout l'orchestre s'éteint sur un point d'orgue *pianissimo*."

53. For an extended discussion of Marx's analysis, see Scott Burnham, *Aesthestics, Theory and History in the Works of A. B. Marx* (Ph.D. diss., Brandeis University, 1988), Chapter 5.

54. Marx, *Beethoven*, 262: "das Allgemeine im energischen Zusammenfassen zu einem einigen Hergang verdichtet, wie die Ilias den zehnjährigen Kampf in eine Spanne von wenigen Tagen."

55. Historical surveys of program music and nineteenth-century narrative interpretations of instrumental works are numerous; the best accounts are those by Carl Dahlhaus, in *Nineteenth-Century Music*, trans. J. Bradford Robinson (Berkeley and Los Angeles: University of California Press, 1989), 236–44; see also Scott Burnham, in *Aesthetics, Theory and History*, Chapters 4 and 5. The work of Kretschmar and Schering, two of the most important narra-

tive critics at the turn of the century, is discussed most recently in the collection of essays edited by Carl Dahlhaus, *Beiträge zur musikalischen Hermeneutik* (Regensburg: Gustav Bosse Verlag, 1975); see also Peter Schleuning, "Beethoven in alter Deutung," *Archiv für Musikwissenschaft* (1987): 165–87.

56. *Mahler: eine musikalische Physiognomik* (Frankfurt am Main: Suhrkamp, 1960), Chapter 4; both Eggebrecht, in *Die Musik Gustav Mahlers* (Munich: Piper Verlag, 1982), and Danuser, in "Konstruktion des Romans bei Gustav Mahler," in *Musikalische Prosa* (Regensburg: Gustav Bosse Verlag, 1975), 87–117, acknowledge Adorno's seminal role in their own writings on musical narrative.

57. See Owen Jander, "The Krentzer Sonata as Dialogue," *Early Music* 16 (1988), 34–38; "Beethoven's 'Orpheus in Hades': the *Andante con moto* of the Fourth Piano Concerto," *19th-Century Music* 8 (1985): 195–212; and Leo Treitler, *Music and the Historical Imagination* (Cambridge: Harvard University Press, 1989), 185–86.

58. Anthony Newcomb, "Once More 'Between Absolute and Program Music': Schumann's Second Symphony." *19th-Century Music* 7 (1984): 234.

59. Treitler, *Historical Imagination*, 57.

60. Newcomb, "Once More," 243–46.

61. Treitler, *Historical Imagination*, 66.

62. Danuser, "Konstruktion des Romans," 93–97.

63. Danuser, following Adorno's sense of Mahler's music as possessing a discursive "distance" (cf. especially *Mahler: eine musikalische Physiognomik*, 106–11), does escape from the notion that music merely *mimes* or *enacts* actions to discuss (for instance) a moment of "epic synthesis" made within the first movement of Mahler's Third Symphony; see Chapter 2.

64. Genette, *Narrative Discourse*, 25.

65. Kaja Silverman, *The Acoustic Mirror*, 3.

66. Adorno, *Mahler: eine musikalische Physiognomik*, 106. Cone, in *The Composer's Voice*, similarly described music as a language of gestures, that enacts by means of "purely symbolic" actions (164).

67. See Jean-Jacques Nattiez, "Y a-t-il une diégèse musicale?" in *Musik und Verstehen*, ed. Faltin and Reinecke, 247–58.

CHAPTER TWO

1. So, at least, runs the ex post facto program written to accompany the first performance of the work.

2. Eco, "Producing Signs," in *On Signs*, ed. Marshall Blonsky (Baltimore: Johns Hopkins University Press, 1985), 145.

3. Hubert Kolland, in "Zur Semantik der Leitmotive in Richard Wagners *Ring des Nibelungen*" (*International Review of the Aesthetics and Sociology of Music* 4 [1973]: 197–211), has evaluated Wagnerian leitmotifs in terms of their iconicity and symbolism (again, in Peirce's sense of the terms), but interprets iconicity in visual and spatial (rather than sonic) terms: thus, the Ring motif is iconic because, in circling back upon itself gesturally, it traces a ring shape. I understand the iconicity of musical motives solely in terms of isosonority

(thus, a motif cannot be an iconic signifier for a plastic object, but can be an iconic signifier of a sound).

4. Nattiez, "Y a-t-il une diégèse musicale," 247–58.

5. Georges Favre, *L'ouvre de Paul Dukas* (Paris: Durand, 1969), 68.

6. See, for example, Carl Dahlhaus, *Richard Wagner's Music Dramas* (Cambridge: Cambridge University Press, 1979), 84–87, and the discussion of Wotan's narrative in *Die Walküre*, 122–24.

7. Italo Calvino, *The Castle of Crossed Destinies*, trans. William Weaver (New York: Harcourt Brace Jovanovich, 1979), 5.

8. The notion that motives with textual associations often recur for largely musical reasons, and are developed musically, without necessarily carrying the baggage of their referential meanings, is another truism of Wagnerian analysis: see Alfred Lorenz, *Das Geheimnis der Form bei Richard Wagner* vol. 1 (Berlin: Max Hesses Verlag, 1924), 73–74; Carl Dahlhaus, "Formprinzipien in Wagners 'Ring des Nibelungen'," in *Beiträge zur Geschichte der Oper*, ed. Heinz Becker (Regensburg: Gustav Bosse Verlag, 1969), 112–13.

9. Perhaps we overlook the significant thing because it is so ordinary: as Poe's Dupin points out in "The Purloined Letter," we are continually duped because we do not expect the things for which we search (a letter, answers, solutions, meaning) to be plainly visible—especially when they are surrounded by exotic hiding places.

10. Asaf'ev's notion of *intonatiya* may clarify this point. Asaf'ev argued that musical ideas originated as expressions of human actions and experiences, but that over historical time they came to express music, to refer to one another and not to things outside the musical universe. To take one elementary example: a fanfare is played by a king's trumpeters to signal his arrival, to exhort and signal the crowd. In the course of time, the musical idea may lose its specific and inevitable expressive meaning and become a "sound formula"; a fanfare in a Mahler symphony refers to other fanfares in hundreds of other symphonies. See B. V. Asaf'ev, *Musical Form as a Process*, trans. J. R. Tull (Ph.D. diss., Ohio State University, 1976), vol. 1, 184–95; vol. 2, 543 and 625–33.

For Asaf'ev, music nonetheless could not be seen as wholly tautological, as a closed, self-referential system—for every fanfare is linked back through history in a chain of innumerable members, and is distantly, subliminally bound by this filament to its origins in referential sound. If I have simplified an elaborate theory, the summary will suffice to suggest how Asaf'ev's thinking impinges on both the notion of musical topos as interpreted by, for example, Frits Noske in *The Signifier and the Signified* (The Hague: Nijhoff, 1977), and the broader tradition of Hegelian musical aesthetics, and the neo-Hegelian tradition of musical hermeneuticists like Kretschmar (whom Asaf'ev occasionally cites).

11. Dahlhaus, *Die Idee der absoluten Musik*, 129.

12. See Harold S. Powers, "Language Models and Musical Analysis," *Ethnomusicology* 24 (1980): 16–25 (on Lévi-Strauss).

13. Roland Barthes, "Introduction to the Structural Analysis of Narra-

tive," *Image. Music. Text*, trans. Stephen Heath (New York: Hill and Wang, 1977), 92.

14. Roland Barthes, *S/Z*, trans. Richard Miller (New York: Hill and Wang, 1974) 29.

15. Ibid., 29.

16. Jean-Jacques Nattiez, "The Concept of Plot and Seriation Process in Music Analysis," trans. Catherine Dale, *Music Analysis* 4 (1985): 107–18.

17. This point is made by Burnham, in *Aesthetics, Theory and History* (Chapter 5).

18. Though the issue is tangential to the argument here, the connection of structuralist narrative theory (with its "minimal units of plot," "narremes," and the like) to linguistics is not irrelevant. The structuralist image of narrative as, so to speak, a sentence writ large has meant a definition of narrative also thrown wide open, potentially able to embrace all forms of utterance. For a brief but cogent and characteristic discussion of the broad applicability of structuralist categories (including Barthes') to other text types—and hence their *insufficiency* as a sign of narrative—see Elizabeth Cowie, "The Popular Novel as Progressive Text—A Discussion of *Coma*—Part 1," in *Feminism and Film Theory*, ed. Constance Penley (New York: Routledge, 1988), 104–40, especially 113–16.

19. "Schumann and Late Eighteenth-Century Narrative Strategies," in *19th-Century Music* 11 (1987): 166.

20. Roman Jakobson, "Language in Relation to Other Communication Systems," in *Linguaggi nella societa e nella tecnica* (Milan: Edizioni di Communita, 1970), 3–16; this approach was also taken up by semiologist Nicolas Ruwet, and is discussed in Jean-Jacques Nattiez, *Musicologie générale et sémiologie*, 147–55. Eero Tarasti, in "Pour une narratologie de Chopin," *International Review of the Aesthetics and Sociology of Music* 15 (1984): 53–75, similarly associates narrativity with the process of comparing specific (Chopinesque) gestures with generalized types.

21. See, for a summary, Harold S. Powers, " 'La solita forma' and 'The Uses of Convention'," *Acta musicologica* 59 (1987): 65–90 (see also note 28).

22. *Reading for the Plot* (New York: Alfred A. Knopf, 1984), 97: "Narrative always makes the implicit claim: to be in a state of repetition, as a going over again of ground already covered: a *sjuzet* (the novel, the discourse) repeating the *fabula* as the detective retraces the story of the criminal." The Russian Formalists' formulation has been challenged by Richard Belknap, who has asked whether the distinction is pointless, as "story" has no reality and is only constituted through "discourse"; see "The Minimal Unit of Plot," in *Literature and History: Theoretical Problems and Russian Case Studies* (Stanford: Stanford University Press, 1986) 221–29.

23. See, for instance, Barbara Herrnstein Smith, "Narrative Versions, Narrative Theories" (cited previously, Chapter 1, note 40).

24. For a summary of narratological definitions, see Jonathan Culler, "Story and Discourse in the Analysis of Narrative," *The Pursuit of Signs* (Ithaca: Cornell University Press, 1981), 169–87.

25. "Narrative Versions, Narrative Theories," 209.

26. Treitler, *Historical Imagination*, 186–91; significantly, the reading is couched in terms of "[giving] an account that will make plausible the sorts of things [narrative metaphors] that were written around 1800 about the experience of this music."

27. Jonathan Kramer, "Multiple and Non-Linear Time in Beethoven's Opus 135," *Perspectives of New Music* 11 (1973): 122–45. Concerning "story and discourse," see also Fred E. Maus, *Humanism and Music Criticism* (Ph.D. diss., Princeton University, 1989), Chapter 3.

28. Dahlhaus's Wagnerian studies—for example, his classic "Formprinzipien in Wagners 'Ring des Nibelungen',"" in *Beiträge zur Geschichte der Oper*, 95–129—suggests this approach for analysis; Anthony Newcomb's interpretation of Schumann's transformation of a basic symphonic model, in *Critical Inquiry* 10 (1984): 614–42, is an exemplary generic interpretation. On the side of Italian opera lie studies such as Philip Gossett, "Verdi, Ghislanzoni, and *Aida*: The Uses of Convention," *Critical Inquiry* 1 (1974): 291–334; and Harold S. Powers, " 'La solita forma' and 'The Uses of Convention' " (see note 21). A case could be made for associating "generic" musical analysis with another literary (or at least linguistic) idea: Umberto Eco's sign-type "replica" and its subclass "stylization" (he gives the example of both literary genre and musical genre, of any given march as a particular, unique replica of the musical type "march"). See *A Theory of Semiotics* (Bloomington: Indiana University Press, 1976), 237–41.

29. Newcomb, "Schumann and Late Eighteenth-Century Narrative Strategies," 165. I think, however, that the connections are perhaps more tenuous than this formulation implies. First, the "narrative structures" of the Russian Formalists and their descendents were ex post facto constructs with no reception history of their own to parallel that of the texts that they interpreted, while sonata, rondo, and all the rest are formal ideas attested to and recognized by the composers who used them, and discussed by contemporary critics as far back as the eighteenth century. A paradigmatic plot, like Lévi-Strauss's paradigm for the Theban myth-cycle, claims to be an ahistorical and indeed mysteriously eternal structure, which seeps through human writers or tellers who are not conscious of its presence. Musical forms such as sonata are historically limited, and consciously exploited. Thus I would argue that the two concepts are not critically or theoretically derived in similar ways, and that they make different epistemological claims. I admit, however, to being uncertain about exactly how *histoire* (*story*) is being used in this context. Newcomb (if I am reading correctly) implies that it is analogous to "deep structure" or "plot paradigm" as an a priori. Yet the "story" of David Copperfield, in terms of the classic *histoire-récit* distinction, is not some "deep structure," some *Bildungsroman* paradigm, but rather a construct, spun out of the discourse, of that untellably rich "real" life of David, its every moment, which his discourse collapses, dilates, turns, and reshapes in the course of retelling.

30. Paul Ricoeur, *Time and Narrative* vol. 2, trans. Kathleen McLaughlin and David Pellauer (Chicago: University of Chicago Press, 1985), 68. Music

seems excluded from this narrative world, certainly by Ricoeur. On pages 29–30, he catalogs (as a rhetorical device) the things that can narrate; music is absent from his list.

31. See, for example, G.W.F. Hegel, *Aesthetik* vol. 2, ed. Friedrich Bassenge (Berlin: verlag das europäische buch, 1985), 474–80.

32. The coinage goes back to Gunther Müller, "Erzählzeit und erzählte Zeit," in *Morphologische Poetik*, ed. Elena Müller (Tübingen: M. Niemeyer, 1968); Genette began his classic *Narrative Discourse* by evoking the distinction with its suggestion of "pseudo-time." For a brief summary, see Ricoeur, *Time and Narrative* vol. 2, 61–99.

33. Peter Brooks, *Reading for the Plot*, 25.

34. Danuser, "Konstruktion des Romans," 105.

35. Indeed, the musical leitmotif is in some sense parallel to Barthes' "code symbolique": the abstract symbols repeated, encountered (in various guises) over the course of the story; each repetition refers backward to previous appearances and forward to future recurrences. The repetitions remind us of the past of our reading, but they are not analogous to the past tense, which does not depend on repetition of the formula over elapsed time to establish pastness, but can evoke pastness instantaneously.

36. This is pointed out by Caryl Emerson in her analysis of Mussorgsky's revisions to Kutuzov's texts for the "Songs and Dances of Death." Composers know what music is and what it can do; music is a marking of experienced time that ends without a narrating survivor who could tell the tale in the past tense. When Mussorgsky eliminates the framing narrator from Kutuzov's poems and changes all past tenses to present, he is compelling language to imitate the condition of music. See Caryl Emerson, "Real Endings and Russian Death: Mussorgskij's *Pesni i pljaski smerti*," *Russian Language Journal* 38 (1984): 199–216.

37. "Das Unheimliche," *Studienausgabe* vol. 4 (Frankfurt am Main: Fischer, 1982), 243–74.

38. It is worth noting that the most concrete interpretive realization of the piece's drama—that with Mickey Mouse in *Fantasia*—confronts this problem (that repetitive generalized motion is boring) with a certain refreshing brashness: a long stretch of the premurder portion of the piece is staged as Mickey's dream of adult power, in which he sets stars and waters dancing from the pinnacle of the Sorcerer's castle. The designer (for one) had a sense that there was something superfluous or extra in the piece, and did not hear it simply as a trace of more trips to the well, more water.

CHAPTER THREE

1. On music's ability to arouse attention, see *What is Art*, trans. Almyer Maude (Indianapolis: Bobbs-Merrill, 1960), 106; that Tolstoy regarded music as dubious in its immediacy is not unrelated to his apprehension that music will continually and unavoidably grasp at the listener's mind.

2. Joseph Kerman, *Opera as Drama*, 174.

3. On allegorical functions of the narrative scene, see Ross Chambers, *Story and Situation: Narrative Seduction and the Power of Fiction* (Minneapolis:

University of Minnesota Press, 1984), 18–49; and Marie Maclean, *Narrative as Performance*, 43–50 and 71–88.

4. Lucien Dällenbach, in *The Mirror in the Text*, trans. Jeremy Whiteley and Emma Hughes (Chicago: University of Chicago Press, 1989), 43 and 44.

5. The recitative is overlooked by many critics, not in the sense of being left unmentioned, but by being treated as if it were equivalent to the trio that surrounds it, and which it so violently interrupts. Tim Carter, who sees the recitative passage as a "joke" (in the sense of being a false recapitulation before the true recapitulation at "Onestissima signora"), thus equates it with the discourse of the trio proper (both are "recapitulations" in a formal design), and makes the shock of the recitative's interruptive force inaudible. See *W. A. Mozart: Le Nozze di Figaro* (Cambridge: Cambridge University Press, 1987), 101.

6. This has been suggested by Stefan Kunze; again, by reading consistency *across* the break into recitative, Kunze, like Carter, passes over the critical moments when the shift is made, first toward recitative, then away from it. See Kunze, *Mozarts Opern* (Stuttgart: Reclam, 1984), 254.

7. Dällenbach, *The Mirror in the Text*, 56.

8. See Carl Dahlhaus, "Über das 'kontemplative Ensemble'," in *Opernstudien: Anna Amalie Abert zum 65. Geburtstag*, ed. Klaus Hortschansky (Tutzing: Hans Schneider, 1975), 189–95.

9. "The Old Man's Toys," in *Music: A View from Delft* (Chicago: University of Chicago Press, 1988), 170.

10. See Siegfried Goslich, *Die deutsche Romantische Oper* (Tutzing: Hans Schneider, 1975), 249–66.

11. Hegel wrote in 1835 of ballad as a lyric genre brushed by the narrative mode of epic: "andererseits aber bleibt der Grundton ganz lyrisch; denn nicht die subjektivitätslose Schilderung und Ausmalung des realen Geschehens, sondern umgekehrt die Auffassungsweise und Empfindung des Subjekts . . . ist die Hauptsache," in *Aesthetik* vol. 2, 474. For Goethe, the poetsinger, mixed epic, lyric, and dramatic elements as needed, in making his ballads, to realize his "prägnanter Gegenstand," yet the strict strophic structure of such poetry is a hallmark of the lyric: "der Refrain, das Wiederkehren ebendesselben Schlußklanges, gibt dieser Dichtart den entscheidenden lyrischen Charakter." See "Ballade, Betrachtung und Auslegung" (1821), in *Goethes Werke: Hamburger Ausgabe* vol. 1, ed. Erich Trunz (Hamburg: Wegner, 1949), 400.

12. See Otto Holzapfel, "Winterrosen: A German Narrative Love Song," in *The Ballad as Narrative* (Odense: Odense University Press, 1982), 103–10.

13. "Ballade, Betrachtung und Auslegung," 400.

14. Jack Stein, *Poem and Music in the German Lied* (Cambridge: Harvard University Press, 1971), 63–65, and Werner-Joachim Düring, *Erlkönig-Vertonungen: eine historische und systematische Untersuchung* (Regensburg: Gustav Bosse Verlag, 1972), 108–9.

15. Düring, *Erlkönig-Vertonungen*, 10.

16. *Opera as Drama*, 58–59.

17. Dällenbach, *The Mirror in the Text*, 61.

18. Barthes said of myth that it "transforms history into nature . . . what causes mythical speech to be uttered is perfectly explicit, but is immediately *frozen* into something natural; it is not read as a motive, but as a reason." Myth in Rimbaud's Ballad has literally *frozen* history, by making of a historical progression (a human being is seduced) a "natural," inevitable, repeated "form" or "structure." *Mythologies*, trans. Annette Lavers (New York: Hill and Wang, 1972), 129.

19. See John Deathridge, Martin Geck, and Egon Voss, *Verzeichnis der musikalischen Werke Richard Wagners und ihrer Quellen* (hereafter *WWV*) (Mainz: Schott, 1986), 120–21.

20. Dieter Borchmeyer, *Das Theater Richard Wagners* (Stuttgart: Reclam, 1982), 182. The entire ballad scene was, in fact, an afterthought for Wagner; in the early surviving prose draft for the opera, the French text sent on 6 May 1840 to Scribe (Bibliothèque Nationale N.a.fr. 22552; published in *La Revue hebdomadaire* 33 [9 August 1924]: 216–19), Senta's obsession with the portrait is presented as only one element in a narrative that describes the past history of her relation with her lover, the young man (later to be called first Georg, then Erik). See Isolde Vetter, *Der fliegende Holländer von Richard Wagner—Entstehung, Bearbeitung, Überlieferung* (Ph.D. Diss., Technical University Berlin, 1982, Microfiche), 10.

21. See Dällenbach, *The Mirror in the Text*, 67.

22. "Gehalt und Zusammenhang . . . vom Subjekte getragen," *Aesthetik* vol. 2, 473.

23. "Eine Mitteilung an meine Freunde," in *Sämtliche Schriften* vol. 4, 323: "es breitete sich nur das empfangene thematische Bild ganz unwillkürlich als ein vollständiges Gewebe über das ganze Drama aus; ich hatte, ohne weiter es zu wollen, nur die verschiedenen thematischen Keime die in der Ballade enthalten waren, nach ihren eigenen Richtungen hin weiter und vollständig zu entwickeln."

24. Carl Dahlhaus, "Zur Geschichte der Leitmotivtechnik bei Wagner," in *Das Drama Richard Wagners als musikalisches Kunstwerk*, ed. Carl Dahlhaus (Regensburg: Gustav Bosse Verlag, 1970), 17–40.

25. Reinhold Brinkmann, "Sentas Traumerzählung," *Bayreuther Programmheft* (Bayreuth, 1984): 4, wrote of "Kristallisationspunkte" (the ballad, the dream narration, and the opening of the Dutchman-Senta duet) alternating with banal and typical operatic conceits (the Spinning Song, the Eric-Senta dialogue-duet, Daland's aria, the final trio). Borchmeyer's interesting reading of scene 2 as a smooth progression from "Dichtung" (ballad) to "Wirklichkeit" (Senta's explosive final line) to "Wahrheit" (the appearance of the Dutchman) (*Das Theater Richard Wagners*, 183) does pass over ambiguous lines such as "ich bin ein Kind und weiss nicht, was ich singe," and hence over Wagner's delaying tactics in the argument over reflexivity.

26. Brinkmann, "Sentas Traumerzählung," 11–16, links the conceit of Senta's prescience, her "magnetic slumber," to contemporary philosophical

and medical speculation on Mesmer's theories of "animal magnetism," and the nature of hysterical ecstasy.

27. *Story and Situation*, 74.

28. This point is made by Anne Ubersfeld, *Lire le théâtre* (Paris: Edition Sociales, 1977), 260–62.

29. See Dällenbach, *The Mirror in the Text*, 75.

30. See Chapter Four.

31. The tale of the versions of *Tannhäuser* is oft-told; for a summary, see Carolyn Abbate, "The Parisian Vénus and the 'Paris' *Tannhäuser*," in *Journal of the Americal Musicological Society* 36 (1983): 73–123.

32. See Carolyn Abbate, "Orpheus in the Underworld," in *Tannhäuser*, ed. Nicholas John (London: John Calder, 1988), 33–50, especially 44–50.

33. In "Richard Wagner der Erzähler," in *Österreichische Musikzeitschrift* 37 (1982): 299, Brinkmann argued that the Rome Narrative's tendency away from the formally structured musical *Satz* toward the through-composed motivic web in a sense presupposed a (nonexistent) collection of symbolic leitmotifs: "Die Formidee der Romerzählung setzt überdies, um zu voller Wirkung zu gelangen, im Grunde das entwickelte Leitmotivgewebe bereits voraus . . . das Fehlen dieser Technik—beziehungsweise ihre musikhistorisch und innerhalb der Entwicklung Wagners erklärbare erst rudimentäre Form—bezeichnet den Bruch zwischen Konzeption und Realisierung des epischen Stils im *Tannhäuser*." Brinkmann also dealt at length with an issue passed over here—the intersection of the Rome Narrative with its orchestral mirror image, the Act III prelude—and with the degree to which musical signs created within the prelude, as well as the structure of the prelude itself, impinge on our hearing of Tannhäuser's narrative (299–302).

34. The first sketch for the Rome Narrative, labeled "Tannh. Pilgerlied," was made on the final sheet of the first (Composition) draft for Act II of *Tannhäuser* (Bayreuth, Richard-Wagner-Gedenkstätte der Stadt Bayreuth, Hs 120/IV/2a). This sketch, as well as the Composition draft for the narrative (Hs 120/III/3a, III/3b, and III/1a), point to an earlier, more formally strophic concept that metamorphosed into a freer form. The very word "Lied"—synonymous for Wagner with strophic design—is an indication of this strophic concept.

Chapter Four

1. This point is explored by Herbert Lindenberger in *Opera: The Extravagent Art* (Ithaca: Cornell University Press, 1984), 139–42.

2. See *The Composer's Voice*, 33; *Music: A View from Delft*, 133.

3. Ibid., 131.

4. Ibid., 135.

5. See Nelly Furman, "The Languages of Love in *Carmen*," in *Reading Opera*, ed. Arthur Groos and Roger Parker (Princeton: Princeton University Press, 1988), 168–83.

6. The image of the wolf derives from Merimée's novel, from Carmen's line "chien et loup ne font pas longtemps bon ménage" ["the wolf and the dog can't get on together for long"].

7. So strong is our impulse to rationalize Beethoven's tragedy, to turn his handicap into strength, that it takes all Beethoven critics to seeming extremes. Maynard Soloman, in *Beethoven Essays* (Cambridge: Harvard University Press, 1988), 93–100, has even speculated that Beethoven's condition may have been partly psychosomatic, born of an overpowering solipcism, a need to shut out the world's noise, to explore some inner world of sound—an explanation that differs from Wagner's only in its imputation of intent, and its evocation of psychological science.

8. *Prose Works* vol. 5, 91–92.

9. Ibid., 111.

10. *Mahler-Briefe 1879–1911*, ed. Alma Mahler (Vienna: Paul Zsolnay Verlag, 1925), 189.

11. On Mahler's program notes for this movement, see Hans Heinrich Eggebrecht, *Die Musik Gustav Mahlers*, 217, and Suzanne Vill, *Vermittlungsformen verbalisierter und musikalischer Inhalte in der Musik Gustav Mahlers* (Tutzing: Hans Schneider, 1979), 241–46. A slightly earlier program note, written in January 1896 to Natalie Bauer-Lechner, describes the same image: "Das im Scherzo Ausgedrückte kann ich nur so veranschaulichen: wenn du aus der Ferne durch ein Fenster einem Tanze zusiehst, ohne daß du die Musik dazu hörst, so erscheint die Drehung und Bewegung der Paare wirr und sinnlos, da dir der Rhythmus als Schlüssel fehlt. So mußt du dir denken, daß einem, der sich und sein Glück verloren hat, die Welt im Hohlspiegel verkehrt und wahnsinnig erscheint.—Mit dem furchtbaren Aufschrei der so gemarterten Seele endet das Scherzo." Natalie Bauer-Lechner, *Errinerungen an Gustav Mahler*, ed. J. Killian (Leipzig: E. P. Tal, 1923), 23.

12. Constantin Floros, *Gustav Mahler III: Die Symphonien* (Wiesbaden: Breitkopf und Härtel, 1985), 60–62.

13. On the musical similarities between Schumann's song and Mahler's scherzo, see Vill, *Vermittlungsformen*, 254–55; and Robert S. Hatten, "The Place of Intertextuality in Music Studies," in *American Journal of Semiotics* 3 (1985): 73–74. M. Tibbe, in *Lieder und Liedelemente in den instrumentalen Symphoniesätzen Gustav Mahlers* (Munich: Piper Verlag, 1971), 58–59, concludes perhaps too quickly that the song "must" have nothing to do with the symphony, because Mahler's program note gives us a protagonist who is deaf but *sees* the dance, while Heine's poem gives us one who *hears* but cannot see.

14. Vill, *Vermittlungsformen*, 254.

15. *Die Musik Gustav Mahlers*, 199–226.

16. Ibid., 206–8.

17. Only in the last program, written for the Dresden performance of the symphony in 1901, does a more general feeling of alienation and disgust replace the instant of "not hearing the music they dance to" as motivation for the scream. See Eggebrecht, *Die Musik Gustav Mahlers*, 217.

18. See Vill, *Vermittlungsformen*, 253–54.

19. *Todtenfeier von Adam Mickiewicz*, trans. Siegfried Lipiner (Leipzig: Breitkopf und Härtel, 1887), 88. All subsequent references in the text are to this edition.

20. Mickiewicz's mirror, an image absent from Heine's poem, was echoed by Mahler in his first program note for movement (the note for Natalie

Bauer-Lechner), in which he refers to "seeing the world through a mirror of hollowness, so that all is inverted." See note 11.

21. The passage is discussed in these terms by Reinhold Brinkmann, "Mythos-Geschichte-Natur," in *Richard Wagner: Von der Oper zum Musikdrama*, ed. Stefan Kunze (Bern: Francke, 1978), 63.

22. Isolde, in Gottfried's romance, is identified as a musician who eventually surpasses her teacher, Tristan, in the art of composition.

23. Wagner wrote that the "Alte Weise" in *Tristan* was inspired by an experience in Venice: he heard from a distance the sound of a gondolier's "mournful song" (see *Prose Works* vol. 5, 73). This has sometimes been taken as evidence that some particular gondolier melody was literally adopted or copied in the "Alte Weise" tune, and Jean-Jacques Nattiez has discovered the source (personal communication). What Wagner describes is of course less some ethnomusicological exercise than the experience of hearing phenomenal music at a distance and outside one's own consciousness. It is the otherness or outsideness, the phenomenality of the gondolier song, that resonates most powerfully into the "Alte Weise."

24. This phenomenon is discussed in greater detail in Carolyn Abbate, "Elektra's Voice," in *Richard Strauss: Elektra*, 107–27.

25. Gilman, *Jewish Self-Hatred* (Baltimore: Johns Hopkins University Press, 1986), 3–21 and 209–19.

26. The most detailed plot-analysis in English is Stephen Hefling, "Mahler's *Todtenfeier* and the Problem of Program Music," in *19th-Century Music* 12 (1988): 27–53; see also Vill, *Vermittlungsformen*, 241–46; Floros, *Mahler* vol. 1, 81–82, and vol. 3, 47–58. There are critics who have rejected specific connections between Mahler's symphonic movement and Mickiewicz's drama—such as Rudolf Stephan, in his handbook on the Second Symphony, *Gustav Mahler: II Symphonie C-moll* (Munich: Fink, 1979), 47–49. Throughout my discussion, I shall refer to the *Todtenfeier* movement and cite the score of the piece in its incarnation as the symphonic movement, not the score of the earlier (slightly different) tone-poem version.

27. Hefling, "The Problem of Program Music," 30–32.

28. Ibid., 32–38.

29. Dahlhaus, "The Musical Work and Sociology," in *Schoenberg and the New Music*, trans. Derrick Puffett and Alfred Clayton (Cambridge: Cambridge University Press, 1987), 243 and 245.

30. Hefling reads this "first" suicide (i.e., Gustav's narration of suicide outside his beloved's wedding, as opposed to the later, terrifying onstage reenactment before the hermit) at measure 200, on the strength of a musical quotation in that measure of the line "Ich wollt' ich läg auf der schwarzen Bahr' " ["Would that I lay upon my black coffin"] from the *Wunderhorn* song "Ich hab' ein glühendes Messer." See "The Problem of Program Music," 36–37.

31. Part III of *Todtenfeier* (which is not discussed here) is the most famous section of the play; its hero is the Polish patriot Konrad.

32. These footnotes appear in Polish and French editions of the play; they do not appear in Lipiner's German edition.

33. The notion that Mahler's symphonies are infused with what Floros calls "Liedhaftigkeit" ("songlikeness"; *Mahler* vol. 2, 131) is, of course, a com-

monplace. Floros summarizes the tradition, and discusses various instrumental vocalisms (though nothing from the *Todtenfeier* movement) in his chapter "Charaktere vokaler Provenienz" (ibid., 111–34); among the types that he enumerates are instrumental imitations of recitative and arioso, and of chorale, hymn, and song. Floros argues generally, as have many before him, that (for instance) certain Mahlerian instrumental melodies possess a "song character," and that symphonies may partake of "song style" when a movement follows the formal patterns of song (rather than those more typical of symphony). The latter point is expanded in Michael Oltmanns, *Strophische Strukturen im Werk Gustav Mahlers* (Pfaffenweiler: Centaurus-Verlag, 1988).

34. Vill, *Vermittlungsformen*, 248–51.

35. This is a Dahlhausian and dialectical notion of form, in which the evocation of a "type" such as sonata must always be defused by demonstration of how the "type" is merely a priori to its own partial collapse or reconstruction.

36. "The Problem of Program Music," 44.

37. I have favored "membrane" over "foil" (the conventional translation) because of its implications of transparency, for Vill is describing how we "see the movement through" distance. I thereby lose the figural meaning (in German and English) of "foil" as "a foil to"—something that sets off, or sets in relief.

38. Vill, *Vermittlungsformen*, 251.

39. Richard Specht, *Gustav Mahler* (Berlin: Schuster and Loeffler, 1913), 219; Paul Bekker, *Gustav Mahlers Sinfonien* (Berlin: Schuster and Loeffler, 1920), 76; Edward R. Reilly, "Die Skizzen zu Mahlers zweiter Symphonie," in *Österreichische Musikzeitschrift* 34 (1979): 281; Floros, *Mahler* vol. 3, 54; and Vill, *Vermittlungsformen*, 248.

40. Floros, made uneasy by the poor "fit" of the movement into "sonata form," drifts nearest to this idea, if only negatively: he must speak plaintively of the movement's "offenses against the rule" of sonata when the first repetition of the gesture occurs in measure 64, the "sharp split" of the development section by the recurrence in measure 244, which forced both him and Specht to write of a "second development." See Floros, *Mahler* vol. 3, 54–55; also Specht, *Mahler*, 227. Michael Oltmanns, *Strophische Strukturen*, 237–47, describes the cyclic form of the movement as "mildly" influenced by strophic song, and reads Mahler's "sonata" forms generally as disrupted and mediated by the strophic forms typical of his orchestral songs.

Chapter Five

1. *Romantic Opera and Literary Form* (Berkeley and Los Angeles: University of California Press, 1977), 27.

2. Ibid., 75.

3. See Caryl Emerson, *Boris Godunov: Transpositions of a Russian Theme* (Indiana: Indiana University Press, 1986), 192–98.

4. Richard Wagner, *Gesammelte Schriften und Dichtungen* vol. 2 (Leipzig: E. W. Fritzsch, 1871), 300.

5. For an account of the music to *Siegfrieds Tod*, see Robert Bailey, "Wag-

ner's Musical Sketches for *Siegfrieds Tod*," in *Studies in Music History: Essays for Oliver Strunk*, ed. Harold S. Powers (Princeton: Princeton University Press, 1968), 459–94; and *WWV*, 404–5.

6. *Richard Wagner: Sämtliche Briefe* vol. 4, ed. Gertrud Strobel and Werner Wolf (Leipzig: Breitkopf und Härtel, 1979), 44.

7. Ibid., 187.

8. Mann's two important essays on the *Ring* are "Leiden und Grösse Richard Wagners" (1933) and "Richard Wagner und *Der Ring des Nibelungen* (1937), published in *Pro and Contra Wagner*, trans. Allan Blunden (Chicago: University of Chicago Press, 1985).

9. The phrase appears in "Leiden und Grösse Richard Wagners," in *Wagner und unsere Zeit*, ed. Erika Mann (Frankfurt am Main: Fischer, 1983), 74; in Thomas Mann, *Pro and Contra Wagner*, it is translated as "distaste for antecedent events that hover unseen behind the action" (102).

10. Mann, *Pro and Contra Wagner*, 186.

11. On dating these sketches, see Otto Strobel, *Skizzen und Entwürfe zur Ring-Dichtung* (Munich: F. Bruckmann, 1930), 201–12; and *WWV*, 406–7.

12. Strobel, *Ring-Skizzen*, 204. At this time, Wagner had abandoned the German custom of capitalizing all nouns; the spelling of "Wodan" was changed to "Wotan" at a later stage. Strobel transcribed the text from a single undated sheet in the Richard-Wagner-Archiv at Bayreuth, whose other side contains a brief text sketch for *Das Rheingold* (NA A II g 1); the date generally assigned to this sheet (around October 1851) is based on a letter to Uhlig from early October, in which Wagner alludes to his plans for *Die Walküre* and *Rheingold*, and on an entry in his *Annalen* at about the same time. See *WWV*, 406.

13. Strobel, *Ring-Skizzen*, 204–5.

14. Ibid., 211. These sketches were made in a small pocket notebook (Bayreuth, NA B II a 4); their date (after December 1851) is based upon their inclusion of elements from Friedrich Heinrich von der Hagen's *Wölsungasaga*, a book that Wagner had requested in a letter of 12 November 1851 to Uhlig, and which he received from Uhlig on 3 December. See *WWV*, 406.

15. Thomas Mann, *Pro and Contra Wagner*, 187–88 (emphasis mine).

16. Ibid., 188–89.

17. Paul de Man, "Genesis and Geneology," in *Allegories of Reading* (New Haven: Yale University Press, 1979), 97–98.

18. Dahlhaus, *Richard Wagner's Music Dramas*, 87.

19. Ibid., 124.

20. Ibid., 123.

21. Anthony Newcomb, "The Birth of Music out of the Spirit of Drama: An Essay in Wagnerian Formal Analysis," in *19th-Century Music* 5 (1981): 42.

22. Joseph Kerman, *Opera as Drama*, 15; he is discussing the final quotation of Cavaradossi's aria "E lucevan le stelle" as a pointless gesture—given that it accompanies Tosca's death leap.

23. This would, for example, be Edward Cone's reading; see *The Composer's Voice*, 43–66.

24. The allegory of the treaty for Valhalla is discussed at length in Deryck Cooke, *I Saw the World End* (Oxford: Oxford University Press, 1979), 53–80.

25. Adorno, *In Search of Wagner*, 28–29.

26. Peter Brooks, *Reading for the Plot*, 25–28.

27. On such long-range tonal arcs in Wagnerian opera, see Arnold Whittall, "The Music," in *Richard Wagner: Parsifal*, ed. Lucy Beckett (Cambridge: Cambridge University Press, 1981), 61–86; Robert Bailey, "The Structure of the *Ring* and Its Evolution," in *19th-Century Music* 1 (1977): 45–61; William Kinderman, " 'Das Geheimnis der Form' in Wagners *Tristan und Isolde*," in *Archiv für Musikwissenschaft* 40 (1983): 74–88.

28. Certainly the notion that repetition (whether exact or varied) constitutes a governing gesture that can structure otherwise unruly music is implicit in Newcomb's brief discussion of the monologue: "the musical procedure in question is the gradual modulation from musically unformed recitative to a musically highly formed aria-like unit [the passage beginning, "nur einer konnte / was ich nicht darf"], the whole set off by two musically similar *pillars* of great intensity (from Wotan's '*O heilige Schmach!*' through his '*zernage ihn gierig dein Neid!*')"; see "The Birth of Music," 42 (emphasis mine). Points of articulation in Wagnerian opera are often referred to in terms borrowed from architecture and structural engineering ("pillars," "cornerstones," "supporting arches")—implying that chaotic forces (the tendency of stones to crash to the ground, the tendency of music toward amorphousness) are controlled or brought into order by a phalanx of physical supports.

29. This is the kind of mingling between musical description and narratological tropes that was reviewed in Chapter 2; for examples, see Roland Barthes, "Action Sequences," in *Patterns of Literary Style*, ed. Joseph P. Strelka (University Park: Penn State University Press, 1971), 5–14; or the essay by Barthes discussed in Chapter 2, "Structural Functions of Narrative," in *Image. Music. Text*, 45–68.

30. Stefan Kunze, "Über Melodiebegriff und musikalischen Bau in Wagners Musikdrama," suggested that Wagner's cadences "play" at suggesting structural arrivals that are neither adumbrated nor followed up in surrounding music. His article is a provocative critique of traditional Wagnerian tonal analysis; see *Das Drama Richard Wagners als musikalisches Kunstwerk*, ed. Carl Dahlhaus, 124–28.

31. Dahlhaus, taking his direction from Schoenberg, has written on the phenomenon of the "motivization" of harmony, citing a "bizarre" Wagnerian chord progression (from Fasolt's warning speech in *Rheingold*), inexplicable in conventional harmonic terms, whose illogical juxtapositions are treated as a self-sufficient thematic idea; see "Tonalität und Form in Wagners 'Ring des Nibelungen'," in *Archiv für Musikwissenschaft* 40 (1983): 169–70.

32. This issue is explored in much greater detail in Carolyn Abbate, "Wagner, 'On Modulation,' and *Tristan*," in *Cambridge Opera Journal* 1 (1989): 33–58.

33. Discussions of "instrumental" forms in Wagner's work go back to Karl Grunsky's "Wagner als Symphoniker," in *Richard Wagner Jahrbuch* 1 (1906):

227–44; later writings that take the same general line include Lorenz's *Das Geheimnis der Form bei Richard Wagner* [cf. volume 1, 73–74]. For other examples of the argument, see Jack Stein's *Richard Wagner and the Synthesis of the Arts* (Detroit: Wayne State University Press, 1960), 157–66; Josef Mainka's "Sonatenform, Leitmotiv, und Charakterbegleitung," in *Beiträge zur Musikwissenschaft* 5 (1963): 11–15; and William Kinderman, "Dramatic Recapitulation in Wagner's *Götterdämmerung*," in *19th-Century Music* 4, no. 2 (1980): 108. The preference for instrumental models is a complex institutional phenomenon—one that I believe has more to do with opera critics' needs to align themselves with pedigreed traditions of musical analysis (which deal almost exclusively with instrumental works) than with the texts at hand; these needs are projected onto Wagner's music, as "discoveries" of instrumental models. Wagner's formal ideas are, of course, mainly operatic in origin; this statement may seem merely commonsensical (Wagner was an exclusively operatic composer whose involvement with instrumental music was limited and peculiar), yet it is also controversial. Wagner's claims to a creative heritage from Beethoven are biographically significant, but, as a clue to some concrete musical-formal similarity between the two composers, largely specious. His polemic has, however, also shaped the conclusions of those Wagnerian critics whose tastes may, in any case, incline them away from "lesser" operatic music and toward the canonized works of the German symphonic tradition.

34. Wagner, *Gesammelte Schriften* vol. 2, 212.

CHAPTER SIX

1. Unpublished letter written 6 September 1875 by Cosima Wagner, reporting Richard Wagner's explanation of the final melody in *Götterdämmerung*. Cited by John Deathridge, in *19th-Century Music* 5 (1981): 84.

2. Quoted from Theodore M. Anderssen, *The Legend of Brynhild* (Ithaca: Cornell University Press, 1980), 27, 30, 137, 237, and 148 (I have used spellings for character names as they appear in Wagner's text, except when the names are substantially different [e.g., Kriemhild and Gutrune], in which case both are given). The politer version of the laughter incident in the *Nibelungenlied* is generally consistent with what Anderssen calls the poem's "more delicate sensibility" as a late, courtly version of much older tales. Anderssen describes fully the arguments concerning the versions of Brünnhilde's story and the mutation of Brünnhilde's character through the medieval tradition, and all citations to sources will be taken from his volume.

3. Richard Wagner, *Gesammelte Schriften* vol. 2, 292–93. I have cited the version in *Siegfrieds Tod*; that in *Götterdämmerung* differs very slightly, though significantly—in the later text, the verbs of hearing are replaced (e.g., "hört' ich ein Horn" becomes "war das sein Horn"; "wild hört' ich weiherte sein Roß" becomes "wild weiherte sein Roß").

4. "The Numinous in *Götterdämmerung*," in *Reading Opera*, ed. Groos and Parker, 211–16; in this essay, Wintle also reviews the patterns underlying the disjunct surface of the scene, and the various local harmonic sequences that integrate the music within its larger context.

5. It is important to remember, of course, that certain poems are lost and have been reconstructed by collating later redactions; when I speak of "versions" (following their content as described in Anderssen, *The Legend of Brynhild*), I am speaking sometimes of these reconstructions, and sometimes of poems that survive fully or partially in manuscript sources (which are not, of course, necessarily contemporary with the text that they preserve). *The Legend of Brynhild* provides a full philological accounting.

6. Anderssen, *Brynhild*, 27–28.

7. Anderssen, in *Brynhild* (238), points out that "because the prior betrothal of Sigurd and Brynhild is fully described only in the Norse *Volsunga saga* and is only partially or dimly hinted at in the German versions (*Thidreks saga* and the *Nibelungenlied*), it has always been assumed that the prior betrothal was peculiar to the Norse version. In fact, it is a specifically German motif and acquired currency in the north only because the *Mieri* poet [one of the poets of the Eddic versions] sought to harmonize the Norse and German variants and because the author of the *Volsunga saga* accepted his harmonization."

8. Ibid., 236–37.

9. Ibid., 242.

10. Ibid., 241.

11. Ibid., 246.

12. Ibid., 78–80; he also theorizes that stories about Sigurd's [Siegfried's] youth were probably added to the tale "because of [Sigurd's] flattering association with such a powerful heroine."

13. *Opera, or the Undoing of Women*, 160. Ruth Berghaus's Frankfurt *Götterdämmerung* staging (1987) well-nigh wrote Clément's image onto the stage; Caterina Ligendza was directed to bid farewell to Siegfried, and then (though slowly and uncertainly, as if unaccustomed to the motions) sit primly on her chair and fold her hands.

14. *Romantic Opera and Literary Form*, 26. One wonders how deeply these negative images of the plot-Brünnhilde have also been conditioned by inept acting and poor stage-presence in live performances.

15. *Opera, or the Undoing of Women*, 156.

16. *Romantic Opera and Literary Form*, 26.

17. See John Deathridge's review of Curt von Westernhagen, *The Forging of the Ring*, in *19th-Century Music* 5 (1981): 84; the text of the letter in which Wagner makes the identification is given at the head of this chapter.

18. *The Legend of Brynhild*, 116 and 242–43.

19. Ibid., 27.

20. Ibid., 30 and 237–38.

21. For an account of this text, see Deryck Cooke, *I Saw the World End*, 20–25; on the manuscripts for the various endings to *Götterdämmerung*, see *WWV*, 393–414.

22. Julia Kristeva, "From Symbol to Sign," in *The Kristeva Reader*, ed. Toril Moi (New York: Columbia University Press, 1986), 67.

23. Ibid., 68.

24. Roland Barthes, "Listening," in *The Responsibility of Forms*, 214 and 215.

25. *The Nibelungenlied*, trans. A. T. Hatto (Harmondsworth: Penguin, 1965), 133. Hatto claims in a footnote to this passage that the shriek is a transmutation, from the older versions, of Brünnhilde's laughter, but (as we have seen) Gutrune's [Kriemhild's] cry counters that laughter even in the oldest sources; it would be better to speak of a *dilation* of the single cry into an extended episode.

26. See Wintle, "The Numinous," 217, for a discussion of the passage, which he hears as one of the "numinous" recurrences of a particular collection of motifs whose center is the rising arpeggio of the sword.

27. Ibid., 219.

28. Carl Dahlhaus, in "Entfremdung und Erinnerung: Zu Wagners *Götter-dämmerung*," notes Siegfried's claim that he did not take the ring from Brünn-hilde but argues that, though he remembers all other details of the second night with Brünnhilde, he forgets about the ring because the ring (as another magical object) inspires enforced forgetfulness in those who touch it. See *Bericht über den internationalen musikwissenschaftlichen Kongreß Bayreuth 1981*, ed. Christoph-Helmut Mahling and Siegrid Wiesmann (Kassel: Bärenreiter, 1984), 419–20.

29. The scene is described in terms of a three-part structure articulated by rhythmic and tonal patterning, in Robert Bailey, "The Structure of the *Ring* and Its Evolution," *19th-Century Music* 1 (1977): 48–61; see 55–58.

30. The Fate motif has its origins in *Walküre* Act I, where it appears (though in a less pointed shape than in the *Todesverkündigung*) at Siegmund's line, "Mißwende folgt mir / wohin ich fliehe" (scene 1), and is repeated (both times with its bass falling through the seventh D–E, a D minor sixth-chord juxtaposed with an E) in scene 2 during his narration: "Unheil lag auf mir." Both appearances are *cadential* forms, and anticipate the motif as it appears at the end of the opera (also bass D–E, D minor to E major), where it is used as a cadential figure to close off the "Magic Fire" music. At the beginning of the *Todesverkündigung*, the motif again begins on bass note D, but the bass falls the half-step to C♯ in a *modulatory* or open form (D minor chord as ♭vi to a dominant seventh on C♯).

31. The phrase is difficult to translate since both *erklingen* and *tönen* are ordinarily rendered as "to sound," "to ring," or "to resound," yet both have a musical overtone (*Klang* as a musical sound or the sound of a bell; *Ton* as a musical pitch) that cannot be captured in English. Hence my whimsical alternative.

32. "Des Stammes Scheite / hieß er sie schichten / zu ragendem Hauf / rings um der Seligen Saal" becomes "Starke Scheite / schichtet mir dort / am Rande des Rheines zuhauf!"

33. Anderssen points out that certain motifs originally attached to Brünn-hilde (such as the bad dream on the night of Siegfried's death) actually become transferred to Gutrune as she assumes greater narrative stature; see *The Legend of Brynhild*, 151–86.

34. See *L'Opéra, ou le cri de l'ange*, 25–31.

35. *Problems of Dostoevsky's Poetics*, trans. Caryl Emerson (Minneapolis: University of Minnesota Press, 1984), 185 and 186.

36. Any soprano who has sung the part knows this high B; a bad note for the voice in any case (it lies on one of the secondary breaks), it comes at the end of a killing solo passage and an exhausting night: it looms as a sinister note for most.

BIBLIOGRAPHY

Abbate, Carolyn. "Elektra's Voice." In *Richard Strauss: Elektra*, ed. Derrick Puffett, 107–27. Cambridge: Cambridge University Press, 1989.

———. "Orpheus in the Underworld." In *Tannhäuser*, ed. Nicholas John, 33–50. London: John Calder, 1988.

———. "The Parisian Vénus and the 'Paris' *Tannhäuser*." *Journal of the American Musicological Society* 36 (1983): 73–123.

———. "Symphonic Opera, a Wagnerian Myth." In *Analyzing Opera*, ed. Carolyn Abbate and Roger Parker. Berkeley and Los Angeles: University of California Press, 1989.

———. "Ventriloquism." (Forthcoming.)

———. "Wagner, 'On Modulation,' and *Tristan*." *Cambridge Opera Journal* 1 (1989): 33–58.

Adorno, Theodor W. *Mahler: eine musikalische Physiognomik*. Frankfurt am Main: Suhrkamp, 1960.

———. *In Search of Wagner*, trans. Rodney Livingstone. London: Verso, 1981.

———. *Quasi una fantasia*. Frankfurt am Main: Fischer, 1963.

Anderssen, Theodore M. *The Legend of Brynhild*. Ithaca: Cornell University Press, 1980.

Asaf'ev, B. V. *Musical Form as a Process* trans. J. R. Tull. Ph.D. diss., Ohio State University, 1976.

Bailey, Robert. "The Structure of the *Ring* and Its Evolution." *19th-Century Music* 1 (1977): 48–61.

———. "Wagner's Musical Sketches for *Siegfrieds Tod*." In *Studies in Music History: Essays for Oliver Strunk*, ed. Harold S. Powers, 459–94. Princeton: Princeton University Press, 1968.

Bakhtin, M. M. *The Dialogic Imagination*, ed. Michael Holquist, trans. Caryl Emerson and Michael Holquist. Austin: University of Texas Press, 1981.

———. *Problems of Dostoevsky's Poetics*, trans. Caryl Emerson. Minneapolis: University of Minnesota Press, 1984.

Barthes, Roland. "Action Sequences." In *Patterns of Literary Style*, ed. Joseph P. Strelka. University Park: Penn State University Press, 1971.

———. "Introduction to the Structural Analysis of Narrative." In *Image. Music. Text*, trans. Stephen Heath. New York: Hill and Wang, 1977.

———. *Mythologies*, trans. Annette Lavers. New York: Hill and Wang, 1972.

———. *The Responsibility of Forms*, trans. Richard Howard. New York: Hill and Wang, 1985.

———. *S/Z*, trans. Richard Miller. New York: Hill and Wang, 1974.

Bauer-Lechner, Natalie. *Errinerungen an Gustav Mahler*, ed. J. Killian. Leipzig: E. P. Tal, 1923.

Bekker, Paul. *Gustav Mahlers Sinfonien*. Berlin: Schuster and Loeffler, 1920.

Belknap, Richard. "The Minimal Unit of Plot." In *Literature and History: The-*

oretical Problems and Russian Case Studies, 221–29. Stanford: Stanford University Press, 1986.

Benveniste, Emile. *Problems in General Linguistics*, trans. Mary Elizabeth Meek. Coral Gables: University of Miami Press, 1971.

Berlioz, Hector. *A Travers chants*. Paris: Michel Lévy frères, 1862.

Borchmeyer, Dieter. *Das Theater Richard Wagners*. Stuttgart: Reclam, 1982.

Brinkmann, Reinhold. "Mythos-Geschichte-Natur." In *Richard Wagner: Von der Oper zum Musikdrama*, ed. Stefan Kunze, Bern: Franke, 1978.

———. "Richard Wagner der Erzähler." *Österreichische Musikzeitschrift* 37 (1982): 299–306.

———. "Sentas Traumerzählung." *Bayreuther Programmheft*. Bayreuth 1984.

Brod, Max. *Prager Sternenhimmel: Musik- und Theatererlebnisse der zwanziger Jahre*. Vienna: Paul Zsolnay Verlag, 1966.

Brooks, Peter. *Reading for the Plot*. New York: Alfred A. Knopf, 1984.

Burnham, Scott. *Aesthestics, Theory and History in the Works of A. B. Marx*. Ph.D. diss., Brandeis University, 1988.

Calvino, Italo. *The Castle of Crossed Destinies*, trans. William Weaver. New York: Harcourt Brace Jovanovich, 1979.

Carter, Tim. *W. A. Mozart: Le Nozze di Figaro*. Cambridge: Cambridge University Press, 1987.

Chambers, Ross. *Story and Situation: Narrative Seduction and the Power of Fiction*. Minneapolis: University of Minnesota Press, 1984.

Chatman, Seymour. "What Novels Can Do That Films Can't (and Vice Versa)." In *On Narrative*, ed. W.J.T. Mitchell, 117–36. Chicago: University of Chicago Press, 1981.

Clément, Catherine. *Opera, or the Undoing of Women*, trans. Betsy Wing. Minneapolis: University of Minnesota Press, 1988.

Cone, Edward T. *The Composer's Voice*. Berkeley and Los Angeles: University of California Press, 1974.

———. *Hector Berlioz: Fantastic Symphony*. New York: Norton, 1971.

———. *Music: A View from Delft*. Chicago: University of Chicago Press, 1988.

Conrad, Peter. *Romantic Opera and Literary Form*. Berkeley and Los Angeles: University of California Press, 1977.

Cooke, Deryck. *I Saw the World End*. Oxford: Oxford University Press, 1979.

Cowie, Elizabeth. "The Popular Novel as Progressive Text—A Discussion of *Coma*—Part 1." In *Feminism and Film Theory*, ed. Constance Penley, 104–40. New York: Routledge, 1988.

Culler, Jonathan. "Story and Discourse in the Analysis of Narrative." In *The Pursuit of Signs*, 169–87. Ithaca: Cornell University Press, 1981.

Dällenbach, Lucien. *The Mirror in the Text*, trans. Jeremy Whiteley and Emma Hughes. Chicago: University of Chicago Press, 1989.

Dahlhaus, Carl. "Entfremdung und Errinnerung: Zu Wagners *Götterdämmerung*." In *Bericht über den internationalen Musikwissenschaftlichen Kongreß Bayreuth 1981*, ed. Christoph-Helmut Mahling and Siegrid Wiesmann, 419–20. Kassel: Bärenreiter, 1984.

———. "Formprinzipien in Wagners 'Ring des Nibelungen'." In *Beiträge zur*

Geschichte der Oper, ed. Heinz Becker, 95–129. Regensburg: Gustav Bosse Verlag, 1969.

———. *Die Idee der absoluten Musik*. Kassel: Bärenreiter, 1978.

———. *Nineteenth-Century Music*, trans. J. Bradford Robinson. Berkeley and Los Angeles: University of California Press, 1989.

———. *Richard Wagner's Music Dramas*, trans. Mary Whittall. Cambridge: Cambridge University Press, 1979.

———. *Schoenberg and the New Music*, trans. Derrick Puffett and Alfred Clayton. Cambridge: Cambridge University Press, 1987.

———. "Tonalität und Form in Wagners 'Ring des Nibelungen'." *Archiv für Musikwissenschaft* (1983): 165–73.

———. "Über das 'kontemplative Ensemble'." In *Opernstudien: Anna Amalie Abert zum 65. Geburtstag*, ed. Klaus Hortschansky. Tutzing: Hans Schneider, 1975.

———. "Das 'Verstehen' von Musik und die Sprache der musikalischen Analyse." In *Musik und Verstehen*, ed. Peter Faltin and Hans-Peter Reinecke, 37–47. Cologne: Arno Volk Verlag, 1973.

———. "Zur Geschichte der Leitmotivtechnik bei Wagner." In *Das Drama Richard Wagners*, ed. Carl Dahlhaus, 17–40. Regensburg: Gustav Bosse Verlag, 1970.

———, ed. *Beiträge zur musikalischen Hermeneutik*. Regensburg: Gustav Bosse Verlag, 1975.

———. ed. *Das Drama Richard Wagners als musikalisches Kunstwerk*. Regensburg: Gustav Bosse Verlag, 1970.

Danuser, Hermann. "Konstruktion des Romans bei Gustav Mahler." In *Musikalische Prosa*, 87–117. Regensburg: Gustav Bosse Verlag, 1975.

———. "Zu den Programmen von Mahlers frühen Symphonien." *Melos/Neue Zeitschrift* (1975): 13–16.

Deathridge, John. Review of Curt von Westernhagen, Richard Wagner. *19th-Century Music* 5 (1981): 81–89.

———, Martin Geck, and Egon Voss. *Verzeichnis der musikalischen Werke Richard Wagners und ihrer Quellen (WWV)*. Mainz: Schott, 1986.

De Man, Paul. *Allegories of Reading*. New Haven: Yale University Press, 1979.

———. *Blindness and Insight*. Minneapolis: University of Minnesota Press, 1983.

———. *The Rhetoric of Romanticism*. New York: Columbia University Press, 1984.

Derrida, Jacques. *Of Grammatology*, trans. Gayatri Chakravorty Spivak. Baltimore: Johns Hopkins University Press, 1976.

Duchez, Marie-Elisabeth. "La représentation de la musique." In *Actes du XVIIIe Congrès de Philosophie de langue française*, 178–82. Strasbourg: Strasbourg University Press, 1980.

Düring, Werner-Joachim. *Erlkönig-Vertonungen: eine historische und systematische Untersuchung*. Regensburg: Gustav Bosse Verlag, 1972.

Eco, Umberto. "Producing Signs." In *On Signs*, ed. Marshall Blonsky. Baltimore: Johns Hopkins University Press, 1985.

Eco, Umberto. *A Theory of Semiotics*. Bloomington: Indiana University Press, 1976.

Eggebrecht, Hans-Heinrich. *Die Musik Gustav Mahlers*. Munich: Piper Verlag, 1982.

Emerson, Caryl. *Boris Godunov: Transpositions of a Russian Theme*. Indiana: Indiana University Press, 1986.

———. "Real Endings and Russian Death: Mussorgskij's *Pesni i pljaski smerti*." *Russian Language Journal* 38 (1984): 199–216.

Faltin, Peter, and Hans-Peter Reinecke, eds. *Musik und Verstehen*. Cologne: Arno Volk Verlag, 1973.

Favre, Georges. *L'ouvre de Paul Dukas*. Paris: Durand, 1969.

Felman, Shoshana. *The Literary Speech Act*, trans. Catherine Porter. Ithaca: Cornell University Press, 1983.

Floros, Constantin. *Gustav Mahler III: Die Symphonien*. Wiesbaden: Breitkopf und Härtel, 1985.

Forster, E. M. *Aspects of the Novel*, 1927. Reprint. New York: Harcourt, Brace, 1955.

Freud, Siegmund. "Das Unheimliche." In *Studienausgabe* vol. 4. Frankfurt am Main: Fischer, 1982.

Fried, Michael. *Realism, Writing, Disfiguration*. Chicago: University of Chicago Press, 1987.

Furman, Nelly. "The Languages of Love in *Carmen*." In *Reading Opera*, ed. Arthur Groos and Roger Parker, 168–83. Princeton: Princeton University Press, 1988.

Genette, Gérard. *Narrative Discourse*, trans. Jane E. Lewin. Ithaca: Cornell University Press, 1980.

Gilman, Sander. *Jewish Self-Hatred*. Baltimore: Johns Hopkins University Press, 1986.

Goethe, Johann Wolfgang von. *Goethes Werke: Hamburger Ausgabe* vol. 1, ed. Erich Trunz. Hamburg: Wegner, 1949.

Goodman, Nelson. *The Languages of Art*. Indianapolis: Bobbs-Merrill, 1968.

Goslich, Siegfried. *Die deutsche Romantische Oper*. Tutzing: Hans Schneider, 1975.

Gossett, Philip. "Verdi, Ghislanzoni, and *Aida*: The Uses of Convention." *Critical Inquiry* 1 (1974): 291–334.

Groos, Arthur, and Roger Parker, eds. *Reading Opera*. Princeton: Princeton University Press, 1988.

Grunsky, Karl. "Wagner als Symphoniker." *Richard Wagner Jahrbuch* 1 (1906): 227–44.

Hatten, Robert S. "The Place of Intertextuality in Music Studies." *American Journal of Semiotics* 3 (1985): 73–74.

Hefling, Stephen. "Mahler's *Todtenfeier* and the Problem of Program Music." *19th-Century Music* 12 (1988): 27–53.

Hegel, G.W.F. *Aesthetik* vol. 2, ed. Friedrich Bassenge. Berlin: verlag das europäische buch, 1985.

Holzapfel, Otto. *The Ballad as Narrative*. Odense: Odense University Press, 1982.

Ingarden, Roman. *The Work of Music and the Problem of Its Identity*, trans.

Adam Czerniawski, ed. Jean G. Harrell. Berkeley and Los Angeles: University of California Press, 1986.

Jakobson, Roman. "Language in Relation to Other Communication Systems." In *Linguaggi nella societa e nella tecnica*, 3–16. Milan: Edizioni di Communita, 1970.

Jander, Owen. "Beethoven's 'Orpheus in Hades': the *Andante con moto* of the Fourth Piano Concerto." *19th-Century Music* 8 (1985): 195–212.

―――. "The Kreutzer Sonata as Dialogue." *Early Music* 16 (1988): 34–48.

Kallberg, Jeffrey. "The Rhetoric of Genre: Chopin's Nocturne in G Minor." *19th-Century Music* 11, no. 3 (Spring 1988): 238–61.

Kerman, Joseph. *The Beethoven Quartets*. New York: Alfred A. Knopf, 1967.

―――. *Opera as Drama*. Revised edition. Berkeley and Los Angeles: University of California Press, 1988.

Kinderman, William. "Dramatic Recapitulation in Wagner's *Götterdämmerung*." *19th-Century Music* 4, no. 2 (1980): 101–12.

―――. " 'Das Geheimnis der Form' in Wagners *Tristan und Isolde*." *Archiv für Musikwissenschaft* 40 (1983): 174–88.

Kivy, Peter. *Sound and Semblance: Reflections on Musical Representation*. Princeton: Princeton University Press, 1984.

Kolland, Hubert. "Zur Semantik der Leitmotive in Richard Wagners *Ring des Nibelungen*." *International Review of the Aesthetics and Sociology of Music* 4 (1973): 197–211.

Kramer, Jonathan. "Multiple and Non-Linear Time in Beethoven's Opus 135." *Perspectives of New Music* 11 (1973): 122–45.

Kristeva, Julia. "From Symbol to Sign." In *The Kristeva Reader*, ed. Toril Moi, 62–73. New York: Columbia University Press, 1986.

Kunze, Stefan. *Mozarts Opern*. Stuttgart: Reclam, 1984.

―――. "Über Melodiebegriff und musikalischen Bau in Wagners Musikdrama." In *Das Drama Richard Wagners*, ed. Carl Dahlhaus, 111–48.

Leibowitz, René. *Le compositeur et son double*. Paris: Gallimard, 1971.

Leppert, Richard, and Susan McClary, eds. *Music and Society*. Cambridge: Cambridge University Press, 1987.

Lindenberger, Herbert. *Opera: The Extravagant Art*. Ithaca: Cornell University Press, 1984.

Lorenz, Alfred. *Das Geheimnis der Form bei Richard Wagner* vol. 1. Berlin: Max Hesses Verlag, 1924.

Maclean, Marie. *Narrative as Performance*. London: Routledge, 1988.

McClary, Susan. "The Politics of Silence and Sound." Afterword to Jacques Attili, *Noise*, trans. Brian Massumi, 154–56. Minneapolis: University of Minnesota Press, 1985.

Mahler, Gustav. *Mahler-Briefe 1879–1911*, ed. Alma Mahler. Berlin: Paul Zsolnay Verlag, 1925.

Mainka, Josef. "Sonatenform, Leitmotiv, und Charakterbegleitung." *Beiträge zur Musikwissenschaft* 5 (1963): 11–15.

Mann, Thomas. *Pro and Contra Wagner*, trans. Allan Blunden. Chicago: University of Chicago Press, 1985.

Mann, Thomas. *Wagner und unsere Zeit*, ed. Erika Mann. Frankfurt am Main: Fischer, 1983.

Marx, Adolf Bernard. *Ludwig von Beethoven* vol. 1. Berlin: Verlag von Otto Janke, 1859. Facsimile reprint. Hildesheim: Georg Olms Verlag, 1979.

Maus, Fred E. "Music as Drama." *Music Theory Spectrum* 10 (1988): 65–72.

Mickiewicz, Adam. *Chefs d'oeuvre traduits par lui-même et par ses fils*, ed. Ladislas Mickiewicz. Paris: Editions Bossard, 1924.

——. *Todtenfeier von Adam Mickiewicz*, trans. Siegfried Lipiner. Leipzig: Breitkopf und Härtel, 1887.

Mitchell, W.J.T., ed. *On Narrative*. Chicago: University of Chicago Press, 1981.

Müller, Gunther. *Morphologische Poetik*, ed. Elena Müller. Tübingen: M. Niemeyer, 1968.

Murnaghan, Sheila. "Voice and Body in Greek Tragedy." *Yale Journal of Criticism* 1/2 (1987): 23–45.

Nattiez, Jean-Jacques. "The Concept of Plot and Seriation Process in Music Analysis," trans. Catherine Dale. *Music Analysis* 4 (1985): 107–18.

——. "Introduction à l'esthétique de Hanslick." In Eduard Hanslick, *Du beau dans la musique*, trans. Charles Bannelier and Georges Pucher. Paris: Christian Bourgois, 1986.

——. *Musicologie générale et sémiologie*. Paris: Christian Bourgois, 1987.

——. "Y a-t-il une diégèse musicale?" In *Musik und Verstehen*, ed. Peter Faltin and Hans-Peter Reinecke, 247–58. Cologne: Arno Volk Verlag, 1973.

Neubauer, John. *The Emancipation of Music from Language*. New Haven: Yale University Press, 1986.

Newcomb, Anthony. "The Birth of Music out of the Spirit of Drama: An Essay in Wagnerian Formal Analysis." *19th-Century Music* 5 (1981): 38–66.

——. "Once More 'Between Absolute and Program Music': Schumann's Second Symphony." *19th-Century Music* 7 (1984): 233–50.

——. "Schumann and Late Eighteenth-Century Narrative Strategies." *19th-Century Music* 11 (1987): 164–75.

——. "Sound and Feeling." *Critical Inquiry* 10 (1984): 614–42.

The Nibelungenlied, trans. A. T. Hatto. Harmondsworth: Penguin, 1965.

Nietzsche, Friedrich. *The Birth of Tragedy*, trans. Walter Kaufmann. In *Basic Writings of Nietzsche*. New York: Random House, 1968.

Norris, Christopher. "Utopian Deconstruction: Ernst Bloch, Paul de Man, and the Politics of Music." In *Music and the Politics of Culture*, ed. Christopher Norris, 305–43. New York: St. Martin's Press, 1989.

Noske, Frits. *The Signifier and the Signified*. The Hague: Nijhoff, 1977.

Oltmanns, Michael. *Strophische Strukturen im Werk Gustav Mahlers*. Pfaffenweiler: Centaurus-Verlag, 1988.

Pfister, Manfred. *Theory and Analysis of the Drama*, trans. John Halliday. Cambridge: Cambridge University Press, 1988.

Poizat, Michel. *L'Opéra ou le cri de l'ange*. Paris: A. M. Métailié, 1986.

Powers, Harold S. "Language Models and Musical Analysis." *Ethnomusicology* 24 (1980): 1–60.

———. " 'La solita forma' and 'The Uses of Convention'," *Acta musicologica* 59 (1987): 65–90.

Reilly, Edward R. "Die Skizzen zu Mahlers zweiter Symphonie." *Österreichische Musikzeitschrift* 34 (1979): 266–84.

Ricoeur, Paul. *Time and Narrative* vol. 2, trans. Kathleen McLaughlin and David Pellauer. Chicago: University of Chicago Press, 1985.

Robinson, Paul. "A Deconstructive Postscript: Reading Libretti and Misreading Opera." In *Reading Opera*, ed. Arthur Groos and Roger Parker, 328–46. Princeton: Princeton University Press, 1988.

———. Review of Catherine Clément, *Opera or the Undoing of Women. New York Times Book Review* (1 January, 1989): 3.

Rousseau, Jean-Jacques. *Essai sur l'origine des langues.* Paris: A. Belin, 1817.

———. *On the Origin of Language*, trans. John H. Moran. Chicago: University of Chicago Press, 1966.

Ruwet, Nicholas. "Typography, Rhyme, and Linguistic Structure in Poetry." In *The Sign in Music and Literature*, ed. Wendy Steiner, 131–37. Austin: University of Texas Press, 1981.

Schering, Albert. *Beethoven und die Dichtung.* Berlin: Junker und Dünnhaupt, 1936.

Schleuning, Peter. "Beethoven in alter Deutung." *Archiv für Musikwissenschaft* (1987): 165–87.

Silverman, Kaja. *The Acoustic Mirror.* Bloomington: Indiana University Press, 1988.

Smith, Barbara Herrnstein. "Narrative Versions, Narrative Theories." In *On Narrative*, ed. W.J.T. Mitchell, 209–32. Chicago: University of Chicago Press, 1981.

Soloman, Maynard. *Beethoven Essays.* Cambridge: Harvard University Press, 1988.

Specht, Richard. *Gustav Mahler.* Berlin: Schuster and Loeffler, 1913.

Stein, Jack. *Poem and Music in the German Lied.* Cambridge: Harvard University Press, 1971.

———. *Richard Wagner and the Synthesis of the Arts.* Detroit: Wayne State University Press, 1960.

Steiner, George. *Real Presences.* Chicago: University of Chicago Press, 1989.

Stephan, Rudolf. *Gustav Mahler: II Symphonie C-moll.* Munich: Fink, 1979.

Strobel, Otto. *Skizzen und Entwürfe zur Ring-Dichtung.* Munich: F. Bruckmann, 1930.

Tarasti, Eero. "Pour une narratologie de Chopin." *International Review of the Aesthetics and Sociology of Music* 15 (1984): 53–75.

Tibbe, M. *Lieder und Liedelemente in den instrumentalen Symphoniesätzen Gustav Mahlers.* Munich: Piper Verlag, 1971.

Tolstoy, Leo. *What is Art*, trans. Almyer Maude. Indianapolis: Bobbs-Merrill, 1960.

Treitler, Leo. *Music and the Historical Imagination.* Cambridge: Harvard University Press, 1989.

Ubersfeld, Anne. *L'Ecole du spectateur: Lire le théâtre II*. Paris: Editions Sociales, 1981.

———. *Lire le théâtre*. Paris: Editions Sociales, 1977.

Vetter, Isolde. *Der fliegende Holländer von Richard Wagner—Entstehung, Bearbeitung, Überlieferung*. Ph.D. diss., Technical University, Berlin, 1982. Microfiche.

Vill, Suzanne. *Vermittlungsformen verbalisierter und musikalischer Inhalte in der
Musik Gustav Mahlers*. Tutzing: Hans Schneider, 1979.

Wagner, Richard. *Gesammelte Schriften und Dichtungen*. Leipzig: E. W. Fritzsch,
1871–1873.

———. "Eine Mitteilung an meine Freunde." In *Sämtliche Schriften* vol. 4,
230–344. Leipzig: Breitkopf und Härtel, 1911–1916.

———. *Prose Works*, trans. William Ashton Ellis. London: Routledge, 1892–
1899. Reprint. New York: Broude Brothers, 1966.

———. *Sämtliche Briefe* vol. 4, ed. Gertrud Strobel and Werner Wolf. Leipzig:
Breitkopf und Härtel, 1979.

———. *Sämtliche Schriften und Dichtungen*. Leipzig: Breitkopf und Härtel,
1911–1916.

———. "Über die Benennung *Musikdrama*." In *Sämtliche Schriften* vol. 9, 302–
7. Leipzig: Breitkopf und Härtel, 1911–1916.

White, Hayden. "The Value of Narrativity in the Representation of Reality."
In *On Narrative*, ed. W.J.T. Mitchell, 1–23. Chicago: University of Chicago
Press, 1981.

Whittall, Arnold. "The Music." In *Richard Wagner: Parsifal*, ed. Lucy Beckett,
61–86. Cambridge: Cambridge University Press, 1981.

Wintle, Christopher. "The Numinous in *Götterdämmerung*." In *Reading Opera*,
ed. Arthur Groos and Richard Parker, 200–34. Princeton: Princeton University Press, 1988.

Wolff, Janet. "The Ideology of Autonomous Art." In *Music and Society*, ed.
Richard Leppert and Susan McClary, 1–12. Cambridge: Cambridge University Press, 1987.

INDEX